From Mecca to Calvary:
Leaving Islam
to Become a Christian

From Mecca to Calvary: Leaving Islam to Become a Christian

Frederick Douglass

Dextera Books
2014

From Mecca to Calvary: Leaving Islam to Become a Christian

Frederick Douglass, Ph.D.

First Printing 2014
ISBN 978-0-9909752-0-5
Dextera Books, LLC
3230 Sycamore Rd, #218
DeKalb, IL, 60115

Dedication

This book is dedicated to all of the individuals

who have made the trip from Mecca to Calvary.

Special acknowledgment is

made for those who lost their lives, endured tortures,

or suffered great emotional and physical losses,

as a result of their faith in Jesus Christ.

Foreword

The purpose of this book is not to conduct a debate between Islam and Biblical Christianity. Others have taken on that job. They have done a far better job than could this author. On the website answering-islam.org (http://www.answering-islam.org/), many authors have contributed articles addressing specific issues of the debate and differences between Muslim and Christian scholars. Similarly, a number of good books – from both sides of the debate - have also addressed this material. From the Christian perspective, I have learned a good deal from three books on this topic: *Islam Revealed,* by Anis A. Shorrosh (Thomas Nelson Publishers, Nashville, TN, 1988); *The Islam Debate*, by Josh McDowell and John Gilchrist (Here's Life Publishers, San Bernadino, CA, 1983); *Seeking Allah, Finding Jesus*, by Nabeel Qureshi (Zondervan, Grand Rapids, MI, 2014). Qureshi's book is highly recommended for its presentation of arguments for and against Christianity and the Bible.

Millions of individuals leave Islam for Christianity every year. Why? This book will answer that question. God revealed vital messages through His ancient prophets, and as we shall see in this book, these truths are faithfully preserved in the pages of the Bible. Moreover, there are strongly compelling reasons to trust the Bible as the source of spiritual truth and guidance. These things are also discussed in the following chapters. Truth is the ultimate goal. The Quran says Jesus Christ was not crucified (Quran 4:157-158), but the Bible says Jesus Christ was crucified, died on the cross, buried in a tomb, and rose from the dead three days later. Which one is correct? What is the truth? As millions of former Muslims have found, the Bible is a trustworthy record of historical events. It is also a pure source of spiritual truth.

Finally, it should be mentioned that quotes from the Quran are from English translations. Every effort has been made to assure that the quotes are the best available translations. Seven different Quran translations were consulted for each passage. Bible passages were mostly from the New King James version. In a few cases, Bible passages are from the New International Version. For archaeological studies, the author relied extensively on the outstanding books by Joseph P. Free (*Archaeology and Bible History*, Zondervan, 1992) and Randall Price (*The Stones Cry Out*, Harvest House Publishers, 1997).

Frederick Douglass
September, 2014

Contents

Preface

This book had its beginning about 20 years ago on a cool, rainy morning in Los Angeles. With a morning flight at Los Angeles International Airport, I called a taxi to drive me to the airport. When I got into the taxi, I noticed a variety of decorations put up by the driver. There were colorful ribbons, fabrics, and hanging beads. And there were statements written in Arabic. I have always thought Arabic was perhaps the most beautiful writing in the world – with elegant loops and swirls of ink. It was very pretty but I could not read a word of it.

As soon as the ride began, the taxi driver said to me, "Allah sends rain today." I sat thinking about the gentleman's statement and I continued to look at all of the unusual decorations within the cab. Then he repeated, "Allah sends rain today, I said."

I felt obliged to respond to the driver's comment. I said to him, "Yes, I heard you. But I am not a Muslim. I am a Christian."

At this point, the driver happily responded by saying, "Oh, you and I believe the same things!"

I was not an expert on Islam at the time, but I was quite certain that the Christian faith was much different than the Islamic faith. I had been a student of the Bible for many years. Moreover, I had the good fortune of sitting under the teachings of some of the best Bible teachers in the world. So instinctively, I replied to him, "Well, that's not true. Christians believe that Jesus Christ is God and the Eternal Creator. Muslims do not believe this."

My driver was pretty irritated by that comment, but confidently replied, "Jesus never claimed to be God."

My carry-on bag was sitting next to me in the cab and I happened to have my study Bible packed in there. I had previously done a study on this very subject, so I opened my Bible to the New Testament gospel book of John. The Bible seemed to open on its own to the tenth chapter. I read the passage where Jesus says (John 10:30),"I and My Father are one," and I continued with the next few verses (John 10:31-33):

> Then the Jews took up stones again to stone Him. Jesus answered them, "Many good works I have shown you from My Father. For which of those works do you stone Me?" The Jews answered Him, saying, "For a good work we do not stone You, but for blasphemy, and because You, being a Man, make Yourself God."

I explained to the driver that the Jewish leaders understood the meaning of Jesus's statements – He was claiming to be God. I went on to explain how Jesus Christ is given the exact same names as the God of the Old Testament. I also mentioned that Jesus accepted prayers and worship from men and He was able to forgive sins. These were qualities only found in God Himself.

By this time, the taxi driver was stunned and silent. I explained that Jesus came to save us from our sins. And He took our sins to the cross and suffered the penalty for them. Finally, I told him that God offers salvation to sinners through a simple command: believe that Jesus died for your sins. You will be saved – free of charge. Not a word from the taxi driver.

We arrived at the airport. He pulled the taxi up to the curb in front of a departure terminal, however the poor fellow was so agitated by the conversation that he literally jumped out of the cab. Evidently, he had not looked out his window, because he jumped in front of an oncoming shuttle van! The van slammed on its breaks and stopped about 1 or 2 feet from my taxi driver. He was almost run over. Following the near-death experience, he went to the back of the taxi and removed my luggage from the trunk. His hands were shaking. I was at a loss for words. I paid the frightened driver and gave him a large gratuity. Finally, I simply told him, "God bless you, sir," and I went on to get my airline flight.

I have thought about the taxi driver many times over the years, praying for him on several occasions. I was struck by his comment that Muslims and Christians, "believe the same things." Did he really think this? Was this man's knowledge of Biblical Christianity that lousy or was he just trying to be non-confrontational to his Christian passenger? In the following years, I learned more about Islam. They do respectfully call Jesus a great prophet. Perhaps this was the common ground between the Islamic and Christian faiths, according to my taxi driver. Nevertheless, I came to one conclusion from the exchange: Muslims know very little about the true messages taught in the Bible.

Prompted by this encounter with the Muslim taxi driver, I began reading books about Islam and I acquired a Quran. I learned about their beliefs and their thoughts on Judaism and Christianity. I also followed the news from around the world and I took notice of their treatment of Christians. I recall hearing of the terrible genocidal attacks on the people of Southern Sudan and the Nuba Mountains, attacks often prompted by the attempted Islamization of this region. It is estimated that up 2 million people died in these attacks.[1] Many of the victims were Christians. Moreover, the Islamic forces from northern Sudan captured as many as 200,000 women and children for use as slaves. I also read of brutal attacks on Christians in countries such as Indonesia, Pakistan, Kenya, Egypt, and other locations.[2,3]

Around this time, I met some Armenian Americans and we discussed the horrible genocide of the Armenians by the Ottoman Turks between 1915 to 1920. Of the roughly 2 million Armenians living in Turkey, about 1.5 million were slaughtered. Based on many studies and eyewitness accounts, this event has been characterized as an attack of Muslim Turks on the Christian Armenians and it involved some of the most grotesque acts of violence seen in modern times.[4,5] Testimony presented in the U. S. Congress characterized it as perhaps the "most colossal crime of the ages."

And then on the morning of September 11, 2001, nineteen Muslim terrorists hijacked four jetliners in the United States and crashed the planes into the World Trade Center in New York City, the Pentagon in Washington, DC, and into a field in Pennsylvania. Nearly 3,000 people were murdered in this single act of Islamic violence. I was among the many people who began to wonder about this religion on that day. What kind of religious faith could prompt a group of men to kill so ruthlessly? Fathers, mothers, children were all indiscriminately killed during these attacks. This event further motivated me to learn about Islam and it moved me closer to writing this book.

I also remember reading newspaper stories of Muslim fathers who would murder their own daughters in "honor killings." These men objected to some manner of behavior of their daughters and they considered this to be worthy of death. In some cases, it was simply a matter of the clothes or hairstyle of the girls. Similarly, I read that some Palestinian mothers would celebrate when their sons were blown to pieces in suicide bombings. In their joy, they would even pass out candy to neighborhood children. I could not help but sympathize for these families. The God of the Bible is one that acts out of love, compassion, and charity. These parents seemed to be so deprived of love that they did not grieve in the deaths of their own children. Truly sad, I thought.

I began writing this book after a brief walk through the woods. Near my place of work, there is a thick forest and I walk through there on my way into work. On this particular morning, I was considering new writing projects. As I walked through the woods, I came to the recreation site near the edge of the woods. I sat on a concrete bench next to a fire pit – smoke rose from the burned up wood and ashes. I sat thinking about new writing projects and I considered all of my Bible studies from the years past. I had also taught adult Bible classes, I owned a very large library of theology books, and I enjoyed my relationship with the Lord. That was it, I would write a book on the Christian faith! With a little more thought, I decided to write a book to Muslims. I remembered my taxi driver. I thought about the parents who commit "honor killings." I even thought about those young men who committed the terrorist acts of September 11. These individuals all needed to know about the love of God – as demonstrated in the life of Jesus Christ. At that moment, the smoldering ashes in the pit caught fire. A flame rose from the blackened wood and grey ashes. As I watched the light of the flame, I smiled and thought of a statement from Jesus Himself (John 8:12):

> Then Jesus spoke to them again, saying, "I am the light of the world. He who follows Me shall not walk in darkness, but have the light of life."

References:

(1)   Sabit A. Alley, "A Brief Overview on: War and genocide in Sudan." As presented at *The 19th Annual Holocaust and genocide Program: Learning Through Experience*, Raritan Valley College, New Jersey, 2001. See also:
http://webarchieve.org/web/20051221045218/http:///www.iabolish.com/today.features/sudan/overview1.htm.

(2)   Raymond Ibrahim, *Crucified Again*, Regnery Publishing, Washington, D.C., 2013.

(3)   Serge Trifkovic, *Sword of the Prophet*, Regina Orthodox Press, Salisbury, MA, 2007.

(4)   John Kifner, "Armenian Genocide of 1915: An Overview," *The New York Times*. Retrieved 22 March 2014, see:
http://www.nytimes.com/ref/timestopics/topics_armeniangenocide.html

(5)   Ara Safarian (ed.), *The Treatment of Armenians in the Ottoman Empire, 1915–1916: Documents Presented to Viscount Grey of Falloden by Viscount Bryce, James Bryce and Arnold Toynbee, Uncensored Edition.* Gomidas Institute, Princeton, NJ, 2000.

Chapter 1

From Mecca to Calvary: start of the journey.

*Keep me, O LORD, from the hands of the wicked; preserve me
from violent men, who have purposed to make my steps stumble.*
Psalm 140:4

An Israeli helicopter took up position in the sky above the West Bank city of Ramalah. Its laser-guided missiles locked on to a distant car in which two men were sitting. One of the men was Mosab Hassan Yousef. In a moment, there would be a flash of light. The men in the car would hear a loud "clank" sound, an instant before the explosion rips into their bodies. The resulting fire would then take their lives and burn up their dead bodies. However, it never happened. The men took a fortunate turn down an alley and no missiles were fired. Mosab nearly lost his life on that day to an Israeli targeted killing.

Mosab's story is told in his best-selling biography entitled, *Son of Hamas*.[1] He was born in Ramallah, just 10 miles from Jerusalem. His grandfather was Sheikh Yousef Dawood, the imam in the town of Al-Janiya (also in the West Bank) and his father is Sheikh Hassan Yousef - an influential leader among Palestinian Arabs, a respected Muslim sheikh, and one of the founders of the Hamas terrorist group. Mosab was raised in the Muslim religion, and in fact, he can accurately be described as being born into "one of the most religious Islamic families in the Middle East".[1]

Because of his relationship to Hamas, Mosab's father spent a considerable amount of time in Israeli prisons. Despite these circumstances, his father was still concerned about raising his family to be good Muslims. When Mosab visited his father in prison, his father always asked him, "How is your relationship with Allah? Did you pray today? Cry? Spend time with Him?".[1]

Even as a youth, he fully expected to wage war against Israel. During the first Intifada, Mosab was arrested by Israeli forces for throwing rocks at Israeli settlers in the West Bank. He was just 10 years old at the time. He saw these battles as a righteous struggle between his people and the Israelis - who were occupying Arab land. As he grew older, his rage also grew. He arranged to purchase some weapons. This led to his arrest by Israeli forces and he was sent to prison.

During his sentence at the Migiddo prison, Mosab witnessed many acts of torture. These were not the Israelis torturing Arab prisoners, but rather these were Muslims torturing Muslims! He saw members of the Hamas security wing (*maj'd*) brutalizing other Muslim prisoners. The horrible brutality and torture was often carried out on perceived enemies and weak individuals in the prison. Observing this behavior had a profound impact on Mosab. Having heard the screams of men being tortured, he wondered, "Was this Hamas? Was this Islam?".[1]

His perspective did not improve much when he was not in prison. He was disgusted by the suicide bombings being carried out, especially those done against civilian targets including women and children. The violence seemed to be escalating to a sickening level. He was also aware of the thoroughly corrupt politics of the Palestinians, both in the Palestinian Liberation Organization (PLO) and in Hamas. Although his own father and grandfather had embraced the most noble elements of Islam - including care for people, love for family, and giving to charities – it was clear that these aspects of Islam were not so important to others who claimed to be Muslims.

Around this time, Mosab was in Jerusalem and he met a British man who was a Christian. This fellow invited Mosab to a Bible study where they read the Scriptures with about 50 other individuals. Someone gave him a copy of the New Testament written in English and Arabic. The message from Jesus Christ struck a cord within Mosab's heart, as he related, "I found that I was really drawn to the grace, love and humility that Jesus talked about".[2]

In particular, Mosab was "thunderstruck" by one message taught by Jesus Christ. The Bible describes the "Sermon on the Mount" given by Jesus about 2,000 years ago. Among the profound statements in the teaching session, Jesus told His listeners:

> "But I say to you, love your enemies, bless those who curse you,
> do good to those who hate you, and pray for those who spitefully
> use you and persecute you." Matthew 5:44

Mosab had never heard such a magnificent teaching, "love your enemies." He could immediately see the great wisdom in the messages from Jesus. As he considered the teachings, he was overwhelmed and he began to cry.

Mosab had hurled rocks at an Isreali Defensive Forces armored personnel carrier, he had dodged bullets shot at him from an Israeli settler, he himself had endured an Israeli interrogation, and he had spent time in the brutal Migiddo prison. He was a tough, strong man. Yet, the Bible and its message reached to his very heart. The truth of the Jesus Christ penetrated even the toughened exterior of this Palestinian from Ramallah. After reading the Bible and thinking about its message, Mosab prayed, "God, show me the truth...I'm confused. I'm lost. And I don't know which way to go".[1]

Eventually, God did show him the truth and Mosab believed. He describes the journey as a six-year process. Like many Christians, it is difficult for him to point to a day and time in which salvation occurred. He struggled with the concept of the deity of Christ, even though his new Christian friends showed him these teachings from the Holy Scriptures. These same friends prayed for Mosab every day – for his salvation and his safety.

One day, Mosab saw a program on television and this was a turning point. On the program was a Coptic priest named Zakaria Botros. This elderly gentleman was systematically analyzing the Quran and Islam. He pointed out the inconsistencies, the problems, the contradictions, and the errors. It was a thorough analysis of the Quran and Mosab's initial response was to "lash out and turn the television off." However, Mosab soon realized that God had answered his prayers: he was being guided into the truth. He considered the points being made by Father Botros. At that moment, he knew that Jesus Christ was "indeed the Son of God." He was baptized a short time later in the Mediterranean Sea. Since his conversion to Christianity, he has immigrated to the United States to begin a new life. His father was told of Mosab's conversion and he cried bitterly at the news. Within a short time however, Sheikh Hassan Yousef disowned his eldest son Mosab.

Mosab completed a most difficult journey: he made the trip from Mecca to Calvary. As every Muslim knows, Mecca is the spiritual center for the Islamic faith. It is the location where the prophet Muhammad established Islam during his lifetime (570-622 A.D.). 793 Miles northwest of Mecca, there is a prominent hill in the old section of Jerusalem. It is called Mount Calvary and it is the site upon which Jesus Christ was nailed to a Roman cross about 2,000 years ago. The crucifixion of Jesus Christ, with His resurrection from the dead three days later, is the basis for the Christian faith. Mount Calvary is considered to be the location where the gospel of Christ was established. Thus, a spiritual journey from Mecca to Calvary is a long, arduous trip for an individual, because it involves leaving the Muslim faith to embrace Christianity.

Despite the great difficulties in the journey from Mecca to Calvary, millions of Muslims make the trip each year.[3] They leave the religion of Islam and find enduring peace in the embrace of a waiting savior, Jesus Christ. Each individual may begin the trip for different reasons, but they all complete the journey for exactly the same reason. Some may want to leave Islam because of the brutal violence carried out by other fellow Muslims, while others leave because of the oppression of women in the Islamic faith. Still others leave for more subtle reasons, like a felling of emptiness or an awareness of sin and the impending judgment from God. Although there may be many factors that provoke a person to leave Islam, there is just one reason for the individual to convert to Christianity: the Christian faith is the truth. Moreover, it is the Christian faith that leads to the forgiveness of sin, a restoration of our relationship with God, and eternal life in Heaven. The trip from Mecca to Calvary must be made, because this journey determines the eternal destiny of a person's soul.

Once a person begins an earnest effort to journey from Mecca to Calvary, it becomes ever more apparent that the gospel of Jesus Christ is life-giving, pure, and true. Invariably, the difficult journey must involve exposure to God's message outlined in the Bible. Just as a physical journey between Mecca and Calvary would require road maps and other means of navigation, the spiritual journey likewise requires a complete set of directions and maps. These "travel directions" are given to us by God Himself and they are found in the pages of the Bible. Not only does the Bible describe why a person should become a Christian, but it also describes how one becomes a follower of Jesus Christ. The Bible is a complete set of instructions on traveling from Mecca to Calvary.

Like a Muslim beginning the trip from Mecca to Calvary, one of the original Apostles of Jesus Christ (2,000 years ago) asked the Him the question, "...how can we know the way?" The answer to this question is found in the Bible, as Jesus Christ replied to Thomas:

> Jesus said to him, "I am the way, the truth, and the life. No one
> comes to the Father except through Me." John 14:6

In this discussion with His disciples, Jesus notes that it is only through Him that a person can have access to God, who Jesus calls "the Father." The journey to Calvary involves a steady walk towards the Savior Jesus Christ, who loves you and who is waiting for you. Furthermore, the God of Heaven has promised to guide you in this journey, as there are many Bible references describing such spiritual journeys. Consider the following passages written by King David:

> For this is God, Our God forever and ever; He will be our guide
> even to death. Psalm 48:14

> You will guide me with Your counsel, and afterward receive me
> to glory (Psalm 73:24; in this passage "You" is referring to God).

Jesus once told His followers that there is joy in Heaven over "one sinner who repents" or changes their thinking (Luke 15:10). In a similar respect, there is joy and celebration in Heaven with every person that completes the journey from Mecca to Calvary. This joy and celebration has been repeated many times in Heaven, as millions of Muslims have looked toward Calvary and completed the difficult journey from Mecca. While these individuals have left Islam for Christianity, hundreds of millions of Muslims still remain followers of Islam. During one of his teaching sessions, Jesus Christ described why the journey is necessary. He points out that many people follow the way that "leads to destruction," which He describes as being similar to a wide road or "way." Fewer individuals are able to find the narrow road that "leads to life," as Jesus taught:

> For the gate is wide and the way is broad that leads to destruction,
> and there are many who enter through it.
>
> For the gate is small and the way is narrow that leads to life, and
> there are few who find it. (Matthew 7:13,14)

The narrow gate and narrow way is the path from Mecca to Calvary. It might be compared to a narrow trial along the side of a mountain, perhaps only a few feet in width. Most people decide against that path, because it appears to be difficult travel. Nevertheless, it is the only path that leads to eternal life in Jesus Christ.

How did the former Muslims find the "narrow path" that leads to life? They heard or read the life-giving messages from Jesus and His Apostles, as recorded in the Bible. Like Mosab Hassan Yousef, they saw the glory of God, demonstrated in the life of Christ and in His death, burial, and resurrection. They began to experience God's infinite love for men and women. These individuals understood and realized that the messages in the Bible are honest and true. These former Muslims saw that the Bible and its messages can withstand all investigation and examination. Its messages are framed in history, reason, and spiritual power.

Anyone can claim to speak for God and countless individuals have claimed to be prophets, Apostles, and even messiahs. However, Jesus Christ and the co-authors of the Bible provided overwhelming confirmation of their divine mission. In the case of Jesus Christ, His message was supported and confirmed by the miraculous works that Jesus accomplished before many thousands of witnesses. This included raising several people from the dead, healing all types of illnesses and disabilities, commanding violent storms to cease, and many other signs. The most important miraculous event was His physical resurrection from the dead, an event that distinguishes the Christian message from every other religion and philosophy - including Islam. These evidences for the Christian faith are described in detail in later chapters, and they can help motivate a person in their trip from Mecca to Calvary. These evidences support the reliability of the "travel directions" found in the Bible and they confirm the absolute truth of the Christian message.

According to the record in the Bible, Jesus Christ and His Apostles said many things regarding salvation for sinners. The entire theme of the Bible is consistent throughout: God calls out to sinners in need of a Savior. One of the most well known passages in the Bible reads:

> For God so loved the world that He gave His only begotten Son, that whoever believes in Him should not perish but have everlasting life. For God did not send His Son into the world to condemn the world, but that the world through Him might be saved. (John 3:16,17)

In this passage, the "Son" is a reference to Jesus Christ, as one of the common titles for Jesus Christ is the "Son of God." The Bible proclaims our need for salvation and it shows that Jesus Christ provides the means of our salvation. So how does one obtain salvation and the eternal blessings described in the Bible? This very question was asked of the Apostle Paul during his imprisonment in the ancient city of Philippi (Acts 16:30,31). As recorded in the Biblical book of Acts, Paul had been jailed for preaching the good news concerning Jesus Christ. During the night, the jailer in Philippi fearfully asked Paul, "What must I do to be saved?" Paul responded by telling him, "Believe in the Lord Jesus Christ and you will be saved."

According to the Bible, salvation from sin and condemnation is very simple: believe and be saved. We are told that Jesus Christ died for our sins. That is to say, Jesus took your sins and my sins (God placed it on Christ) and it was all punished in Him. It was His cross, but it was your sin that was punished. When Jesus Christ was raised from the dead three days later, this was a confirmation from God that the sin debt had been paid. The great sacrifice of the Savior has been accepted by God and now God offers salvation (free of charge!) to anyone who will accept the infinitely gracious gift. When a person believes this message, God has promised to save their soul from sin and He gives many eternal blessings to the individual. For the former Muslim, this represents completing the journey from Mecca to Calvary.

Unfortunately, the majority of Muslims will never undertake the trip from Mecca to Calvary. Some may look to the northwest and wonder about Calvary. They may briefly consider the claims of Jesus Christ and the messages that are contained in the Bible. But they have been told by their imams and Islamic scholars that the trip from Mecca to Calvary should never be considered. Rather than leading to eternal life in Jesus Christ, they claim that the journey will instead cause a person to lose all hope of reward in the afterlife. And if this threat is not enough to dissuade the Muslim from looking towards Calvary, they point to Quran itself.

They remind everyone of the message of the Quran: leaving Islam for Christianity is worthy of death.[4] This is not an idle threat. This threat has been carried out against many people who have made the trip from Mecca to Calvary. Sadly, the murders of these individuals are sometimes committed by members of their own families. With these warnings, threats, and intimidation, most Muslims then turn away from Calvary. They place their eternal destinies in the trust of their imam and reject the message of the Bible without question.

Since the Bible calls all men and women to Calvary, and the Quran calls all men and women to Mecca, the question becomes: which message and calling should be followed? Which is the reliable and truthful message from God? To which revelation (and book) should a person entrust their soul and eternal destiny? These questions make the assumption that both books cannot be the inerrant message from God. Since the two books have contradictory messages, only one book can be the truth. In the discipline of logic, this is related to the law of non-contradiction.

Of course, Islamic teachers claim that the Bible is corrupted from its original message originating in God. They boldly claim that the Bible is no longer an accurate message from Heaven. In the chapters of this book, it will be shown that this is a blatant lie. Several lines of evidence will demonstrate that the Bible has been well preserved and that it has the true qualities of Divine revelation. For the Muslim looking towards Calvary from Mecca, this book should help reassure the individual that the Bible is truthful and it is an accurate set of "travel directions" to get from Mecca to Calvary, a trip that will end in the forgiveness of sin and eternal life.

References

(1)   Mosab Hassan Yousef, *Son of Hamas*, SaltRiver, 2009.

(2)   Matthew Kaminski, "They Need to be Liberated from Their God." *Wall Street Journal*, 5 March, 2010. Retrieved 5 March 2010.

(3)   James M. Arlandson, "Six Million African Muslims Leave Islam per Year." Retrieved from othodoxytoday.org on 22 March 2014. See: http://www.orthodoxytoday.org/view/six-million-african-muslims-leave-islam-per-year

(4)   See, for example: Quran 4:89.

Chapter 2

From Mecca to Calvary: an introduction to the Bible.

Let all the earth fear the LORD; let all the inhabitants of the world stand in awe of Him. For He spoke, and it was done; He commanded, and it stood fast.
Psalm 33:8,9

Another man to journey from Mecca to Calvary was the Indonesian Muslim scholar, Hamran Ambrie.[1] He was very active in the Muslim community. As a young man, he taught regularly at the mosque, he was appointed to a leadership position in a regional Muslim Congress, he was a Muslim clergy member in the army of Indonesia (at Banjarmasin), and he published articles in Muslim periodicals. In his zeal for the Islamic faith, he also provided moral support for those who aggressively fought against Christians in Indonesia. By all accounts, Hamran was a well-grounded, hard working, and intelligent man of Islam.

A turning point in his life came during a study of the Quran. He was preparing a sermon for a teaching session at his mosque, when he came to the passage *Sura Al-Ma'ida* 5:68, which states:

> "Say, O people of the Book! You will be nothing unless you uphold the Torah and the Gospel, and all that is revealed to you from the Lord."

He had read this passage many, many times. But on this occasion, Hamran recognized something new: this passage refers to the Bible. Although he had owned a Bible for many years, he had never actually studied the Jewish and Christian Scriptures to see their messages. Hamran would later acknowledge that God Himself "whispered to my soul" and the Lord used this verse in the Quran to lead him into the Biblical Scriptures.

From his training in Islam, Hamram believed that the Bible was falsified and that its original contents were hopelessly lost. He also believed that the true messages of the Jewish and Christian prophets were summarized in the Quran. So how could he now be directed to examine the contents of the Bible? This was an epic struggle in his mind, so he turned to the Lord God in prayer. He appealed for guidance as he read the Bible. He asked God to shut the Bible if its messages were false. He earnestly desired for God to reveal only truth to him and to guide him away from error. Having made many prayers, Hamram opened his Bible to study its message.

According to his own written account of these events (or testimony),[1] Hamram did not consult with any teachers or scholars - Christian or Muslim. His search involved only the Muslim Scriptures, the Biblical Scriptures, and the guidance of the Almighty God. His first study of the Bible was in Deuteronomy 18. He was already very familiar with this passage because it was supposed to be a Biblical prophecy predicting the arrival of Muhammad. On this day, Hamram gave this passage considerable thought.

The key passage reads, "The LORD your God will raise up for you a Prophet like me from your midst, from your brethren. Him you shall hear (Deut. 18:15)." Hamram carefully analyzed this verse. His attention focused on the promise of a Prophet like Moses. Who was more like Moses - Jesus or Muhammad?

Hamram first noticed how both Moses and Jesus had their lives threatened as babies. Pharaoh tried to kill all of the baby boys among the Jews (including Moses), while King Herod specifically tried to kill baby Jesus who was born "King of the Jews." He then noticed that both Moses and Jesus were given the power to conduct miracles in support of their Divine messages and revelation. Further study showed how Moses and Jesus both led people to out of slavery and into freedom. Moses had brought Israel out of Egyptian slavery, while Jesus is said to have freed people from slavery to sin. These observations made Hamram conclude that the passage in Deuteronomy 18 was describing Jesus and not Muhammad!

Despite seeing this truth, Hamram could not accept other doctrines commonly taught by Christians. He thought about the Islamic teachings that "there is no God but Allah" and "those who say Allah is the third of the three are heathen." These doctrines certainly argued against the Biblical messages of Jesus being the Son of God and the idea of a Divine Trinity. Regarding the accounts of Jesus' death, he remarked,

> "If Jesus, or "Isa al-Masih" was a prophet, the loving, faithful messenger of God, or the "Son of God" as the Christians called him, how could the Jews easily torture and hang him on the cross until he died? Why did God not defend him, but let him die on the cross? Suppose I saw my own son tortured, or even hanging on a cross, I would surely fight those people who tortured him in order to save him, whatever the consequences. How could Allah lose his authority over the Jews?"[1]

With these lingering issues, Hamram decided to investigate why Jesus is said to have died. He also sought to determine why the Jews wanted to kill Jesus. Other questions arose regarding Jesus and the purpose of His ministry. He continued to pray for guidance into God's truth.

In his studies of the death of Jesus, Hamram noticed that the Bible contained four eyewitness accounts of the death, burial, and resurrection of Jesus. These records were put down in the New Testament gospel books of Matthew, Mark, Luke, and John. While one or two good eyewitness testimonies are usually considered reliable in legal affairs, here the Bible has four witnesses. They all state that Jesus was crucified, buried, and rose from the dead three days later. When Hamram examined the messages in Quran describing Jesus, he concluded it to be an "unconvincing supposition, because the writer did not witness it" (the Quran was written about 600 years after the crucifixion).

He further analyzed the crucifixion. Traditional Muslim teachings suggest that Judas or someone else was crucified in place of Jesus Christ. There were several reasons why this appeared to make no sense. Hamram noted that following the death of Jesus on the cross, Joseph of Arimathea asked the Roman ruler, Pilate, for the body of Jesus. Joseph of Arimathea was a wealthy man and he had built a new tomb, so he desired to place the body of Jesus in the tomb. Certainly, Joseph would have no interest in placing the body of Judas or some other criminal in his new tomb! He would have rejected the imposter. Likewise, the Jews asked Pilate to guard the tomb after Jesus was buried. Had the wrong person been crucified, the Jews would not need to make such a request. With further thought, Hamram concluded that Jesus Christ was in fact crucified according to the description in the Bible.

Why was just Jesus crucified? Many passages of the Bible answered this question from Hamram. In the gospel book of John, Jesus is quoted and explained two important elements of the crucifixion:

> "I am the good shepherd; and I know My sheep, and am known by My own. As the Father knows Me, even so I know the Father; and I lay down My life for the sheep...No one takes it from Me, but I lay it down of Myself. I have power to lay it down, and I have power to take it again. This command I have received from My Father." John 10:14-15,18

This passage showed that Jesus knew of His upcoming death and that He allowed Himself to be slain for the sake or benefit of His "sheep." In the Bible, the term sheep often refers to those people who follow God's message (see, Psalm 23). Other specific statements regarding the death Christ are found in both the Old Testament (Isaiah 53) and New Testament. For example, the Apostle Paul wrote,

"Christ died for our sins according to the Scriptures (1 Chorinthians 15:3)." This is why Jesus was crucified.

He also wrestled with the idea of the Trinity. Hamram considered the passage, *Sura Al-Ma'ida* 5:73 which states, "Truly these are the unbelievers who say that God is the third of the three." Then he wondered about the Bible teaching of God being Father, Son, and Holy Spirit. He clearly saw that Christians rejected pantheism (belief in many gods), but he also thought that they believed in three gods. During this time, he visited some Christian churches. He knew that pantheistic religions often require the worship of idols and images. He saw that there was no such worship being carried out in the churches. He further studied the Bible, prayed, and attended a Christian church. For a period of time, Hamram would carryout his duties at the mosque on Fridays, but then attend the Christian church on Sunday.

With further study, Hamram saw that the Bible teaches monotheism (i.e., one God) with a God having three parts or personalities. This idea is similar to an egg. It is a single egg, but it has a shell, a yoke, and the egg white. He concluded, "the oneness of the Trinity of God in Christianity does not violate the doctrine of *Tauhid*, and it does not mean a unity of several Allahs or gods." Bible passages echoed this concept, such as John 14:8-9, where one of Jesus' disciples asks Him to show them God the Father:

> Philip said to Him, "Lord, show us the Father, and it is sufficient for us." Jesus said to him, "Have I been with you so long, and yet you have not known Me, Philip? He who has seen Me has seen the Father; so how can you say, 'Show us the Father'?

In passages like this, Jesus clearly teaches that He is co-equal with the Father. Other passages (John 17:11) quote Jesus that He and God the Father are one. God's call to Hamram seemed to be growing louder, as he became more aware of the truth in the Bible and he became accepting of the truth.

Following his extensive survey, Hamram was ready to accept Jesus Christ as his Lord and Savior. However, there was initially a hesitation. He was convinced regarding the merits of Christianity and Bible truth, but he thought about his conversion. He loved his wife very much and he wondered if she would leave him. In his own words, he was "haunted by fear and anxiety." Nevertheless, Hamram accepted the offer of salvation from sin. Jesus gladly saved this Muslim man and gave him eternal life. For sometime, Hamram kept his new faith a secret. No one in his family, not even his wife, knew that he had been given new life in Christ. One day his fears came to an end, as his wife said that she wanted to become a

Christian! Soon after, Hamram, his wife, and his eight children became Christians. Remarkably, his son was also secretly attending a Christian church, but he did not wish to tell his father - the Muslim leader who was about to become a Christian himself! Together, the entire family completed the trip from Mecca to Calvary.

Hamram described the impact of Christianity of his family. Their family had so much joy that their neighbors thought that they might be getting wealthy. In a sense, they had become wealthy, but not in rupiahs (Indonesian currency). They had been blessed with the priceless wealth of God's love and kindness in Christ. Because he was a leading Muslim figure, Hamram's conversion to Christianity was big news. The news and commentary regarding his conversion appeared in regional newspapers and magazines in Indonesia during the early 1970s. Commentary from the Muslim community was in the form of attacks, often accusing Hamram of leaving Islam for Christianity for some kind of financial gain. Despite these slanderous attacks, Hamram stood up for his faith and he declared that his conversion was the result of the "guidance of God." He continued to grow in faith and minister to the people of Indonesia and other parts of the world.

Hamram's journey from Mecca to Calvary began with his Quran and Bible open before him. As an initial step in the journey from Mecca to Calvary, it is important to see that the Bible is a reliable and trustworthy record of God's revelation to mankind. If we are to entrust our eternal destiny to a book and its message, then we must thoroughly examine its credentials. In the next five chapters, we will examine the credibility of its message and the preservation of the Bible. This will involve studies of:

1. The Crucifixion (chapter 3)
2. The Resurrection (chapter 4)
3. The New Testament (chapter 5)
4. The Old Testament (chapter 6)
5. The Jewish Temple (chapter 7)

Following these studies, we will examine the evidence for the spiritual truth of God's messages found in the Bible. This will involve studies of:

1. Prophecy (chapter 8)
2. Progressive Revelation (chapters 9, 10)
3. Miracles and Testimonies (chapter 11)

The Bible

Since readers of this book may be unfamiliar with the Bible itself, it may be useful to provide a brief description of the book. The Bible is divided into two basic parts, the Old and New Testament. The Old Testament was written by the ancient Jewish prophets between the years of about 1450 B.C. and 450 B.C. and it is a collection of books written by more than 30 different men. These authors include men such as, Moses, Isaiah, and David. The purpose of the Old Testament was to prepare the way for the Savior Jesus Christ. The Old Testament itself can be further divided into sections, such as historical and prophetical books.

The prophetical books contain many predictions or prophecies of future events, including the arrival of Jesus Christ. Indeed, this is one of the strongest pieces of evidence to demonstrate that the Bible is the true revelation from God. As the Old and New Testaments were being written in ages past, the Lord spoke through these men. This idea is summarized in Peter's second New Testament book (2 Peter 1:21): "For prophecy never had its origin in the will of man, but men spoke from God as they were carried along by the Holy Spirit." Although this passage in Peter's letter is referring to the entire Bible, it is especially true for the prophecies.

In the book of Isaiah, chapter 46, we read that the God of the Bible has told the "end from the beginning." These prophecies distinguish the Bible from all other religious books. The God of the Bible makes a challenge to other religions and false gods: only He can see into the distant future, so who compares to Him? No other religious book contains anything similar to the hundreds, and even thousands, of prophecies in the Bible. These prophecies predict, hundreds of years in advance, the events that are to come to pass. They are often very specific. For example, the Jewish prophet Micah wrote in the Old Testament that the Messiah or Savior would be born in Bethlehem.

> "But you, Bethlehem Ephrathah, though you are small among the clans of Judah, out of you will come for me one who will be ruler over Israel, whose origins are from of old, from ancient times."
> Micah 5:2

This was written about 800 years prior to the birth of Jesus Christ. Centuries after Micah's prophecy, it came to pass. Jesus Christ was born in Bethlehem. In fact, the Old Testament contains several hundred prophecies concerning various aspects of the life, death, and eternal reign of the Savior Jesus Christ. A more thorough description of the Biblical prophecies is given in Chapter 8.

The New Testament was written shortly after the arrival of Jesus. It contains 27 books written by eight different men between the years 50-95 A.D. (Figure 1).

Figure 1. Dates of authorship for the Old and New Testaments.

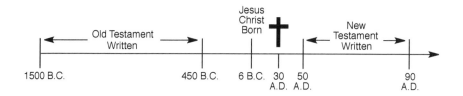

Like the Old Testament, the New Testament consists of several different sections. The four gospel accounts (Matthew, Mark, Luke, and John) contain eyewitness accounts of the events related to the lifetime of Jesus Christ, as well as His death, burial and resurrection.

The book of Acts is also a historical type of book. It describes the beginning of the Christian age and the setting aside of Israel. Other parts of the New Testament describe spiritual truth and future events (prophetical material). It is important to realize that the New Testament accounts of Jesus Christ contain multiple records of eyewitnesses to these events. The New Testament accounts are written by <u>men who were with Jesus Christ or contemporaries with Him</u>. As noted by Hamram, this gives their writings credibility that the Quran does not possess.

Among the striking observations from the study of Christian Scriptures, one immediately notes that the Bible contains no Islamic religious doctrines. How can this be explained? Islamic scholars have suggested that the Bible was systematically corrupted or changed around 100-300 A.D., and indeed, this was Hamram's belief prior to his journey from Mecca to Calvary. Ancient Bible manuscripts argue against this suggestion (see chapters 4-5), but nevertheless it is worthwhile to consider this possibility.

First of all, who could have done this? Who would have been able to corrupt the Scripture? Why is there no evidence in the Bible for "Islamic revelations" from Moses, Jesus, or any of the other prophets? The canon of Scripture (books of the Bible) was completed around or before 90 A.D. Old and New Testament books came from several different locations - Jerusalem, Rome, and other places. Because of intense persecution from the Romans and Jews, the early Christians did not have a large organized structure, but were dispersed into small enclaves and groups. If there were "Islamic Bibles" or "Islamic revelations" in ancient times, none of the Christians could have organized the massive revision of Scripture that has been suggested by the Muslim clerics. This would have involved retrieving thousands of Bible books or chapters from libraries, synagogues, and personal collections, all separated by hundreds of miles. If there were "Islamic revelations" or "Islamic Bibles" at some point history, it would have been impossible to blot out all of the references to Allah, and then to insert the name "God of Abraham, Isaac, and Jacob." It would have been impossible to revise the copies of Scripture to remove references to Islam and Muslims.

In a similar respect, the Jews could not have organized such a huge revision of Scripture. Their nation was destroyed by the Romans in 70 A.D., and its population was dispersed throughout the known world. Around the Roman Empire, the individual Jewish synagogues had neither the ability to change all the copies of Scripture, nor would they have desired to do so! The ancient Jews had a great reverence for the messages from the prophets of God, so they would not have even attempted to corrupt Scripture on such a large scale. The Jewish scribes would wash their hands before even writing the name of God and they had careful routines to count letters and words on copied pages – all to preserve the written message of Scripture. If a copied page had even one error, the scribes would usually toss it into a fire. Even if the Jews or Christians had revised copies of Scripture to make them "non-Islamic," it would have been impossible to accomplish this task. There would always be some copies of "unrevised" versions and this would create competing accounts and versions of Scripture. As such, we would have some old copies of Scripture (or fragments) with references to Allah and Muslims. There are, however, no such references even in the oldest copies of Scripture!

With these considerations, it seems unlikely that the Bible could have been corrupted or systematical changed during the time period from 100 A.D. to 300 A.D. From this time period onward, there exist many hundreds of copies and fragments of the Bible and none contain Islamic theology or ideas. This means that Moses, Jesus, Isaiah, and the other Biblical prophets, said nothing about Islam. It also means that Muhammad alone spoke the message of Islam, and moreover, this message contradicted the revelations taught for 1,500 years through the pages of Jewish and Christian Scriptures!

Evaluating the Bible

For the sake of argument, let's ignore the fact that no group could have changed all of the Bibles. Is there any means by which we can determine if the Bible has been corrupted through the ages? The answer is - yes. This involves a search through the most ancient Biblical manuscripts to see if there is evidence for corruption and decay of the original messages from God. Moreover since the Bible contains many references to historical events, these can be used as internal checks for corruption in the Old and New Testament text. In this regard, we can examine if the historical records of the Bible are confirmed by archaeology and non-Biblical historical texts, or if the historical records of the Bible are shown to be in error. This is a useful test for the honest and objective individual. A Bible with gross error and corruption - as Muslims claim - should not contain accurate historical records, but a Bible with accurate historical references is not likely to have been corrupted through the ages.

Our analysis of the integrity of the Bible will begin by considering how a fair evaluation can be done. Bible scholars and Biblical historians have used many approaches to conduct this study. The most important pieces of evidence come from ancient artifacts and written texts that date to the time of Biblical events. By digging deep enough (and in the proper locations), archaeologists have been able to retrieve many objects that date to the times of Biblical events and writing (between about 1400 B.C. and 100 A.D.). The following items have been particularly important in the evaluation of the Bible and its text:

Ancient copies of the Bible and Biblical text. There have been many old manuscripts and manuscript fragments that have been discovered through the past several centuries. Perhaps the most notable examples are the Dead Sea Scrolls, copies of the Biblical Old Testament books that date to about 300 B.C. to 100 A.D. Older examples of recovered Bible text date back to 600 B.C., while many hundreds of complete, intact Biblical manuscripts predate the lifetime Muhammad (ca. 670 A.D.). These ancient copies of Scripture may be compared to our modern-day Bibles to examine for errors and corruption of the text.

Clay tablets and ancient inscriptions. Many of the ancient nations and regional powers kept records with inscriptions on pieces of clay, often called tablets. Some of the tablets recorded important historical events, such as wars or the reign of a particular king. The inscriptions on tablets also recorded religious events, agricultural affairs, and economic and business records. Most of the important political powers during Biblical times kept official records, or chronicles, on clay tablets. Over the past two centuries, thousands of these clay tablets have been discovered by archaeologists (dating even before the time of Abraham). Once the tablet inscriptions are translated, their messages or information can be compared with Biblical events. This can be used to examine the accuracy of historical records in the Bible.

Monuments and Stelae. It was the custom in ancient times to inscribe large stone and clay monuments to commemorate events and people. This was often done to provide a permanent written memory of these things. Archaeologists recovered several important stelae, often from Israel's ancient enemies. The Taylor Prism is a typical example of this type of artifact. Recovered from ancient Assyria, it is an inscribed clay pillar measuring about 15 inches in height. It describes the wars of

Assyria against the ancient Jewish cities in about 700 B.C. The inscriptions on the stelae can be compared with records in the Bibles, and since they are non-Biblical historical records, they represent powerful and independent evaluations of the Biblical record. It is important to note that some stelae were inscribed in multiple languages (i.e. Greek and Egyptian hieroglyphics), so scholars are able to accurately read and translate the inscriptions.

Bas Relief Carvings and Tomb Paintings. If a ruler wished to commemorate an event on a larger scale than with a stele, then a bas relief carving was often done. These bas reliefs are images carved directly into stone slabs, or in some cases onto the side of stone mountains (i.e., the image of Darius the Great, carved into the mountain in Behistun, Iran). Besides images on the carvings, the bas reliefs can also have inscriptions that describe the events. A similar type of ancient artwork was commonly done in Egyptian burial chambers or tombs. The Egyptians painted (historical) images on the walls of their tombs. Both types of images, bas relief and tomb paintings, can be used to check Biblical historical records.

Ostracon or Potshards. In Biblical times, it was common to use broken pieces of pottery as a surface on which notes were written. The osctraca were a form of "scratch paper" in ancient times, because paper or papyrus was relatively rare. Archaeologists have recovered many of these artifacts from the ruins of Biblical cities and they can often be accurately dated by the type of pottery fragment. The writing on the ostraca can be translated and compared with historical elements described in the Bible.

Papyrus Fragments and Manuscripts. Prior to the development of paper, ancient documents were often written on papyrus, a paper-like material derived from the papyrus plant. While papyrus documents had a short lifetime in damp, rain-soaked locations, they are almost indefinitely stable in desert-like locations (i.e., around Egypt or the Dead Sea). There have been many discoveries of papyrus documents that date to Bible time periods, some of which contain portions of Biblical text. Other papyri contain records of various events and business activities. The papyrus documents may be accurately dated using carbon dating techniques (^{14}C radioactive decay). The documents are useful for evaluating many aspects of the Bible, including language usage, customs and culture, and even the integrity or preservation of the Biblical text.

Inscriptions. Archaeologists have discovered many important inscriptions from Bible time periods. Inscriptions were generally carved or chiseled into a stone surface or clay object. They were often used in the dedication of buildings, on monuments, and to show ownership of objects. For example, King Herod was the King of Israel when Jesus was born. Archaeologists have found Herod's Dead Sea fortress and the pottery at this location is inscribed with King Herod's name.[2,3] Inscriptions can be used to place an individual at a particular place and time. This information can also be used to evaluate the accuracy of Biblical records of history and geography.

Coins. Historians believe that the coinage of precious metals began around 700 B.C.[4] Since the names and images of kings were often pressed into the ancient coins, they have been useful for comparing Biblical dates and other historical information.

Other Historical Books. The historical records contained in the Bible are also compared with other ancient historical documents. The Greeks and Romans produced several important historical accounts, some of which describe Bible-era events. Likewise, the Jews produced several non-Biblical ancient historical records. This includes the writings of Josephus (ca. 100 A.D.) and the completion of the *Mishnah* (ca. 200 A.D. and 500 A.D., Parts 1 and 2).

Miscellaneous Archaeological Findings. Many other types of archaeological findings can be used to measure the accuracy of the Biblical text. This can range from small clay buttons to entire civilizations that have been lost to history. The Hittites are one example of a lost civilization. Their cities and artifacts had been buried and forgotten for thousands of years. Of this civilization, the only surviving record was a few passages in the Old Testament of the Bible. Archaeologists eventually caught up with the Bible and this once great civilization was rediscovered, buried in the sands of modern day Turkey.[5]

Even a small clay button can be a significant archaeological discovery. Clay buttons, or bullae, were used by ancient scribes to seal scrolls and parchments. They often had the name of the scribe pressed into the clay. In several instances, archaeologists have discovered bullae from scribes mentioned in the Bible.[6] The location of the bullae can then be compared with historical records in the Bible (i.e., did this scribe work in Jerusalem during a particular time period?). Other times, archaeologists can determine the date that an ancient city was destroyed. The date of destruction can be compared with the dates given in the Bible. Sometimes even the method of destruction is apparent, such as when the city is burned to the ground. These types of details can also be compared with the Bible text.

It is often said that the stories in the Bible are rooted in history. This can be contrasted with the Hindu faith, where thousands of "deities" are said to exist. Their mythological stories are not connected to real cities, time periods, and historical figures or people. In the case of the Bible, there are historical figures and time periods described. The historical aspect of the Bible allows us to evaluate its accuracy and preservation. For example, all four New Testament gospel books (Matthew, Mark, Luke, and John) describe how Jesus Christ was judged and condemned to death by a Roman ruler named Pontius Pilate. Several non-Biblical sources have confirmed that this ruler governed during the lifetime of Jesus Christ in the region of Judea (Israel):

1. The name and title of Pilate has been found inscribed on the ruins of a building in Cesearea (a first century city in Israel).[7]
2. The Roman historian Tacitus wrote around 100 A.D. and he confirms the Biblical account. In his work titled *Annals*, he wrote a section describing the Roman persecution of Christians under Nero, and regarding Jesus Christ, it specifically states, "was executed at the hands of procurator Pontius Pilate in the reign of Tiberius."[8]
3. Philo of Alexandria (a Jewish philosopher) wrote about the rule of Pilate.[9]
4. The Jewish historian Josephus wrote around 100 A.D. and he described Pilate's brutal rule in Judea.[10]

This type of agreement from ancient historical sources is extremely rare and it argues for the accuracy of the historical Bible account.

Why is it important to verify the historical references in the Bible? First of all, it is strong evidence against the Muslim claim of a corruption of Biblical text. If the Bible had been corrupted through the ages, then archaeological discoveries would not confirm the details found in the Bible. For example, a corrupted Bible might have Pilate's name spelled incorrectly, or even worse, it might have an entirely incorrect ruler named for the lifetime of Jesus Christ. If ancient Jewish scribes or Christian monks altered the text of God's revelation in the Bible, then historical references would have been altered, too. However, there is no evidence for this type of large-scale corruption or modification of the Biblical text! As described in the next several chapters, Biblical historical references are overwhelmingly accurate. This fact is seen in the comments of leading scholars and archaeologists over the years:

Joseph Free once declared, "I do not know of any cases where the Bible has been proved wrong."[11]

Regarding the Old Testament, Green commented, "It may safely be concluded that no other work of antiquity has been so accurately transmitted."[12]

Truthful Theology

What about the spiritual messages in the Bible? Is there evidence for corruption of the written messages from the prophets and from Jesus Christ Himself? To the follower of Islam, accurate and truthful theology is far more important than knowing that the Bible correctly records historical information (i.e., the name of a Roman ruler). Upon examination, our modern day Bible is found to have no references to the deity named Allah, it has no references to Islam or Muslims, and it says nothing regarding the arrival of a future prophet out of the Quraysh tribe near Mecca. Neither does the Bible contain messages describing the "Five Doctrines of Islam" or "The Five Pillars of Islam." The Bible contains vastly differing messages than the Quran and hadith. Does this mean that the spiritual messages and theology of the Bible are corrupted from their original writings? What evidence supports the Bible's claim to be a true source of God's message to mankind?

As noted above, prophecy is one of the seals of authenticity found in the Bible. Prophecy will be thoroughly examined in chapter 8. Fulfilled prophecy could only have occurred through the vision and revelation of the eternal God. By themselves, men cannot predict events centuries in advance. Moreover, a corrupted Bible would not have accurate prophecies! If the Jews or Christians had altered Scripture in the past, then they would have also changed prophecies. Instead, we find that the predictions of future events have been amazingly accurate. Still further confirmation of the message is found in the miracles demonstrated by Jewish prophets, Jesus Christ, and the early Christian prophets or Apostles. As described later, these supernatural events confirm the spiritual truth of the Bible.

Finally, we will examine how the Bible was carefully produced through a 1,500 year period - a process in which God used around 40 different prophets. This process has often been called progressive revelation. It will be examined in later chapters and this represents further evidence that the Bible's spiritual message is accurate, complete, and truthful. Progressive revelation is perhaps similar the Arabic concept of *wahy*, but in contrast to the Quranic revelations, the Old and New Testament revelations fit perfectly with one another. Taken together, these considerations provide convincing evidence for the skeptical Muslim reader – evidence for the absolute truth of the Biblical message.

References

(1)   Hamran Ambrie, *God Has Chosen Me For Eternal Life*, The Good Way Publishing, 2010.   Available for download at: http://the-good-way.com/.

(2)   Duane W. Roller, *The Building Program of Herod the Great*, University of California Press, Berkeley and Los Angeles, 1998.

(3)   Hilary Appelman, "Archaeologists Unearth Wine Jug Used by King Herod," *Associated Press,* 8 July 1996. Available for download at: http://www.apnewsarchive.com

(4)   G. Davies, *A History of Money: From Ancient Times to the Present Day*, University of Wales Press, Cardiff, 1994.

(5)   O. R. Gurney, *The Hittites*. Penguin Books, Baltimore, Md., 1966

(6)   Robert Deutsch, *Biblical Period Hebrew Bullae. The Josef Chaim Kaufman Collection*, Archaeological Center Publications, Tel Aviv, 2003.

(7)   Jerry Vardaman, "A New Inscription Which Mentions Pilate as 'Prefect'," *Journal of Biblical Literature*, Vol. 81, 1962. pp 70–71. This artifact – the "Pilate Stone" - may be viewed at the Israel Museum in Jerusalem.

(8)   Donald R. Dudley, *The Annals of Tacitus*, Mentor Book, NY, NY, 1966.

(9)   Philo, *On The Embassy of Gauis*, Book XXXVIII 299–305.

(10)   Flavius Josephus, *Jewish Antiquities*, 18.3.1, 18.4.1,2.   See also, William Whiston, *The Works of Josephus,* Hendrickson Publisher, Peabody, MA, 1987.

(11)   Joseph P. Free, *Archaeology and Bible History*, Zondervan Publishing House, Grand Rapids, MI, 1992; p. 114.

(12)   William H. Green, *General Introduction to the Old Testament*, Scribner's Sons, New York, NY, 1899; P. 81.

Chapter 3

The Crucifixion of Jesus Christ

...understand what the will of the Lord is. Ephesian 5:17

Ester was born to Pakistani parents in the Untied States.[1] She was raised Muslim, and even at a young age, she had an enthusiasm for the Islamic faith and the Quran. In grade school, she was often the only Muslim in her classes. She remembers arguing with another third grader (8 year old) about the truth of Islam over Christianity. However as she grew older, she was troubled by the awareness of her own sins and the judgment of God. From the Quran, she had learned about the torments of Hell. Islam provided her no assurance that she would be forever in paradise and avoid the condemnation of Hell. This was very depressing to young Ester, but she kept studying, fasting, and praying.

In her teenage years, she read *Surah* 4:34, which commanded husbands to beat their wives if they were disobedient. Shocked by this passage, she sought the advice of her father, but he could not explain the passage. Even as a 14 year-old girl, Ester recognized the problems with this teaching. Indeed, this is called domestic assault in western countries and men have gone to jail for this crime.

When she began her college studies, Ester found Muslim friends and enrolled in a college class dealing with the history and theology of Islam. She enjoyed studying the Quran and hadith - "all familiar territory" in her words. As the college course progressed however, Ester became deeply bothered by the wars and conquests of early Islam. These were offensive wars waged by Muslim armies. She was alarmed by the treatment of Jews and Christians who would not convert to Islam. Having believed Islam to be a religion of peace, she was particularly bothered by the slaughter of Qurayza Jews.

Ester was further troubled as she read Muhammad ibn Ismail al-Bukhari's hadith collection, *Sahih al-Bukhari*. She was again bothered by the status and treatment of women. This included the description of the "deficiency of a women's mind" (*Sahih al- Bukhari*, Volume 3, Book 48, Number 826) and plain statements about Hell being filled mostly by women! The prophet Muhammad is quoted as saying,

> "... I also saw the Hell-fire and I had never seen such a horrible sight. I saw that most of the inhabitants were women." (*Sahih al-Bukhari*, Volume 2, Book 18, Number 161)

It also became difficult to understand the Quran's allowance for men to have up to four wives, but then Muhammad himself had at least 10 wives simultaneously and other "concubines" or sex slaves. This list included Aesha (an 8 or 9 year old girl) and Zaynab of Jahsh who was Muhammad's daughter in law (through his adoptive son Zaid).

Ester was reduced to tears by these teachings from the hadith. They described Muhammad much differently than the image she had been taught – the great prophet dressed in white. She knew that God existed, but she also had a feeling that God was not revealed in Muhammad. How could God be revealed by the actions of this man?

She began a search for the truth. Being on a college campus in the United States, almost every religion could be found. After some time, a friend gave her a Bible to look over. She was initially confused by the messages in Genesis and the Old Testament books, but a friend suggested that she read the New Testament books of the Bible. Together they read the book of Matthew (a historical account of Jesus Christ) and a great sense of peace came over her. As she recalls,[1]

> "We read aloud the first twelve chapters of Matthew. I felt enormously secure, as if God Himself was in the room with me, holding me. The words of Christ filled my dry and parched soul like refreshing water. The way that He spoke was with such authority!"

Shortly after this reading of the Bible, one of Ester's friends reminded her that, "He died for you." Ester had never heard that Jesus Christ had given His life to save her from her sins. But that day she heard it for the first time and it touched her heart. She remembered that it "filled me with a love I had never known." Ester realized that God truly loved her and He showed this love by sending His only Son, Jesus Christ.

Ester's search for the truth came to a point that many people have experienced (including this author). She prayed to the Lord for guidance and help in determining the truth. This is a prayer that God is eager to answer and it was answered for Ester. Several days after praying for guidance, she received a letter from an old friend. It described how this friend had become a Christian. The letter continued and stated,[1] "All I know is that I must tell you to believe in the Lord Jesus Christ and you will be saved!"

Ester completed the journey from Mecca to Calvary and she became a Christian. She has now been a Christian for more than 20 years. Looking back she now realizes - that even as a devoted Muslim - she was not on her way to Heaven or

Paradise. She understands that no one can enter Heaven and stand before the Holy and Almighty God in their sins. Only through the blood of Christ can someone be truly cleansed from their sins. Ester brought her sins to the cross of Calvary. They were judged and punished on that cross - when Jesus Christ was crucified.

The next two chapters consider the most important events in the entire Bible: the crucifixion and resurrection of Jesus Christ. We will examine the evidence for these two historical events. Before beginning the analysis, it may be helpful to consider why these two events are so important. First of all, the Bible proclaims that the death of Jesus Christ is the basis for our salvation from sin and condemnation. We read that Jesus "…died for our sins." The message of the Bible clearly teaches that our sin will be judged and punished by God, either on the cross of Calvary or in the fires of Hell. With such great spiritual importance in the crucifixion, it is necessary to examine the evidence for its historical truth (as recorded in the Bible). This examination is also essential because the Quran directly contradicts the Biblical record, as the Quran states that Jesus was not crucified.

The resurrection of Jesus Christ is also a critically important message in the Bible. As the Christian Apostle Paul stated, the Christian faith is meaningless if Jesus Christ did not rise from the dead. However if it is true, the resurrection of Jesus Christ from the dead sets Christianity apart *and above* every other religious faith. All other religions were established or created by men who eventually died and their mortal remains returned to the Earth. Their bones remain buried to this day. However, the Bible teaches that the resurrection is evidence for the truth of the gospel or good news of Jesus Christ. The God of Heaven used the resurrection to show us that Jesus Christ is the Son of God and Savior of mankind.

Crucifixion of Jesus Christ

The Muslim apologist Ahmed Deedat (died in 2005) was fond of using the term "cruci-fiction" when commenting on the death of Christ.[2] Like most Muslim scholars, Deedat openly denied the historical truth of the crucifixion and resurrection. Their claim is based on descriptions in the hadith and one or two passages from the Quran, most notably *Sura Nisaa* 4:157-158. From an English translation, part of this passage reads:

> But they killed him not, nor crucified him, but it was made to
> appear to them so,

Based on this text, the entire New Testament account of the crucifixion of Jesus is said to be unreliable. Archaeological evidence supports the historical

24

accuracy of the New Testament (see chapter 5), yet despite this fact, men like Deedat dismiss the Biblical accounts of the crucifixion and resurrection of Jesus Christ. Is this reasonable? The Bible has four written accounts of these events in the gospel books of Matthew, Mark, Luke, and John. The events are also described by eyewitness accounts recorded in the book of Acts. Some of these written records are from individuals who were at the trials of Jesus, present at His crucifixion, visited the empty tomb, and even met the resurrected Christ. Thus, the Bible contains eyewitness accounts by several men who were at these events, and it is essentially discarded based on one or two verses in Quran, passages which were written more than 600 years after the crucifixion! As described in this chapter, an honest and reasonable person will recognize the truth in the Bible's account of the crucifixion and resurrection. For Muslim clerics to argue that it did not occur, it requires an almost delusional attitude towards the study of history, the examination of evidence, and the use of sound reasoning.

Most Islamic schools teach that someone other than Jesus Christ was nailed to cross or that He never really died on the cross.[3] When the facts are actually examined however, these theories are shown to be complete nonsense. The crucifixion of Jesus Christ is perhaps the most well documented event of ancient history. In the following section, we will review four lines of evidences arguing for the crucifixion of Jesus Christ as described in the Bible. It should again be noted that the text of the New Testament - especially the gospel accounts - are known to be very accurate in its descriptions of historical people, places, customs, and other things. Therefore, this same level of accuracy should also be expected in the descriptions of Jesus Christ and His death, burial, and resurrection.

Prophecies of the crucifixion

In the Old Testament, the Jewish prophets and writers spoke of a coming Messiah or Savior. These prophets were conveying a message from God Himself, and as such, they were able to look into the distant future. In the centuries after they wrote, they predicted the arrival of a Savior, one who would suffer horribly for the people. This line of prophecy can be followed throughout the Old Testament and they are described as the "suffering servant" group of prophecies.

It is in our age and time that we are able to see the true meaning of these ancient prophecies or predictions: they were describing the crucifixion of the Messiah or Savior (which occurred in about 30 A.D.). When Jesus Christ spoke to the Jewish leaders of His day regarding the Old Testament books, He said, "You search the Scriptures, for in them you think you have eternal life; and these are they which testify of Me (John 5:39)." As part of the Old Testament, one finds several references to the Savior being slain or killed. These passages of Scripture were testifying about Jesus Christ. They are the first line of evidence for the crucifixion of Jesus Christ.

The Old Testament prophecies described the crucifixion of Jesus Christ hundreds of years before His birth. For example, the 22nd Psalm was written by King David about 1,000 years before the arrival of Jesus Christ. It begins with the statement, "My God, My God, why have You forsaken Me?" This was the exact statement uttered by Jesus Christ as He hung upon the cross. Indeed, Jesus Christ intended to be forsaken by God through the death of the cross. This was a necessary condition for Him, as He took the penalty for our sins. The psalm continues with a description of the crucifixion (written in the first person tense), including accurate statements such as:

> "But I am a worm, and no man; a reproach of men, and despised by the people. (Ps 22:6)"
> "...all My bones are out of joint...(Ps 22:14)"
> "...They pierced My hands and My feet...(Ps 22:16)

Each of these statements describes aspects of the crucifixion. In particular, verse six uses the Hebrew word for worm that is transliterated, *towla'*. This type of Middle Eastern worm (*coccus ilicis*) attaches its body to a tree as part of its natural reproductive cycle.[4] Upon the worm's death, a red fluid stains the wood of the tree. This represented a vivid picture of the future crucifixion of Jesus Christ, because His blood stained the wood of the cross. Moreover, this shed blood provides spiritual life to those who turn to Christ. The psalm continues with an accurate picture of the death of Christ on the cross, as nails were used and they pierced Christ's hands (or wrists) and feet.

Other explicit prophecies from the Old Testament are connected to the crucifixion of Jesus Christ. The prophet Isaiah wrote in 800 B.C. and the 53rd chapter of Isaiah's book describes the Savior's work on the cross:

> But He was wounded for our transgressions, He was bruised for our iniquities; the chastisement for our peace was upon Him, and by His stripes we are healed (Isaiah 53:5)
>
> ...it pleased the LORD to bruise Him (Isaiah 53:10)
>
> ...He poured out His soul unto death, and He was numbered with the transgressors, and He bore the sin of many, and made intercession for the transgressors (Isaiah 53:12)

These passages not only describe the physical punishment that Christ bore, but they describe His actual death. For example in verse 12, Isaiah accurately predicted a unique aspect of the crucifixion – that Jesus Christ would be put to death along with two thieves (who were crucified side-by-side with Jesus Christ, see Matthew 27:38). The prophecies also indicate why the Savior would go to the cross: to accept "the sins of many" people. Your sins were taken and placed on Jesus Christ. He accepted the judgment and punishment for these sins. By this sacrificial work, "we are healed."

The Old Testament foretold of the violent death of Israel's long-awaited Savior. The passages above even provide details that could only be fulfilled by crucifixion, such as joints being out of socket, great bodily thirst, hands and feet being pierced, and spilled blood. The Apostle Peter makes reference to these prophecies in one of his New Testament books by declaring: the prophecies "testified beforehand the sufferings of Christ and the glories that would follow (1 Peter 1:11)." While these Old Testament prophecies by themselves offer compelling reason to believe in the cross of Calvary, there is far more evidence for the crucifixion of Jesus Christ.

Jesus Christ predicted His own death

In another type of prophecy, Jesus Christ made several predictions regarding His death. These passages of Scripture present a real problem for the Muslim skeptic, because even Muslim theology considers Jesus to be a prophet. So why would a prophet of God repeatedly make incorrect statements regarding His impending death if God did not intend for Him to die? This makes no sense. A prophet of God would not make such statements if they were not going to come to pass. Instead, the Bible passages should be considered accurate and truthful evidence for His walk towards the cross of Calvary.

All four gospel accounts quote Jesus Christ predicting His death, and in two cases, He even indicates that it will be crucifixion. Two passages from Matthew and Mark evidently describe the same statement by Jesus (Gentile means non-Jewish person or nation):

> "Behold, we are going up to Jerusalem, and the Son of Man will be betrayed to the chief priests and to the scribes; and they will condemn Him to death, and deliver Him to the Gentiles to mock and to scourge and to crucify. And the third day He will rise again." Matt 20:18,19

> "Behold, we are going up to Jerusalem, and the Son of Man will be betrayed to the chief priests and to the scribes; and they will condemn Him to death and deliver Him to the Gentiles; and they will mock Him, and scourge Him, and spit on Him, and kill Him. And the third day He will rise again." Mark 10:33,34 (see also Mark 8:31)

The term "Son of Man" was a title known for the Messiah and Savior. It was specifically used by the ancient Jewish prophet Daniel (Daniel 7:13,14). In the gospel records, Jesus Christ is repeatedly referred to as the Son of Man, as He is in these passages of Scripture. Here we have two first-hand, eyewitness accounts of a statement made by Jesus Christ. The good agreement between the two writers is strong evidence for this statement by Christ. Similar quotes can be found in the books of Luke and John. For example, Luke wrote:

> Then He took the twelve aside and said to them, "Behold, we are going up to Jerusalem, and all things that are written by the prophets concerning the Son of Man will be accomplished. For He will be delivered to the Gentiles and will be mocked and insulted and spit upon. They will scourge Him and kill Him. And the third day He will rise again." Luke 18:31-33

The passages in John indicate that Jesus Christ was willingly laying down His life (for you and I). In chapter 10, He emphasizes that no one is taking His life, but rather He is laying it down on His own:

> "Therefore My Father loves Me, because I lay down My life that I may take it again. No one takes it from Me, but I lay it down of Myself. I have power to lay it down, and I have power to take it again...John 10:17,18a

Jesus Christ again predicts that He will die by crucifixion, when he refers to Himself being "lifted up from the earth." He stated:

> "...and I, if I am lifted up from the earth, will draw all peoples to Myself." This He said, signifying by what death He would die. John 12:32-33

We have four independent eyewitness accounts that quote Jesus Christ and they all say the same thing.[5] Jesus Christ clearly knew that He would be crucified and He explicitly stated this fact. There is no indication from His messages that someone other than Jesus would be crucified, nor did He suggest that He would come down from the cross badly wounded but alive. As described in Jesus Christ's own words, He would "rise on the third day." This would make no sense, if He were not actually dead. Jesus Christ Himself predicted that He would be crucified. This is the second major line of evidence for the crucifixion.

Multiple accounts from New Testament authors

Matthew, Mark, Luke, John, Paul, and Peter, all wrote books in the New Testament and their writings are in perfect accord on this topic. They all make statements consistent with the fact that Jesus Christ had been crucified, died, buried, and He was raised bodily. Beside specific descriptions of the crucifixion, there are many references to His death, His sacrifice, how He "gave Himself," and so on. Moreover, there are countless references to His resurrection from the dead. This brings forth an obvious question: how could Jesus Christ be raised from the dead if He never died? The New Testament contains six independent accounts or view points of the same event. By the Law of Moses and even by modern legal standards, a reliable account is one that is supported by two or three witnesses. Here we have essentially six witnesses to Christ's death, burial, and resurrection. Consequently, there is very strong support for the Biblical authority on these historical events.

From the four gospel records, the Bible has eyewitness accounts of the crucifixion. In each of these passages, the writer clearly teaches that Jesus Christ died on the cross. Nevertheless, there are Muslim clerics who suggest that someone other than Jesus died on the cross.[3] What do the gospel records state? A particularly striking description is found in the gospel of John. John stood at the foot of the cross with Mary the mother of Jesus (John 19:25-27). From the cross, Jesus instructs John to take care of Mary from that day onward. If someone other than Jesus were hanging upon the cross, wouldn't Mary the mother of Jesus recognize him as a different person? John was also the closest Apostle to Jesus, wouldn't he recognize a different person? They were both at the cross and they both knew it was Jesus Christ who was crucified and died. Over the years, Muslim teachers have suggested that it was actually Judas who was crucified. This is utter nonsense. Why would Judas instruct the Apostle John to care for Mary, the mother of Jesus? None of those witnessing this event (including Jesus Christ's own mother!) indicated any doubt as to who was on the cross. It was Jesus.

In what appears to be a case of divine providence, the question of His identity was answered by Pontius Pilate himself, as he had a sign nailed to the top of the cross identifying the man hanging from the cross. In Roman law, it was the custom to use a sign or placard to indicate the charges against the condemned man or woman.[6] Upon sentencing Jesus to die on the cross, Pilate had a sign made with this information and the name of the man. As if to speak directly to the Muslims of the future, the sign said, "THIS IS JESUS."

There is perfect agreement among all the witnesses of this event: Jesus Christ was crucified. He died and was buried. Then He rose from the dead to be with God the Father in glory. To determine what happened, we will consider the testimony of the first century gospel records and the authors of these books. Matthew's records does not appear to have leave any doubt regarding the person who died on the cross of Calvary:

Matthew's record	
Matt 27:35	Then **they crucified Him**…
Matt 27:37	And they put up over His head the accusation written against Him: **THIS IS JESUS** THE KING OF THE JEWS.
Matt 27:46	And about the ninth hour Jesus cried out with a loud voice, saying, "Eli, Eli, lama sabachthani?" that is, "My God, My God, why have You **forsaken** Me?"
Matt 27:50	And Jesus cried out again with a loud voice, and **yielded up His spirit**.

Similarly, Mark's account is consistent with Matthew's account. Mark also testifies that Jesus Christ was crucified and He died:

Mark's record	
Mark 15:25,26	Now it was the third hour, and **they crucified Him**. And the inscription of His accusation was written above: THE KING OF THE JEWS.

The gospels written by Luke and John are also in accord with earlier accounts. There is nothing to suggest that Jesus survived the crucifixion or that someone else was crucified:

Luke's record	
Luke 23:33,34a	And when they had come to the place called Calvary, there **they crucified Him**, and the criminals, one on the right hand and the other on the left. Then Jesus said, "Father, forgive them, for they do not know what they do."
Luke 23:46	And when Jesus had cried out with a loud voice, He said, "Father, into Your hands I commit My spirit." Having said this, **He breathed His last**.

John's record	
John 19:17,18	And He, bearing His cross, went out to a place called the Place of a Skull, which is called in Hebrew, Golgotha, where **they crucified Him,** and two others with Him, one on either side, and Jesus in the center.
John 19:30	So when Jesus had received the sour wine, He said, "It is finished!" And bowing His head, **He gave up His spirit**.

Although it is clear that all four gospel accounts teach that Jesus Christ was crucified, the accounts do vary somewhat, as one would expect from eyewitness testimony. One writer states that Jesus "breathed His last" while another states that "He gave up His spirit." This should not be a problem with the consistency of the testimonies. For example, two individuals may be looking at the same sunset, but one says the sky is orange while the other says the clouds are dark blue. Do they contradict each other? Does this suggest there was never a sunset? No, they are making their own observations of the sunset. Likewise, the four gospel writers are recording what was important from their perspective. It should also be noted that the name Calvary is equivalent to Golgotha (one named is derived from the Latin and the other from the Hebrew), so John's description is in agreement with Luke's description.

Two other individuals wrote books in the New Testament and they mentioned the death of Jesus Christ. Both Peter and Paul were Apostles, appointed by God and Christ for positions of special leadership among the early Christians. Peter knew Jesus during His lifetime, while Paul was one of the individuals who met the resurrected Christ. Their books of Scripture do not have the same detailed descriptions of the life of Christ as the gospel accounts. However their contributions to the New Testament also serve as testimony to the truth of the crucifixion. Paul wrote many things about the death of Christ and His glorious resurrection:

Paul's testimony	
Romans 5:8	But God demonstrates His own love toward us, in that while we were still sinners, **Christ died for us**.
Romans 6:8	Now if we **died** with Christ, we believe that we shall also live with Him
1 Cor 1:23	…we preach Christ **crucified**…
1 Tim 2:5,6	For there is one God and one Mediator between God and men, the Man Christ Jesus, who **gave Himself** a ransom for all, to be testified in due time
Gal 1:3,4	Grace to you and peace from God the Father and our Lord Jesus Christ, who **gave Himself for our sins**, that He might deliver us from this present evil age, according to the will of our God and Father

The story of Paul's conversion to Christianity was described by Luke in the book of Acts. He had been a leading Jew, belonging to a strict group of religious Jews (the Pharisees). Following the death, burial, and resurrection of Jesus Christ, Paul became Christianity's greatest opponent. He led the persecution of early Christians - dragging Christians to jail - and helped to martyr these individuals. Yet, Jesus Christ had mercy on Paul. The resurrected Christ appeared to Paul and his response was nothing less than miraculous (see Chapter 11). This man who killed Christians, became the man who loved Christians. Paul then became perhaps the most important Christian in history, writing thirteen books of New Testament and leading countless individuals to salvation in Jesus Christ. Paul had been appointed by God to communicate the message of God's forgiveness and mercy in Jesus Christ. As shown above, Paul confirmed that Jesus Christ was crucified.

Peter also wrote passages of Scripture that mention the death of Christ and they are consistent with the gospel accounts. Like Paul's writing, the Apostle Peter wrote from the perspective of the death, burial, and resurrection being an accomplished fact. He also wrote to describe the spiritual implications and results of Christ sacrifice. Peter's opinion on the matter is well described by his speeches before the other Jews and the Jewish leadership, as recorded in the book of Acts and in his own books of Scripture.

In summary, the New Testament writers present a consistent message regarding the death, burial and resurrection of Jesus Christ. All of these men were alive at the time of Jesus Christ. At least one was at the trial of Jesus and the Apostle John even stood at the cross as Jesus Christ was crucified. This is strong

Peter's testimony	
Acts 2:22-24 (speech at the Jewish feast of Pentecost)	"Jesus of Nazareth, a Man attested by God to you by miracles, wonders, and signs which God did through Him in your midst, as you yourselves also know - Him, being delivered by the determined purpose and foreknowledge of God, you have taken by lawless hands, have **crucified**, and put to death; whom God raised up, having loosed the pains of death, because it was not possible that He should be held by it."
1 Peter 3:18	For Christ also suffered once for sins, the just for the unjust, that He might bring us to God, being **put to death** in the flesh but made alive by the Spirit

evidence in support of the Biblical account. These six men are reliable witnesses and their written words speak for themselves: it was Jesus Christ who died on Mount Calvary.

External evidence

Besides the clear passages from the Bible, there are a number of records or accounts from non-Biblical sources that state Jesus Christ was crucified. Flavius Josephus was a Roman historian of Jewish lineage and he authored several important first century historical books. In *Testimonium Flavianum* by Josephus, he writes that Jesus "wrought surprising feats" (i.e., miracles), "many people believed that he was the Christ, that a leader named Pilate had him crucified," and that his followers claimed that "he appeared to them restored to life."[7] A Roman historian named Tacitus wrote in 115 A.D., noting that Nero persecuted Christians, whom he further describes as followers of Christ, a man crucified under Pontius Pilate, during the reign of Tiberius.[8]

Even Roman law indirectly supports the Biblical account. The Romans had severe penalties for soldiers and jail keepers who mishandled prisoners.[9] If a condemned person were to have survived a crucifixion, or somehow escaped alive, then the executioners would themselves be put to death. The Roman soldiers would not have let Jesus Christ down from the cross before He had actually died. Their own lives would have been at risk! Nor would they have been fooled into crucifying the wrong individual, Judas or someone else. Their job was to crucify a man named Jesus of Nazareth and they successfully completed this task.

Moreover, the Romans crucified thousands of Jews around the time of Christ. It is likely that the soldiers on Mount Calvary were experienced professionals, having crucified – to death - many other individuals before nailing Jesus Christ to the cross. They most certainly accomplished this task with Jesus Christ, too. No evidence suggests He could have survived the crucifixion. A medical pathologist even analyzed the crucifixion several years ago and the report was published in the prestigious *Journal of the American Medical Association*.[6] Based on modern medical knowledge, the authors concluded that Jesus Christ "was dead when taken down from the cross."

Besides the historical accounts found in the Bible, these events and ideas were recorded at an early date (ca. 100-200 A.D.) in the writings of early Christian leaders (often called church fathers). The writings of the "church fathers" were non-Biblical letters and documents that have been found and studied. They are an indication that the events were fully described and known even at these early dates. Because they describe the death, burial, and resurrection of Christ, we know that these were not stories which were added or developed centuries after the time of Christ. Rather, the historical accounts were already in place during the times of the "church fathers", having been committed to writing in the New Testament books by eyewitnesses and contemporaries of Jesus Christ. These writings are not limited to a single individual, but include authors such as, Clement of Rome, Ignatius, Polycarp, Barnabas, and others.[10] In one important example, Ignatius confirmed the orthodox Christian doctrines of the deity of Christ, the humanity of Christ, and the crucifixion of Christ by Pontius Pilate in a letter written before 117 A.D.[11]

Regarding the actual Biblical accounts, some have claimed the Bible must be in error because the gospel records describe Jesus Christ's body being carefully embalmed and wrapped - then His body was laid in a newly carved tomb (Joseph of Arimethia's tomb). To some critics, the Bible's description must surely be in error. A crucified person, such as Jesus Christ, would not have been buried in a dignified location like Joseph's tomb. Since crucifixion was considered the most disgraceful, even "cursed," method of death, these individuals would often end up in a common grave or open pit.[12] Archaeological evidence however supports the Bible regarding the crucifixion of Jesus Christ.

A recent archaeological dig in Jerusalem uncovered dozens of crucified first century Jews.[13] One of the corpses still had a seven-inch nail lodged in his foot and a piece of olive wood was attached to the nail. The remains of this crucified Jewish man were found in an ossuary (a stone burial box) and it bore the inscription of the man's name: Yohanan ben Ha' galgol. The individual was about 30 years old at the time of his death by Roman crucifixion. The discovery is notable for several reasons. First, it shows that crucified individuals were sometimes given proper and respectable burials. Burial in an ossuary was a dignified end for a person's mortal remains. Secondly, bones of this individual still had a nail lodged in the ankle. This demonstrates that the Romans used nails in their crucifixions of first century

Jews, as described in the crucifixion of Jesus Christ. This supports the record in the New Testament - that Jesus Christ was nailed to the Roman cross, He died, and He was given an honorable burial.

Conclusions

Muslim skeptics have a mountain of evidence before them. Old Testament prophecies described Israel's future messiah suffering and dying. Several of these prophecies even seem to describe crucifixion itself – hundreds of years in advance. During the earthly lifetime of Jesus, He foretold of His impending death and He specifically said that He would be crucified. Furthermore, the Bible contains six eyewitness accounts (John, Matthew, Luke, Mark, Paul, and Peter) of the crucifixion and resurrection. These were men who were actually present during these events! The testimony found in the Bible is also found in several non-Biblical history books from the period of 100-200 A.D. All of these sources declare that Jesus Christ died on the cross of Calvary.

However the Muslim skeptic might be struck with the thought, "How can a loving God allow His only Son to be tortured and killed on a cross?" On several occasions, this question was answered by Jesus Christ Himself. Jesus told His first century disciples,

"Greater love has no one than this, than to lay down one's life for his friends" John 15:13

If we return to the Muslim skeptic's question, "How can a loving God...?" The emphasis here should be on love. Jesus Christ loved you so much that He gave His life for you, and moreover, God the Father loved you so much that He was even willing to send the unique Son of God to pay this great price. There was no other way to save us from our sins.

References:

(1)   Based on a published testimony or account. Downloaded March 3, 2011 from the Internet at:
        http://www.answering-islam.org/Testimonies/esther.html.
(2)   Ahmed Deedat, *Crucifixion or Cruci-fiction?*, Adam Publishers, New Delhi, 2006.
(3)   Josh McDowell, *The Islam Debate*, Here's Life Publishers, San Bernardino, CA, 1981.

(4)   George Shaw and James Francis Stephens, *General Zoology or Systematic Natural History, Volume IV, Part 1*, George Kearsley Publishing, London, 1806; pp. 193-194.

(5)   According to many scholars, Mark's gospel account was based on the testimony or eyewitness account of the Apostle Peter. Though it is unlikely that Luke was present during Christ's ministry on Earth, his gospel account is considered to be a collection of eyewitness testimonies from those who were present and did observe these events.

(6)   William D. Edwards, Wesley J. Gabel, Floyd E. Hosmer, "On the Physical Death of Jesus Christ." *Journal of the American Medical Association*, 1986, vol. 255, pp 1455-1463, and references cited therein.

(7)   Flavius Josephus, *Antiquities*, 18.3.63. See also, William Whiston, *The Works of Josephus,* Hendrickson Publisher, Peabody, MA, 1987; p. 480.

(8)   Tacitus, *Annals*, 15.44. See also, Robert E. Van Voorst, *Jesus Outside the New Testament*, William B. Eerdmans Publishing, Grand Rapids, MI, 2000.

(9)   C. E. Brand, *Roman Military Law*, University of Texas Press, Austin, TX, 2013.

(10)   Hebertus R. Drobner, *The Fathers of the Church: A Comprehensive Introduction*, Hendrickson Publishers, Peabody, MA, 2007.

(11)   Lee Strobel, *The Case for Christ*, Zondervan, Grand Rapids, MI, 1998; p. 89. See also: David Hugh Farmer, "Ignatius of Antioch" in *The Oxford Dictionary of the Saints*, Oxford University Press, Oxford University Press, Oxford, UK, 1987.

(12)   John Dominic Crossan, *Jesus: A Revolutionary Biography*, HarperCollins, NY, NY,1994; p. 140.

(13)   E. M. Blaiklock, *The Archaeology of the New Testament*, Thomas Nelson Publishers, Nashville, TN, 1984, p. 160.

Chapter 4

The Resurrection of Jesus Christ

Mercy, peace, and love be multiplied to you. Jude 1:2

Mutee'a Al-Fadi was born and raised in Saudi Arabia.[1] His family was devoted to the Muslim faith, belonging to the *Wahabbi* branch of Sunni Islam. Before his teenage years, he had already memorized half of the Quran. His beliefs were solidly grounded, as he describes his upbringing, "I grew up as a very devout Muslim follower who adhered and applied the teachings of Islam into every aspect of my life."

He thoroughly believed the teachings of Islam. Most notably, Mutee'a was convinced that Islam was "the only acceptable religion to God." As the "final religion on Earth," it was the only "way to Heaven" and those who were not Muslims were of course "doomed to Hell." The authority of Muhammad was absolute. He believed that all people were required to follow God's prophet Muhammad, otherwise they would be condemned to eternal punishment in Hell. As a result of his Muslim faith, he also concluded that "Muslims are superior to all others" and Christians were infidels. In his zeal for Islam, Mutee'a even considered travelling to Afghanistan to join with the *mujahedeen* alongside Osama bin Laden. He believed that the most certain pathway to Heaven involving dying in *jihad*. Fortunately, the love from his mother interceded. She convinced him not to follow this grim - and probably violent - pathway to eternal reward.

Despite his dedication to Islam, Mutee'a saw something that disturbed him. He began to think about the messages in the Quran and he saw a great deal of contempt and hatred towards non-Muslims. Even as a teenage, he recognized this element of Islam. It was filled with hatred. As he remarked,[1] "I could not believe that God can hate His own creation simply because they do not accept Him. I thought God's compassion and love should be bigger than that and above all that."

Mutee'a began his university studies in Saudi Arabia. Following graduation, he wanted to pursue graduate studies at a university in the west, either in Europe or the United States. He was accepted at a prestigious university and he moved away from his home land of Saudi Arabia. Upon his arrival in graduate school, he heard of a program matching international students with a local host family. Mutee'a was paired with a young married couple. They were to help him adjust to his new life.

The couple really took care of Mutee'a and demonstrated a genuine love for him. This was surprising to Mutee'a because the couple was even more kind to him than fellow Muslims! He began to wonder. What made them so caring? Why did they have such a great sense of peace and joy? Several months later, he was invited to their home for a traditional Thanksgiving dinner. They asked Mutee'a if they could pray and give thanks for their dinner. The prayer came as a shock to him, after which he realized that the kind-hearted couple were actually Christians! They had never mentioned anything about religion or the Bible, but instead they simply cared for Mutee'a out of love for him. He left the dinner felling a bit depressed, because he had been taught that Christians were filled with contempt for Muslims. Yet, he saw the exact opposite in this couple. Something was not right in his own thinking. He concluded,[1]

> "On that day, I walked out of their house with great doubts about my faith and my teachings. I vowed to research Christianity to learn more about this Jesus that can make such a profound difference in someone's life, the one that can give them such visible peace and joy, something I have never ever seen or even experienced before, the one that was the source of the light that was shining out of them."

Years later Mutee'a had finished college and he was working for a company. One of his co-workers stood out. This fellow was kind and considerate. He was always joyful and uplifted. His demeanor was noticeably different than other men in the firm. Mutee'a became friends with this co-worker, as this gentleman was a very likeable guy. During one holiday season, Mutee'a was invited to his co-worker's home for Christmas dinner. Mutee'a immediately noticed that his co-worker's wife and children were just like him, filled with a joy that almost defied understanding. His curiosity prompted a question about the co-worker's life, background, and source good spirits. He told Mutee'a that he was a "born-again" Christian, and with salvation in Jesus Christ, God produces joy and peace in his heart. This is a by-product or "fruit" of his Christian faith. It came as a surprise to Mutee'a and he was reminded of the married Christian couple that he met in college.

He was also troubled by the events of that evening. He began to wonder why his faith did not produce joy and peace like he saw in these people. Mutee'a had been a devoted follower of Islam all of his life, but God never produced any "fruit" from his faith. It seemed as though his religion was only capable of making him feel the "ugliness of his inner being." Moreover, he reflected on some of the troubling times he had experienced in life. It seemed as though the Allah was "nowhere to be found" and he provided no comfort or peace to Mutee'a.

These thoughts prompted Mutee'a to do something completely radical: he attended a Christian church service. This was not something he did carelessly or without great consideration. He knew that such an act would be considered a terrible sin by his fellow Muslims. Nevertheless, his heart was moved to investigate the Christian faith. He thought the best place to do so was at a Christian church. After attending the church for sometime, he began to understand the messages of the Bible and he learned more about Jesus Christ. They were studying the New Testament book of John and he comments, "I learned who Christ truly was. And slowly and gradually, His deity began to unfold right before my eyes, and the message of salvation became so clear to me, and I felt how helpless I was and how desperately I needed to be saved."

Mutee's was confronted by his sin, but he was also introduced to the Savior. He accepted Jesus Christ as his Savior and Mutee'a became a Christian. He notes that besides salvation from sin and death, the Lord gave him a new heart. Whereas he was an "arrogant, self-righteous, and prideful man," God has worked to change him into a more humble and gentle individual. Indeed, people around him even noticed a positive change in his character.

As someone who was born and raised in Saudi Arabia, Mutee'a truly did go from Mecca to Calvary. Even as he looks back on his journey, he considers all the millions of people still following Islam. He now knows that Muhammad is not mentioned in the Bible. Neither are the "scientific miracles" in the Quran genuine. Neither is the Bible corrupt. As Mutee'a has discovered, these are simply lies spread throughout the Muslim world.

Mutee'a grew up not far from the holiest sites to the Islamic faith, including the "Mosque of the Prophet" in Medina, Saudi Arabia. At this site, Muhammad's bones are buried. Like the founders of every other religious faith, his mortal remains lie in a tomb or beneath the ground of the Earth. The exception to this rule is Jesus Christ. The Bible describes how He died on the cross and He was buried in Joseph's tomb, but then He was raised bodily from the dead. This was a miracle of the first-order, being announced to His followers by the angels of God. Then Jesus Christ Himself physically appeared to many of the early Christians. The resurrection sets Biblical Christianity apart from every other religious faith.

Yet, most Muslims refuse to believe the truth of the death, burial, and resurrection of Jesus Christ. A short distance away from Muhammad's tomb, there lies an empty grave intended for the bodily remains of Jesus Christ. According to Islamic tradition, Jesus will be buried there when He returns from Heaven and dies a human death. Again, we see a stark contrast between the message God revealed in the Bible and the message taught in the Islamic faith. *Islam says*: Jesus Christ never died but was taken to Heaven. *The Bible says*: Jesus Christ went to the cross to die for our sins - He died and He was buried. *Islam says*: Jesus Christ will return to Earth and die a human death. *The Bible says:* Jesus Christ rose from the dead and He is seated in Heaven, but He will return in judgment and wrath, and He will never die. What did Jesus Himself say about this? The Lord Jesus Christ spoke to the Apostle John in a vision saying, "I am He who lives, and was dead, and behold, I am alive forevermore. Amen (Revelation 1:18)."

In the following chapter, the resurrection of Jesus Christ will be examined. It will be shown that the resurrection of Jesus Christ is a fact of history and the Biblical account is a reliable spiritual truth. The empty grave in the "Mosque of the Prophet" will never contain the deceased body of Jesus, but rather it remains itself a testimony that Jesus Christ rose from the dead!

The Biblical Record of the Resurrection

Before considering some of the evidence for the resurrection of Jesus Christ from the dead, it is worthwhile to consider what the Bible actually says about this event. The reader can consider for themself the merits of the Biblical accounts. It should first be noted that the resurrection is a major part of the Christian Scriptures or New Testament. It was not just mentioned once or twice in vague or confusing terms. When the eyewitness accounts (found in the gospel books and in the book of Acts) are actually examined, one finds clear descriptions of the miraculous event and there are multiple references and testimonies regarding its truth.

In the New Testament books, there are at least 60 separate references to this event, coming from six different authors of Scripture. The descriptions use term such as "raised," "risen," "resurrection," and Christ being "alive." Leaving no doubt regarding the nature of the resurrection, both the Apostles Paul and Peter specifically state that Jesus Christ was "raised from the dead" (see, 1 Thessalonians 1:9,10; 2 Timothy 2:8a; 1 Peter 1:21b; 1 Peter 1:3).

The most thorough descriptions of the resurrection are found in the four gospel accounts (Matthew, Mark, Luke, and John). Like the accounts of His crucifixion, the descriptions of Christ's resurrection are in excellent agreement (Tables 1-6). All four gospel books describe how a man named Joseph of Arimethia went to Pilate to ask for the body of Jesus Christ. The records continue with Jesus' body being taken down from the cross, wrapped in linen and embalmed, and then being laid in a sealed tomb (Table 1). Matthew's account also describes how the Jewish leaders requested that a Roman guard be placed at the tomb.

It is important to note that a sizable number of people were present at this burial. This argues against the possibility that Jesus could still be alive when He was laid in the tomb - someone would have noticed and exclaimed, "He is still breathing!" It is also important to note that Mary Magdalene and the other women were present at the burial and we find these same women as the initial witnesses to the resurrection. Why is this important? Because it insures that there was no confusion either at the burial site (i.e., that somehow they were at the wrong grave on the day of the resurrection) and they are witnesses to the entire miraculous event – from beginning to end. The four gospel records also state that Jesus Christ was raised from the dead on the third day (Table 2). This was the day after the Sabbath and it was after the Passover feast was completed. There is also excellent agreement in this detail of the historical account.

From the disciples and followers of Jesus Christ, several women arrived first at the tomb on the day after Passover. They had came to anoint the body with fragrant spices. The women found the tomb opened and they saw angels from Heaven. As seen in the following passages, the angels announced the resurrection of Jesus Christ. The accounts all describe angels speaking to the women (Table 3),

Table 1.	Burial of Jesus Christ's body in tomb
Matt 27:59-61	When Joseph had taken the body, he wrapped it in a clean linen cloth, and **laid it in his new tomb** which he had hewn out of the rock; and he rolled a large stone against the door of the tomb, and departed. And Mary Magdalene was there, and the other Mary, sitting opposite the tomb.
Mark 15:44-47	Pilate…granted the body to Joseph. Then he bought fine linen, took Him down, and wrapped Him in the linen. And **he laid Him in a tomb** which had been hewn out of the rock, and rolled a stone against the door of the tomb. And Mary Magdalene and Mary the mother of Jesus observed where He was laid.
Luke 23:52-55	This man went to Pilate and asked for the body of Jesus. Then he took it down, wrapped it in linen, and **laid it in a tomb** that was hewn out of the rock, where no one had ever lain before. That day was the Preparation, and the Sabbath drew near. And the women who had come with Him from Galilee followed after, and they observed the tomb and how His body was laid.
John 19:40-42	Then they took the body of Jesus, and bound it in strips of linen with the spices, as the custom of the Jews is to bury. Now in the place where He was crucified there was a garden, and in the garden a new tomb in which no one had yet been laid. So **there they laid Jesus**, because of the Jews' Preparation Day, for the tomb was nearby.

Table 2.	Bodily resurrection on the third day
Matt 28:1a	Now after the Sabbath, as the first day of the week began to dawn...
Mark 16:1	Now when the Sabbath was past, Mary Magdalene, Mary the mother of James, and Salome bought spices, that they might come and anoint Him.
Luke 24:1	Now on the first day of the week, very early in the morning, they, and certain other women with them, came to the tomb bringing the spices which they had prepared.
John 20:1	Now on the first day of the week Mary Magdalene went to the tomb early, while it was still dark, and saw that the stone had been taken away from the tomb.

Table 3.	Appearance of angels, witnessed by multiple individuals
Matt 28:2,5-6	...an angel of the Lord descended from heaven...the angel answered and said to the women, "Do not be afraid, for I know that you seek Jesus who was crucified. He is not here; for He is risen..."
Mark 16:5,6a	And entering the tomb, they saw a young man clothed in a long white robe sitting on the right side; and they were alarmed. But he said to them, "Do not be alarmed. You seek Jesus of Nazareth, who was crucified. He is risen!"
Luke 24:4-6	And it happened, as they were greatly perplexed about this, that behold, two men stood by them in shining garments. Then, as they were afraid and bowed their faces to the earth, they said to them, "Why do you seek the living among the dead? "He is not here, but is risen! "
John 20:11,12	But Mary stood outside by the tomb weeping, and as she wept she stooped down and looked into the tomb. And she saw two angels in white sitting, one at the head and the other at the feet, where the body of Jesus had lain.

though it should be noted that there were encounters both outside and inside the tomb. According to Matthew's record, a single angel was responsible for the stone being rolled away from the opening of the tomb. The angel's appearance was evidently so striking that the Roman guards at the tomb "fainted" or lost consciousness out of fear. Then, as the women looked into the tomb, other angels appeared to them and they also proclaimed that Jesus Christ was risen from the dead. It is significant that these angels spoke to more than one woman at the same time, because this rules out the possibility of a dream or hallucination. The Bible then describes how these women hurried to tell the other followers of Christ the good news, "He is risen!"

When Jesus Christ was placed in the tomb, a very large stone was rolled in front of the grave. Pilate and the Jewish leadership secured the grave with a seal and a Roman guard (a few armed soldiers). On the morning of the resurrection, the followers of Christ discovered that the stone had been moved or rolled away. All four gospel accounts describe this observation and Matthew's book specifically states that one of the angels moved the stone (Table 4).

Table 4.	Burial stone rolled away
Matt 28:2-4	And behold, there was a great earthquake; for an angel of the Lord descended from heaven, and came and rolled back the stone from the door, and sat on it. His countenance was like lightning, and his clothing as white as snow. And the guards shook for fear of him, and became like dead men.
Mark 16:4	But when they looked up, they saw that the stone had been rolled away—for it was very large.
Luke 24:2	But they found the stone rolled away from the tomb.
John 20:1	Now on the first day of the week Mary Magdalene went to the tomb early, while it was still dark, and saw that the stone had been taken away from the tomb.

The gospel accounts continue and describe how the disciples and followers of Christ went into the tomb and the body of Jesus Christ was no longer in the tomb (Table 5). John's book details the scene most thoroughly. It describes how the burial garments of Jesus were laying in the empty tomb. In the gospel accounts, there are both proclamations from angels, "He is not here," as well as observations made by the Apostles Peter and John. It is significant that John is said to have examined the empty tomb, because we know from other passages of Scripture that

Table 5	Body gone
Matt 28:5-7a	But the angel answered and said to the women, "Do not be afraid, for I know that you seek Jesus who was crucified. "He is not here; for He is risen, as He said. Come, see the place where the Lord lay. And go quickly and tell His disciples that He is risen from the dead."
Mark 16:6	But he said to them, "Do not be alarmed. You seek Jesus of Nazareth, who was crucified. He is risen! He is not here. See the place where they laid Him.
Luke 24:3	Then they went in and did not find the body of the Lord Jesus.
John 20:6,7	Then Simon Peter came, following him, and went into the tomb; and he saw the linen cloths lying there, and the handkerchief that had been around His head, not lying with the linen cloths, but folded together in a place by itself.

he was present at the cross. He knew that Christ died, having directly observed His death.

All four gospel records then describe how the risen Lord Jesus Christ began to appear in physical form after the resurrection (Table 6). According to Mark's record, Jesus first met Mary Magdalene. Then He began to meet other disciples. They were able to touch Him and they ate meals with Him. This verified that the risen Jesus Christ was a physical being and not a hallucination or ghostly spirit. He met with individuals and with groups of followers. These appearances of the risen Christ are more fully described later in this chapter.

While many other details are described in the gospel accounts, the passages listed above highlight the most important points. The resurrection itself was announced by angels and several people witnessed this supernatural event. Moreover, the accuracy of this story is supported by the four separate gospel records, which are based entirely on eyewitness testimony.

The resurrection was clearly apparent to these first century observers, as the tomb had been opened and the body of Jesus Christ was gone. Although the disciples did not at first realize that Jesus Christ was to rise from the dead, they soon saw and believed. Jesus Christ met with His followers, disciples, and Apostles, over the next several weeks after His resurrection.

Table 6.	Risen Christ meets frightened disciples and followers
Matt 28:9,10	…behold, Jesus met them, saying, "Rejoice!" So they came and held Him by the feet and worshiped Him. Then Jesus said to them, "Do not be afraid. Go and tell My brethren to go to Galilee, and there they will see Me."
Mark 16:9a	Now when He rose early on the first day of the week, He appeared first to Mary Magdalene…
Luke 24:33,34	So they rose up that very hour and returned to Jerusalem, and found the eleven and those who were with them gathered together, saying, "The Lord is risen indeed, and has appeared to Simon!"
John 20:18,19	Mary Magdalene came and told the disciples that she had seen the Lord, and that He had spoken these things to her. Then, the same day at evening, being the first day of the week, when the doors were shut where the disciples were assembled, for fear of the Jews, Jesus came and stood in the midst, and said to them, "Peace be with you."

Despite the detailed historical accounts given by four authors, some still refuse to believe that Christ rose from the dead. Skeptics suggest that Jesus Christ's body was simply stolen by His followers. As the most intimate associate of Jesus Christ, the Apostle John certainly would have known if the body had been removed by other followers of Jesus. However, John's testimony is clear. He describes the event in unmistakable terms, "…He was raised from the dead (John 21:17)."

There is also the suggestion that the resurrected Christ was a hallucination, a spirit, or some other kind of non-physical being. While a single person might have a hallucination - or imagine seeing an angel - it is impossible for a group of people to see the same "hallucination." With sizable groups of people having seen the resurrected Christ, it becomes implausible to say that they were just having a hallucination. As noted previously, the Apostles had meals with the risen Jesus Christ. The writer Luke describes one of the early encounters with the risen Christ:

Now as they said these things Jesus Himself stood in the midst of them and said to them "Peace to you." But they were terrified and frightened and supposed they had seen a spirit. And He said to them, "Why are you troubled? And why do doubts arise in your hearts? Behold My hands and My feet that it is I Myself. Handle Me and see for a spirit does not have flesh and bones as you see I have." When He had said this He showed them His hands and His feet.

But while they still did not believe for joy and marveled, He said to them "Have you any food here?" So they gave Him a piece of a broiled fish and some honeycomb. And He took it and ate in their presence.[4]

By eating food, He intended to show them that His resurrected body was an actual physical body. This is one of several events in which the Apostles and followers of Christ handled Him or demonstrated that His resurrected body was similar to the body of Christ before His death.

What about the Islamic idea that Christ was never on the cross, but someone else died on the cross? In John's account, we find the resurrected Jesus showing the Apostle Thomas the wounds in His hands and side (John 20:27). Until this time, Thomas did not believe Jesus had risen from the dead. But upon seeing the wounds in Jesus' hands and torso (both from the crucifixion), Thomas believed in the resurrection. This is clear evidence that Jesus was the man on the cross – where he received those wounds – and He still retained the wounds after His resurrection from the dead. Interestingly, some Old Testament prophecies describe Israel's Messiah with large pierce wounds. When the resurrected Jesus returns in the future, it is said the Jews will "look on Me whom they pierced" (Zechariah 12:10). This passage was written 500 years before Jesus Christ was born. It is a prophecy describing the resurrected Jesus Christ still bearing the wounds from the cross!

Testimony of many witnesses

The four gospel books of Matthew, Mark, Luke, and John, represent four independent accounts or descriptions of the same group of events. The gospel books describe the lifetime of Jesus Christ and His death, burial, and resurrection. They contain eyewitness accounts and the gospel books can be considered the testimony of four very good sources. In a court of law, judges and attorneys will often bring forward witnesses to describes events of the past. The goal is to establish a truthful, historically accurate picture of the past. When more than one witness recounts the same story - with agreement among even the smallest details - then a clear picture of the past emerges. The historical accuracy becomes well established. In the Bible, we are presented with testimony from many witnesses to the events related to Jesus Christ. Moreover, these eyewitnesses are in perfect agreement: Jesus Christ died on the cross of Calvary, He was buried in a tomb, and He physically rose from the dead and appeared to His followers.

46

Besides the four gospel books, there are several other lines of evidence to support the Biblical account of the resurrection. In the book of Acts, the author Luke has preserved the "court transcripts" from two trials of early Christians. Both the Apostles Paul and Peter were arrested and testified at court hearings. After restoring sight to a blind man and then preaching about Jesus Christ in Jerusalem, Peter was arrested and brought before the Jewish ruling council. He spoke before the council in his own defense. This testimony is recorded in the book of Acts. Peter testified:

> Then Peter, filled with the Holy Spirit, said to them, "Rulers of the people and elders of Israel: If this day we are judged for a good deed done to a helpless man, by what means he has been made well, let it be known to you all, and to all the people of Israel, that by the name of Jesus Christ of Nazareth, whom you crucified, whom God raised from the dead, by Him this man stands here before you whole." Acts 4:8-10

This passage of Scripture represents eyewitness testimony from the Apostle Peter as he delivered it in a formal court proceeding. It is important to note that the miraculous healing of the blind man is evidence from God Himself that Peter's testimony is true. If Peter had been propagating a lie (or deception), then the God of Heaven would not have performed the miracle. This idea is proclaimed in an earlier verse, where Luke writes (Acts 4:33), "And with great power the Apostles gave witness to the resurrection of the Lord Jesus." This "great power" through miracles was evidence for the resurrection.

Another testimony is given by the Apostle Paul, as recorded in the twenty-sixth chapter of Acts. Paul had been arrested in Jerusalem and he appeared before a royal tribunal with King Agrippa (the Roman ruler of Judea). Paul testified,

> "Therefore, having obtained help from God, to this day I stand, witnessing both to small and great, saying no other things than those which the prophets and Moses said would come— that the Christ would suffer, that He would be the first to rise from the dead, and would proclaim light to the Jewish people and to the Gentiles" Acts 26:22, 23

Paul was one of the most well-educated individuals of his day, so his testimony should be considered reliable and accurate. Christ rose "from the dead." It is also important to realize that Paul's testimony was being made in a Roman court of law. Deceiving or lying (committing perjury) in a Roman court was an offense that could be severely punished (even by death),[2] so Paul would not have knowingly told a false story about Jesus Christ. Even in the first century, court proceedings were serious events. Therefore, testimonies of Peter and Paul should be considered reliable historical accounts, rather than fanciful stories of spiritual legend. With the excellent agreement between their testimonies, we can be assured that the Biblical record of is truthful.

In the book of Acts, there are also records of Peter's and Paul's speeches before fellow Jews at religious services. Religious services were particularly important events for first century Jews. It is not likely that these two men would have blatantly lied in this serious and solemn environment. Paul was invited to speak in the synagogue in Antioch on a Sabbath day, where he proclaimed about Jesus:

> "Men and brethren, sons of the family of Abraham, and those among you who fear God, to you the word of this salvation has been sent. For those who dwell in Jerusalem, and their rulers...asked Pilate that He should be put to death. Now when they had fulfilled all that was written concerning Him, they took Him down from the tree and laid Him in a tomb. But God raised Him from the dead. He was seen for many days by those who came up with Him from Galilee to Jerusalem, who are His witnesses to the people." Acts 13:26-31

Paul's testimony leaves no uncertainty. He confirms that Christ died on the cross, He was laid in the tomb, and He was raised alive from the dead. Paul continues by noting that the risen Christ appeared to a number of people and these people are witnesses to the events. Likewise, Peter spoke before a group of Jews at the Jewish feast day referred to as Pentecost:

> "Men of Israel, hear these words: Jesus of Nazareth, a Man attested by God to you by miracles, wonders, and signs which God did through Him in your midst, as you yourselves also know—Him, being delivered by the determined purpose and foreknowledge of God, you have taken by lawless hands, have crucified, and put to death; whom God raised up, having loosed the pains of death, because it was not possible that He should be held by it." Acts 2:22-24

Peter's testimony is also clear and unmistakable: Jesus Christ died and God raised Him up from the dead. Both Peter's Pentecost speech and Paul's Sabbath speech are preserved for us in the book of Acts. This book and its author Luke are known to be a very good source of documented historical records (see chapter 5). This strongly suggests that these accounts are accurately preserved - we have "heard" for ourselves the speeches of Peter and Paul. Peter himself concludes (Acts 2:32), "this Jesus, God has raised up, of which we are all witnesses." These two first century eyewitnesses confirm the truth of the resurrection.

Besides the "court records" and "solemn speeches" given in Acts, the testimonies of Peter and Paul are amply described in their books of Scripture. These references also leave no doubt regarding the death, burial, and resurrection of Jesus Christ. The Apostle Paul wrote 14 books of Scripture in the New Testament and he constantly refers to the resurrection as an accomplished event. For example, the Apostle Paul wrote:

> Remember that Jesus Christ, of the seed of David, was raised from the dead...2 Timothy 2:8a

> ...you turned to God from idols to serve the living and true God, and to wait for His Son from heaven, whom He raised from the dead, even Jesus who delivers us from the wrath to come.
> 1 Thessalonians 1:9,10

> ...Christ who died, and furthermore is also risen, who is even at the right hand of God, who also makes intercession for us.
> Romans 8:34

Paul makes many other specific references to the resurrection in his books of Scripture (more than 20 separate references). All of his writings indicate that Christ died, He was buried, and He rose from the dead. Paul's testimony does not allow for any other interpretation of these events, most notably the ridiculous Muslim teaching that Jesus never died, but he will die a human death sometime in the future.

Peter's books of Scripture likewise echo this truth. Peter was one of the original twelve Apostles of Jesus Christ. According to the records in the gospel books and the book of Acts, Peter was with Jesus Christ from the beginning of His ministry, until the resurrection, and He led the early Christian church in Jerusalem. Peter himself authored two New Testament books, 1 Peter and 2 Peter, and he was eventually put to death for his faith in Christ. Peter wrote:

...God, who raised Him from the dead and gave Him glory, so that your faith and hope are in God. 1 Peter 1:21b

Blessed be the God and Father of our Lord Jesus Christ, who according to His abundant mercy has begotten us again to a living hope through the resurrection of Jesus Christ from the dead, 1 Peter 1:3

...through the resurrection of Jesus Christ, who has gone into heaven and is at the right hand of God, angels and authorities and powers having been made subject to Him. 1 Peter 3:21b,22

In these passages, the leader of the very earliest Christians (the Jerusalem church) is repeatedly describing how Jesus Christ "raised" from the dead. The Apostle Peter would certainly have known if (somehow) Jesus Christ escaped death and He were still alive. Had the body of Jesus had been stolen by the followers of Jesus Christ, Peter would have likely known about such an act. But Peter's narrative clearly describes Jesus Christ in terms of once "dead" and now alive through "resurrection."

By careful examination of the Bible, one finds that a large number of the early followers of Christ met the risen Savior. These individuals are often referred to as witnesses to the resurrection of Jesus Christ. For the Muslim, this raises important questions, such as: how many witnesses confirmed the supernatural events in Muhammad's life? Were there dozens of people who saw the angel Gibril (Gabriel) speak to Muhammad at the beginning of his ministry? Were there multiple witnesses who saw Muhammad's "night journey" from his bed to Jerusalem to Heaven and back? How many witnesses saw the angels who brought messages to the prophet of Islam?

In contrast to the *missing witnesses* of Islam, the death, burial, and resurrection of Jesus Christ was done openly before many, many witnesses. The Christian Apostles and the writers of Scripture (Matthew, Mark, Luke, John, Peter, and Paul) are the primary witnesses in this great testimony of spiritual truth. But as one reads through the New Testament of the Bible, the list of resurrection witnesses grows immense. These involved many independent witnesses to whom the risen Christ appeared in a physical body, including:

1. To Mary Magdalene (John 20:10-18)
2. To the other women (Matthew 28:8-10)
3. To Cleopas and another disciple on the road to Emmaus (Luke 24:13-32)
4. To the eleven discples and others (Luke 24:33-49)
5. To the eleven Apostles, with Thomas absent (John 20:19-23)
6. To Thomas and the other Apostles (John 20:26-30)
7. To seven Apostles (John 21:1-14)
8. To the disciples (Matt 28:16)
9. With the Apostles on the Mount of Olives before His ascension (Luke 24:50-52 and Acts 1:4-9).
10. To about 500 people at once (1 Corinthians 15)

Peter confirmed to Cornelius that he and others "ate and drank" with Jesus Christ after the resurrection (Acts 10:41) and He was "handled" by His followers, indicating that He was in a real, physical body. The identity of the risen Christ was not in doubt, as He showed His followers the severe wounds in His resurrected body, including the wounds to his wrists, feet, and side (where His body had been pierced by the Roman spear).

In summary, the Bible presents the testimony of many witnesses to the resurrection of Jesus Christ. Some of these individuals were martyred for claiming that Jesus Christ was raised from the dead. Their faith in Christ resulted in persecution and death by Roman and Jewish authorities. Indeed, both the Apostles Paul and Peter were put to death shortly after they wrote their books of Scripture. Would these men and women have given their lives for the Christian faith, had they known that Christ never really died? Would they have gone through the tortures and execution, if they knew that Jesus Christ did not actually die, but instead someone else was nailed to the cross? Absolutely not! The witnesses to the resurrection gave their lives, because they stood with the truth and their risen Lord stood with them.

Indirect evidence for the truth of the resurrection

Following the arrest and crucifixion of Jesus Christ, His followers were scattered and fearful. In the gospel of Mark, the author describes the nighttime arrest of Jesus and he states (Mark 14:50), "Then they all forsook Him and fled." Except for a few brave individuals, most of the disciples went into hiding (the Apostle John and several of the women were at the cross). This fear was also apparent in Joseph of Arimathea, the man who asked Pilate for the body of Jesus Christ, following His death. John describes Joseph as (John 19:38) "being a disciple of Jesus but secretly for fear of the Jews." Before the followers of Christ had seen their resurrected Savior, they cowered in fear behind closed doors. The book of John describes the scene (John 20:19a), "the doors were shut where the disciples were assembled for fear of the Jews."

As the historical book of Acts shows, something dramatic changed the followers of Christ. Their leader, teacher, and beloved Savior, had been executed by Roman crucifixion – a brutal and humiliating death. Rather than rallying around Jesus as a martyr, the opposite occurred. They hid behind closed doors and undoubtedly questioned their decision to follow the crucified Jesus. But then something occurred to inspire these men and it gave them tremendous spiritual power.

The Apostle Peter is a good example. He followed the group of soldiers the night that they had arrested Jesus.[3] He followed the group all the way to the Jewish council chambers, where he stood outside with a crowd. There in the darkness, Peter was confronted by three individuals and each accused him of being a follower of Jesus Christ. One of these individuals was even described as a teenage girl. But Peter denied even knowing Christ. Peter was fearful and he would not admit to following Jesus.

Yet a short time later, Peter is standing before a crowd at the Pentecost feast and boldly proclaimed Christ. Peter even declared Christ in the Jewish Council, and despite being threatened with physical punishment, Peter continued to openly proclaim the death, burial, and resurrection of Jesus Christ! What happened? What caused Peter to become emboldened in his speech and actions? It was the bodily resurrection of Jesus Christ from His burial tomb! Peter met His resurrected Savior and he became a new man – a powerful voice proclaiming Jesus Christ to the nation of Israel, as he was directed by the very Spirit of God.

This is indirect evidence for the resurrection. The early followers of Christ were hiding in fear, but soon boldly proclaiming the resurrection of the Savior. Would these men have rallied behind a crucified man, if they knew the resurrection was a hoax or somehow faked? Not likely. By preaching Jesus Christ in first century Israel, the Apostles and disciples of Christ were arrested, imprisoned, tortured, and even executed, for their witness and testimony to the resurrection. Consider the reaction of the Jewish religious leaders, when they heard the followers of Christ proclaiming the resurrection. Luke gives the account that the Jewish leaders were "… greatly disturbed that they taught the people and preached in Jesus the resurrection from the dead (Acts 4:2)." These men and women proclaimed the good news of the resurrection because *they knew it was the truth*! This was clearly evident by the changes it brought to their lives.

The Apostles, disciples, and other early Christians, were not likely to be fabricating stories and lies regarding a crucified man. They did not become wealthy from their message. Nor did they gain power. The early Christian leaders all suffered horribly for believing in the salvation of Jesus Christ. There was no real motive for them to spread a new false religion. The same cannot be said for the early days of Islam. The early leaders of this new faith became wealthy and powerful, as the Muslim armies spread the message from town to town, province to province, and nation to nation. With each new town and city conquered by Muslim militias, women were enslaved and the wealth of the town was pillaged. After this, severe taxes were then placed on the surviving inhabitants. This is a much different picture than the spread of Christianity at its beginning. The early Christians did not spread their faith in the hopes of gaining wealth or power, but rather their desire was to tell the story of a Savior. For these early Christians, their primary motive was to spread the truth.

It is also important to realize that most of the disciples of Jesus Christ were skeptical about His resurrection. Despite having observed Jesus healing sick people and raising several people from the dead, the followers of Christ did not initially believe the miracle of the resurrection. For example, Mary Magdelene first met the risen Jesus and ran to tell the disciples the good news. As Matthew describes (Matt 16:11):

> "And when they heard that He was alive and had been seen by her, they did not believe."

Likewise, Jesus met with the eleven Apostles, but Thomas was not present. When the Apostles told Thomas about the appearance of the risen Lord, he said (John 20:25), "unless I see in His hands the print of the nails and put my finger into the print of the nails and put my hand into His side I will not believe." A few days later, the risen Christ again appeared to the disciples, but Thomas was present. According to John's account (John 20:27), Jesus said to Him, "Reach your finger here and look at My hands; and reach your hand here and put it into My side. Do not be unbelieving but believing." Thomas believed from that point onward that Jesus Christ was resurrected from the dead.

It is important to realize that these men were skeptical witnesses. The gospel accounts describe them as cautious and "unbelieving." This gives their testimony even more credibility, because they were not likely to be tricked into believing a hoax or an elaborate series of lies. Nor were they simply delusional in their grief and the loss of their leader. The gospel accounts make it very clear: <u>the disciples believed in the resurrection because they knew that the Jesus Christ had died and they met Him after the resurrection.</u>

The resurrection of Jesus Christ was also taught by His followers at an extremely early date, essentially as soon as it occurred. The Biblical record describes the Apostle Peter and others boldly proclaiming the resurrection shortly after the ascension of Jesus Christ to Heaven. From non-Biblical sources, the creeds of the early Christian church can be dated to within several generations of the resurrection of Jesus Christ.[5] These creeds state that Christ rose from the dead. Moreover, the writings of the "church fathers" contain the resurrection account.[6] Some of these letters date to the early second century A.D. Why is it important to realize that the resurrection was taught at an early date? By being a fundamental doctrine at an early date, we can be assured that it was not simply a legend or story devised by the Christian church at a later date. It was the truth then, as it is the truth now.

In summary, these considerations represent indirect evidence for the resurrection of Jesus Christ from the dead. They add to an already large amount of evidence found in the New Testament accounts of the Bible, including eyewitness testimonies concerning the resurrection.

Old Testament Prophecies Related to the Resurrection

As described more thoroughly later, the Bible contains many Old Testament prophecies concerning the arrival of Israel's Messiah. These prophecies were written by ancient Jewish prophets and they looked centuries ahead to the arrival of Jesus Christ, the Messiah and Savior of Israel. The Old Testament has a number of passages that point ahead to the resurrection of Jesus Christ. Among the many prophecies concerning Jesus Christ, King David wrote a passage in Psalm 16 which points directly ahead to the resurrection. This Scripture was written about 1,000 years before Jesus Christ was crucified, buried, and resurrected. It states (Psalm 16:10):

> For You will not leave my soul in Sheol nor will You allow Your
> Holy One to see corruption.

In this passage, David first states that God would not allow Jesus Christ to remain in Sheol (the Hebrew word for Hell or Hades) and he continues with a specific statement from David regarding the resurrection of Jesus Christ. This reference to "corruption" refers to the decay or decomposition of the body upon death and burial. The Apostle Peter pointed directly to this ancient prophecy in his speech at the Feast of Pentecost after the death, burial, and resurrection of Christ,

"Men and brethren, let me speak freely to you of the patriarch David, that he is both dead and buried, and his tomb is with us to this day. Therefore, being a prophet...foreseeing this, spoke concerning the resurrection of the Christ, that His soul was not left in Hades, nor did His flesh see corruption. This Jesus God has raised up, of which we are all witnesses" Acts 2:29-32

Peter correctly notes that even the great King David was dead and buried. He contrasts this with Jesus Christ and His being "raised up." But he also points out that this king from ancient Israel was a prophet from God. In David's Psalm, he made a prediction regarding Israel's future Messiah, stating, "...nor will You allow Your Holy One to see corruption." It is abundantly clear from other Biblical passages that Jesus Christ was uniquely given the title of God's *Holy One*. For example when the angel Gabriel met Mary and announced that she would be the mother of baby Jesus, he said to her (Luke 1:35), "The Holy Spirit will come upon you and the power of the Highest will overshadow you; therefore also that Holy One who is to be born will be called the Son of God." Thus, the prophecy (Psalm 16:10) could only be referring to Jesus Christ.

Besides the explicit prophecy of Psalm 16:10, there are many implicit prophecies concerning the resurrection of Christ. While an explicit prophecy describes the resurrection directly and it uses obvious terms related to Christ rising, an implicit prophecy is found in a more subtle presentation. These types of prophecies imply the Messiah will rise from the dead, but they do not specifically state this fact.

As described more thoroughly in Chapter 8, the ancient Jewish rabbis noticed two types of Messianic prophecies in the Old Testament Scriptures. One major group of prophecies describes the "suffering servant." As noted previously, these prophecies (i.e., Isaiah 53) describe the crucifixion with the Messiah being "wounded for our transgressions" and "sins being placed on Him." Another group of prophecies describe the Messiah as the glorious King, someone who will take King David's throne in Jerusalem and eventually rule the world for all eternity. With these two lines of prophecies, some of the old Jewish rabbis thought that there must be two different Messiahs coming to Israel.

We can now see that these two lines of prophetic writings make up a major type of implicit prophecy concerning the resurrection of Jesus Christ (Table 7). In other words, there are not two Messiahs described in the Old Testament prophecies, but one Messiah and Savior – the Lord Jesus Christ! The first line of prophecies (suffering servant) describes His crucifixion two thousand years ago. The second line of prophecies (glorious King) describes Jesus Christ *after the resurrection* and

His return to reign as King of Israel and the world. This is still a future event. In order for Jesus Christ to return to Earth, it was necessary for His body to be resurrected. As described by the Apostle Paul, Jesus Christ is now seated in Heaven at the place highest honor, as He waits for the appointed time of His return. These constitute the great implicit prophecy concerning the resurrection of Christ. They were all written more than 600 years before the death, burial, and resurrection of Jesus Christ.

Table 7. Parallel lines of prophecies concerning Jesus Christ, His death and resurrection.

Bible passage	Suffering Servant	Glorious King and Savior	Bible passage
Isaiah 53:3-5	And we hid, as it were, our faces from Him; He was despised, and we did not esteem Him. Surely He has borne our griefs And carried our sorrows; Yet we esteemed Him stricken, Smitten by God, and afflicted. But He was wounded for our transgressions, He was bruised for our iniquities; The chastisement for our peace was upon Him, And by His stripes we are healed.	"And your house and your kingdom shall be established forever before you. Your throne shall be established forever." According to all these words and according to all this vision, so Nathan spoke to David.	2 Samuel 7:16,17
Psalm 22:6	But I am a worm, and no man; A reproach of men, and despised by the people.	Lift up your heads, O you gates! And be lifted up, you everlasting doors! And the King of glory shall come in.	Psalm 24:7
Daniel 9:26a	And after the sixty-two weeks Messiah shall be cut off, but not for Himself	I will make the lame a remnant, and the outcast a strong nation; So the LORD will reign over them in Mount Zion from now on, even forever.	Micah 4:7

There is abundant evidence to support this concept of the implicit prophecies of the Old Testament. For example, the resurrected Jesus Christ was described meeting two disciples on the "road to Emmaus." He taught the disciples from the Old Testament Scriptures regarding the Messiah. Jesus told the disciples (Luke 24:25-27),

> "O foolish ones, and slow of heart to believe in all that the prophets have spoken! <u>Ought not the Christ to have suffered these things and to enter into His glory?</u>" And beginning at Moses and all the Prophets, He expounded to them in all the Scriptures the things concerning Himself.

He specifically noted that it was necessary for the Savior to suffer first and then enter into His glory. This concept is stated elsewhere in the New Testament. For example in describing the ancient Jewish prophets, the Apostle Peter wrote (1 Peter 1:10,11),

> Of this salvation the prophets have inquired and searched carefully, who prophesied of the grace that would come to you, searching what, or what manner of time, the Spirit of Christ who was in them was indicating when <u>He testified beforehand the sufferings of Christ and the glories that would follow.</u>

In this passage, one finds the Old Testament prophets did not fully understand the truth that was being revealed by God through them, as they made prophecies concerning the future Messiah, Jesus Christ. Neither did these prophets understand that the Savior would die to pay for our sins and then enter into His glory. It is only now that these truths have been fully revealed by the writers of the New Testament. Nevertheless, we can look back at these two lines of prophecies, the suffering servant and glorious King, and see these Scriptures pointed centuries ahead to the death, burial, and resurrection of Jesus Christ.

Jesus Christ predicted His resurrection prior to the crucifixion
In the previous chapter, we saw Jesus Christ Himself predicted that His life would end upon a Roman cross. Many of these same verses also predict the resurrection. Jesus Christ Himself predicted His death, burial, and resurrection, and yet Muslim clerics boldly proclaim that it never occurred! On the one hand, Muslims will admit that Jesus was a prophet of God, but then turn around and claim that His statements and predictions were not truthful! This is utter nonsense,

because a true prophet speaks God's message to mankind. Regarding the nature of God in the Bible, the Apostle Paul states (Titus 1:2), "…God, who cannot lie…" A true prophet of God does not make repeatedly false, incorrect, or deceptive statements. When Jesus Christ predicted His own death, burial, and resurrection, He was making a genuine, truthful prophecy about an event that God Himself would bring to pass.

Jesus Christ made these predictions to His disciples and to the religious leaders of Israel (the same men who would eventually force His crucifixion). For example, the Apostle John describes an exchange between Jesus and the rulers of the Jewish Temple. Jesus had just chased away the money exchangers and merchants (who should not have been in the Temple area) and the Jewish leaders confront Him (John 2:18-21),

> So the Jews answered and said to Him, "What sign do You show to us, since You do these things?" Jesus answered and said to them, "Destroy this temple, and in three days I will raise it up." Then the Jews said, "It has taken forty-six years to build this temple, and will You raise it up in three days?" But He was speaking of the temple of His body.

In this passage, Jesus tells the Jewish leaders that His body would rise again – alive – three days after it gets "destroyed." Of course, the body of Jesus was destroyed – not in an absolute sense where it ceased to exist – but in the sense of severe physical punishment. After His arrest, He was beaten by the Temple guard, brutally whipped (scourged) and beaten by the Roman soldiers, and then nailed to the cross to die. In fulfillment of the prediction by Jesus, His body was raised up at the resurrection - three days after it was destroyed.

Moreover, it is clear that the Jewish leaders understood the prophecy by Jesus Christ, because they repeated it to the Roman leader Pontius Pilate. After Jesus had been crucified and buried, they approached Pilate and asked for Roman soldiers to guard the tomb:

> …the chief priests and Pharisees gathered together to Pilate, saying, "Sir, we remember, while He was still alive, how that deceiver said, 'After three days I will rise.' Therefore command that the tomb be made secure until the third day, lest His disciples come by night and steal Him away, and say to the people, 'He has risen from the dead.' So the last deception will be worse than the

first." Pilate said to them, "You have a guard; go your way, make it as secure as you know how." Matt 27:62-65

Despite the presence of Roman soldiers, Jesus Christ rose from the dead (Matt 28:2-4). Not even a group of tough Roman soldiers could withstand the power and glory of an "angel of the Lord" and the resurrection became an accomplished event of history!

The followers of Jesus Christ also heard predictions of His resurrection. All four gospel accounts describe how Jesus predicted His own death, burial, and resurrection. As shown previously in the quotes (Matt 20:18,19; Mark 10:33,34; Luke 18:31-33; John 10:18), Jesus Christ is on record in the Gospel books saying, "...the third day He will rise again." Although the disciples did not understand these predictions before the crucifixion, they understood and believed the statements following the resurrection. Not only did Jesus Christ predict His resurrection, but He also included in these prophecies statements describing how He would be manifest or appear after the resurrection. The night before His arrest, Jesus told His disciples (Matt 26:31,32),

> Then Jesus said to them, "All of you will be made to stumble because of Me this night, for it is written: 'I will strike the Shepherd, and the sheep of the flock will be scattered. But after I have been raised, I will go before you to Galilee."

A very similar quote is recorded in the book of Mark. These records indicate that Jesus was to meet His disciples in the region of Galilee after His resurrection. Indeed, the angel who met the women at Christ's empty tomb said to them (Matt 28:2-7),

> "Do not be afraid, for I know that you seek Jesus who was crucified. He is not here; for He is risen, as He said. Come, see the place where the Lord lay. And go quickly and tell His disciples that He is risen from the dead, and indeed He is going before you into Galilee; there you will see Him."

Jesus told the disciples that He would rise from the dead and meet them in Galilee, and this statement was confirmed by the visions of angels on the very day of the resurrection. The Gospel of John describes one of these appearances of the resurrected Christ in Galilee, where it states (John 21:1): "After these things Jesus showed Himself again to the disciples at the Sea of Tiberias, and in this way He showed Himself..." The city of Tiberias was in the region of Galilee, and the Sea of Tiberias is also known as the Sea of Galilee.

In summary, there are very specific statements by Jesus Christ (prior to the cross) stating that He would rise from the dead in His resurrection. These are further evidence for this event and the truth of the New Testament.

Spiritual or theological significance of the resurrection.

This chapter has examined the overwhelming evidence in support of a physical resurrection of Jesus Christ from the dead. However, the resurrection itself is evidence for many other elements of the Christian faith and truth of the Bible. In this final section, the overall significance of the resurrection of Jesus Christ will be summarized, as it is described in the Christian Scriptures. A brief description does not adequately cover this immensely important topic. Entire chapters, books, and volumes have been devoted this subject.[7] However within the context of this book, a Muslim reader may wonder why this is an important event to Christians. This section will highlight the significant aspects of the resurrection.

The resurrection reveals something very special about Jesus Christ and His death on the cross. It can be considered a "seal of authenticity" for Christianity and the message of the Bible. The resurrection offers convincing proof that the spiritual messages in the Bible are true. It provides assurance to the Muslim: the theology in the Old and New Testament is the truth of God. It is a confirmation from God Himself that Jesus Christ is the Savior and His death saved us from our sins. It confirms His claims to be the one and only Son of God. This concept is explicitly revealed through the Apostle Paul, who wrote (Romans 1:3,4):

> ...concerning His Son Jesus Christ our Lord, who was born of the seed of David according to the flesh, and <u>declared to be the Son of God with power according to the Spirit of holiness, by the resurrection from the dead.</u>

The Apostle Paul continues to describe the resurrection in the book of Romans, where we read (Romans 4:24,25):

> ...but also for us, to whom God will credit righteousness - for us who believe in him who raised Jesus our Lord from the dead. He was delivered over to death for our sins and was raised to life for our justification.

Jesus Christ died on the cross to pay for our sins and all of our sins were punished in Him. In the last part of the passage, God and Paul tell us that Christ's resurrection is "for our justification." Thus, God has accepted Christ's sacrifice on the cross and we are justified by His cross work (i.e., God can declare you to be a "just" or "righteous" person). The physical resurrection of Christ can be considered evidence that we are justified - or declared righteous in God's judgment - as Christians. The God of Heaven has used the resurrection to demonstrate the truth of the Biblical message of the Savior Jesus Christ.

The New Testament has many important passages describing the resurrection of Jesus Christ. In particular, the resurrection is often used as an evidence for different types of spiritual blessings that God bestows upon followers of Jesus Christ. The resurrection itself is linked to "spiritual results" described below:

God promising to give us *new life*...
> But if the Spirit of Him who raised Jesus from the dead dwells in you, He who raised Christ from the dead will also give life to your mortal bodies through His Spirit who dwells in you. Romans 8:11

God promising to *raise us up* (after death)...
> And God both raised up the Lord and will also raise us up by His power. 1 Corinthians 6:14

> ...knowing that He who raised up the Lord Jesus will also raise us up with Jesus...2 Corinthians 4:14

God promising to *save us* from sin and condemnation...
> ...if you confess with your mouth the Lord Jesus and believe in your heart that God has raised Him from the dead, you will be saved. Rom 10:9

God promising to *deliver us* from His wrath...
> ... you turned to God from idols to serve the living and true God, and to wait for His Son from heaven, whom He raised from the dead, even Jesus who delivers us from the wrath to come. 1 Thes. 1:9,10

God promises that Jesus Christ will *intercede for us*...
> ...Christ who died, and furthermore is also risen, who is even at the right hand of God, who also makes intercession for us. Romans 8:34

These passages describe some of the spiritual results that (directly or indirectly) arise from the resurrection of Jesus Christ. With the resurrection, the God of Heaven is able to release tremendous blessings upon the human race. As the Apostle Paul describes it, we are blessed "with every spiritual blessing" because of the work of Jesus Christ. His sacrificial death on the cross removes the judgment of sin and impending wrath of God directed towards lost and hopeless sinners. Without the resurrection, there would be no assurance that our sin debt had been paid. The Apostle Paul even wrote in the New Testament (1 Corinthians 15:17), "...if Christ is not risen, your faith is futile; you are still in your sins." He essentially says without the resurrection, there is no such thing as Christianity. It would be an empty, meaningless faith! But thankfully, Jesus Christ did rise from the dead.

Besides the spiritual blessings, we are told that God the Father raised Jesus Christ from the dead and gave Him the position of highest honor, glory, and power in all of Heaven. At least three New Testament sources have testified regarding the exalted position given to the resurrected Jesus Christ. They describe Him in terms of great glory, power, and honor, using language that could only be applied to God Himself. For example, the Apostle Paul wrote (Ephesians 1:17, 20-21):

> God of our Lord Jesus Christ, the Father of glory...raised Him from the dead and seated Him at His right hand in the heavenly places, far above all principality and power and might and dominion, and every name that is named, not only in this age but also in that which is to come.

When the writers describe Jesus as sitting at God's "right hand," this is actually a statement of position, honor, and authority. It is not meant to describe an actual physical location. In the ancient world, the most important individual was given the "right-hand position" in royal chambers, feasts, or banquets. To be seated at the "right-hand" of the king, meant that this person was given the highest honor. The passage from Ephesians also describes how Jesus Christ is now in a position "far above" all other individuals, either men or angels. The Apostle Peter also describes the glory given to Jesus Christ the Son of God. Peter's message echoes the truth stated by Paul, stating:

> ...who raised Him from the dead and gave Him glory, so that your faith and hope are in God (1 Peter 1:21b).

62

...through the resurrection of Jesus Christ, who has gone into heaven and is at the right hand of God, angels and authorities and powers having been made subject to Him (1 Peter 3:21b,22).

The Apostle John has also confirmed that Jesus Christ was raised to the position of greatest honor and authority in Heaven. This Apostle received a vision of Heaven and future events, and the vision prompted him to write the last book in the Bible, the book generally titled, *Revelation*. At the very beginning of the book, John states the purpose of the book,

> The Revelation of Jesus Christ, which God gave Him to show His servants—things which must shortly take place. And He sent and signified it by His angel to His servant John, who bore witness to the word of God, and to the testimony of Jesus Christ, to all things that he saw. (Rev. 1:1, 2)

John is making the plain statement about the appearance of an angel of the Lord and the role of John as an eyewitness to "all that he saw." As we read John's testimony, it is immediately clear that his intention is not to boast in himself or to bring attention to John the Apostle. But rather, John is describing things that he observed and his role is that of a neutral observer.

John sees the risen Jesus Christ in His glory as the Son of God and fell at His feet "as dead." Evidently, the glory of the risen Lord was so great that it overwhelmed even the Apostle. The Lord then said (Revelation 1:17), "Do not be afraid; I am the First and the Last. I am He who lives, and was dead, and behold, I am alive forevermore. Amen. And I have the keys of Hades and of Death." This statement supports both the death and resurrection of Jesus Christ, as the glorified Lord identifies Himself by stating that He "was dead" but "alive forevermore." The passage (Rev. 1:14,15) describes His appearance as "...white like wool, as white as snow, and His eyes like a flame of fire" and His voice is described as "the sound of many waters." Although even the angels from Heaven have glory and produce a terrifying response in most men, the glory of Jesus Christ goes far beyond the bright light of a mere angel. The glory and power of the risen Lord Jesus Christ causes even the angels and saints to bow down and worship Him.

The witness and testimony of John continues in the book of Revelation, as Jesus Christ Himself returns to Earth one day to crush Satan and his followers. These events are still future and they will fulfill the Old Testament prophecies concerning the Lord's role as the Savior of Israel and mankind. The message in the book of Revelation is in very good agreement with Old Testament prophecies, many of which were written more than 1,000 years prior to the death burial, and resurrection of Christ (and before the writing of Revelation). The Apostle John described scenes in Heaven and on the Earth in which Jesus Christ is seen in magnificent glory and power.

Conclusions

As some Muslims read through this chapter, they will undoubtedly wonder, "What does this have to do with me? Why should I care about all these quotes from the Jewish and Christian Scriptures?"

There is one passage from the Bible that should speak directly to the disinterested Muslim: the account of the rich man and Lazarus. This story is found in Luke's gospel account (Luke 16:19-31).

Jesus Christ described these two men: one was a wealthy individual and one was a poor man named Lazarus. Following their deaths, the two men were confined to a place the Bible calls Hades, described as a temporary holding place for the dead of this world. Moreover, Jesus told of two regions of Hades roughly corresponding to the common ideas of Paradise and a fiery Hell.

The rich man was sent to the place of anguish and pain, while Lazarus "was carried by the angels" to the side of Paradise. At some point, the rich man appeals to Abraham for some type of relief from the fiery torment, but Abraham responds that it is impossible. The rich man then begs Abraham to send a message to his family members, warning them of the place of torment.

Abraham responds (Luke 16:29), "They have Moses and the prophets; let them hear them." The rich man responds, "No, father Abraham; but if one goes to them from the dead, they will repent." Here the rich man suggests that his family will repent, or change their ways of thinking, if one were to return from the dead. However, notice Abraham's response:

> "If they do not hear Moses and the prophets, neither will they be persuaded though one rise from the dead."

Remarkably, Abraham's responses turned out to be completely correct. Not only do most Muslims reject the clear messages of Biblical Scriptures, but neither are they persuaded by the physical resurrection of Jesus Christ!

While the vast majority of Muslims may reject the writings of Moses and the prophets, ignore and deny the resurrection of Jesus Christ, this does not mean that you should reject these truths. By the resurrection of Jesus Christ, the God of Heaven declared that Jesus Christ is the Son of God and that His sacrifice on the cross satisfies the righteousness of God. The resurrection confirmed and verifies the basic message of Christianity, that Christ died for our sins...believe and be saved.

References:

(1)   Based on a published testimony or account. Downloaded February 24, 2011 from the Internet at:
http://www.answering-islam.org/authors/alfadi/testimony.html

(2)   Perjury under Roman Law: Philo Judaeus, *A Treatise On the Honor Commanded To Be Paid to Parents*, Chapter IX; Norval Morris and David J. Rothman *The Oxford History of the Prison: The Practice of Punishment in Western Society*, Oxford University Press, Oxford, UK, p. 14. For the attitude towards perjury in the Jewish culture and religion, see: Exodus 23:1 and Leviticus 19:11,12

(3)   John 18:25-27 and Mark 14:66-72.

(4)   Luke 24:36-43

(5)   Lee Strobel, *The Case for Christ*, Zondervan, Grand Rapids, MI, 1998; p. 98.

(6)   Hebertus R. Drobner, *The Fathers of the Church: A Comprehensive Introduction*, Hendrickson Publishers, Peabody, MA, 2007.

(7)   Charles F. Baker, *A Dispensational Theology*, Grace Bible College Publications, Grand Rapids, MI, 1971, pp. 376-377 and references cited therein.

Chapter 5

Accuracy of New Testament Scriptures

*Prophecy never came by the will of man, but holy men of God
spoke as they were moved by the Holy Spirit. 2 Peter 1:21*

Hassan was raised in the Malaysian city of Kuala Lumpar.[1] Although many years have passed since he fled his homeland, he still has painful memories of the night local security forces broke into his family's home. On that dark night, his mother was beaten to death. Hassan's family was punished simply because they had converted to Christianity. A short time later Hassan's father would also lose his life to Islamic security forces. Although Hassan is comforted in knowing that his parents are in Heaven with their Savior Jesus Christ, he also has firsthand knowledge of the perils of a journey from Mecca to Calvary.

Hassan's story is told in Caner and Pruitt's book *The Costly Call.*[1] Like many Malaysians, his family practiced the Muslim religion. They attended the local mosque, at least until his father learned about Jesus Christ. Hassan's father was a successful business owner and an influential man. His business interests brought Hassan's father into contact with a gentleman from Europe and this man shared the good news of Jesus Christ. Hassan's father recognized the spiritual truth, believed the message, and became a Christian. He completed the journey from Mecca to Calvary when Hassan was about 11 years old.

Shortly after his conversion, Hassan's father was arrested by the Malaysian police. They broke through the door to their home, handcuffed his father, and beat him with wooden clubs. Hassan did not understand what was happening at the time, but he soon would know. His father was arrested, beaten, and thrown in prison for one year. His only offense: leaving Islam to become a Christian.

Hassan's father was forced to sell many of their families assets, as he was heavily fined. Upon his return home, Hassan's father soon led both Hassan and his mother to a relationship with Christ. They made the journey from Mecca to Calvary as a family. However, Malaysian officials again paid their family a visit. They demanded that the family begin attending the local mosque, or they would "pay dearly" for their decision to follow Christ. Hassan's father was deeply committed to his faith and he made this known to the officials. He was arrested again and a large fine levied against him for his release. These fines were not so much payment of restitution or a fine for breaking the law, but they were more like extortion or blackmail.

Unfortunately, some Muslim government officials were not content with fines and excessive taxes levied against Hassan's family. They wanted to completely destroy this group of "infidels." Soon, security forces returned once more. They broke into their home at night. Instead of attacking Hassan's father however, the police went for his mother. She was beaten so badly that she died the same night. With severe wounds to her skull, she had little chance of surviving. Hassan was placed in the custody of his Muslim grandparents, while his father was imprisoned again. His grandparents worked hard to bring Hassan back to Islam, but he stayed firm in his convictions.

Eventually, Hassan's father was released from prison after paying another large fine. Hassan left his grandparents home and he returned to live with his father. Facing relentless persecution for their faith, Hassan and his father tried to flee the country of Malaysia. The authorities would not provide Hassan with a visa and his father's visa was revoked. Nevertheless, they attempted to flee the country by boat to Singapore. They were caught during their escape and Hassan was arrested. When asked about his religious faith, Hassan boldly admitted to being a believer in Jesus Christ. This resulted in an imprisonment and terrible beatings, despite Hassan being only a fourteen year-old boy.

Hassan's father bargained for the release of his son by signing over their home to a Malaysian official. Both Hassan and his father had been arrested and tortured for their faith in Jesus Christ. Since there was little hope for the persecution to subside, Hassan's father again sought to escape the country. According to Hassan's account, the police "continued, however, to keep a close eye on us."

His father contacted a trusted European friend and they arranged for passage aboard a fishing boat. On the evening of their planned escape, the two men went down to the seashore. A small boat was launched from the fishing vessel and it approached the shore to pick up Hassan and his father. At some point, gunfire came from behind a grove of palm trees. Their freedom was just a short distance off shore, but several bullets hit Hassan's father. His father told Hassan to swim to the boat. As his father lay dying on the shore, Hassan made his way to the fishing vessel and eventually to the freedom of a European nation.

Hassan lived with his father's European friend, and later, he attended college. He is committed in his relationship with Jesus Christ. Over the years, he has ministered to others who have made the journey from Mecca to Calvary. Having lost his own mother and father to Muslim persecution of Christians, he has been driven to provide "protection for ex-Muslims on the run."

As one considers Hassan's experience, several New Testament verses come to mind. God warned Christians from the very beginning that their faith could lead to attacks. The Apostle Paul wrote, "In fact, everyone who wants to live a godly life in Christ will be persecuted (2 Timothy 3:12)." And Jesus Himself warned His disciples, "…if they persecuted Me, they will persecute you also…(John 15:20)." These New Testament passages were written almost 2,000 years ago, however they are stunning in their accuracy. For many Christians living in Muslim-controlled countries, these passages of the Bible are all too real. Muslim persecution of Christians continues unabated to this day. But this also raises an important question: how could the ancient writers of the New Testament have known about the conditions for Christians of the modern day?

The answer to this question is simple – the Bible is God's message for mankind. God was able to foresee the pressures His followers would experience in the centuries ahead. This includes the persecution of Christians by Muslim security forces, militias, and thugs. These types of predictions could only come from a Bible that has been well preserved. In other words, a corrupted Bible would not have accurate prophecies and predictions of the future. Neither would a corrupted Bible have accurate historical references. If Christian or Jewish scribes had revised and altered the messages from God's prophets, then they would have also introduced errors in the historical records found in the Bible. But this never occurred!

God's message has been remarkably well preserved in the pages of the Bible. Indeed, the Bible has all of the hallmarks of a trustworthy record. In this chapter, we study the preservation of the New Testament Scriptures. Several lines of evidence will be shown to confirm the integrity and preservation of the God's messages in this part of the Bible. The importance of this study cannot be overstated, because the Quran and the New Testament have vastly different messages. For example, the Quran quotes Jesus as saying, "…we bow to Allah as Muslims (5:111)." The New Testament thoroughly describes His life and ministry, and yet in this part of the Bible, Jesus Christ says nothing about Allah, Islam, or Muslims! Did the writers of the New Testament accurately record the things they heard and saw? Are the words and messages of Jesus Christ preserved in our modern Bibles? Or did Muslim scribes invent these quotes from Jesus to give support to their new religion in 700 A.D.? These questions will be answered by looking at ancient copies of the Biblical books, archaeological records, and looking in the Bible itself.

Has God allowed the Bible to be corrupted? The Muslim reader is encouraged to consider a message from the Old Testament where God promised to preserve His message "forever." Through the writing of His prophet David (ca. 1000 B.C.), God states,

The words of the LORD are pure words, like silver tried in the furnace of earth, purified seven times. You shall keep them, O Lord, You shall preserve them from this generation forever.
Psalm 12:6,7

This passage of Scripture would make no sense if God allowed the Jewish and Christian scribes to alter the messages of His prophets. Jesus Christ Himself told His followers that, "...My words will by no means not pass away (Luke 21:33b)." Although Jesus spoke these words more than 2,000 years ago, they seem to be directed straight to modern-day Muslims! He is telling the Muslim skeptic that "by no means" would His messages be corrupted or altered or changed. The messages of Jesus Christ and His Apostles would be preserved by the very power of God. Indeed, God repeated this concept several times through the centuries (Table 1). So when the pages of the New Testament say nothing about Islam, it is not because the Bible was corrupted, rather it is because Jesus Christ said nothing about Allah, Islam, or Muslims!

Table 1. Bible passages on the preservation of Old and New Testament Scriptures.

Person	Date of Statement	Passage
David	1000 B.C.	"The entirety of Your word is truth, and every one of Your righteous judgments endures forever." Psalm 119:160
Isaiah	800 B.C.	"The grass withers, the flower fades, but the word of our God stands forever." Isaiah 40:8
Jesus	30 A.D.	"Heaven and earth will pass away, but My words will by no means pass away." Matt. 24:35
Peter	65 A.D.	"But the word of the LORD endures forever. Now this is the word which by the gospel was preached to you." 1 Peter 1:25

Trustworthy Records
As described in the previous chapters, the New Testament was written based on eyewitness accounts of historical events. In the first four books of the New Testament, the different writers (Matthew, Mark, Luke, and John) provide four accounts or records of the life and ministry of Jesus Christ. These four writers are in excellent agreement on the details of the life and ministry of Jesus Christ. The

writers were witnesses and their goal was to accurately record the events that they had seen with their eyes. This is clear from the book of 1 John, where he writes (1 John 1:1):

> That which was from the beginning, which we have heard, which we have seen with our eyes, which we have looked upon, and our hands have handled, concerning the Word of life.

In this passage, John refers to Jesus Christ as the "Word of life" and he clearly describes his role as a witness to the events. The Apostle Peter was one of the closest associates of Jesus Christ and the head of the early Jerusalem Christian church. He wrote two books of the New Testament and evidently dictated the gospel book to Mark (which bears Mark's name). Peter also affirms the eyewitness accounts of the New Testament with his statement (2 Peter 1:16):

> For we did not follow cunningly devised fables when we made known to you the power and coming of our Lord Jesus Christ, but were eyewitnesses of His majesty.

These New Testament passages may be contrasted with the accounts of Muhammad's life in the hadith. No first-hand witnesses documented the statements or events from Muhammad's lifetime. In fact, the stories in the hadith pass through many generations before they were recorded. For example, the following passage precedes Ibn Sa'd's description of Muhammad's night journey:

> Muhammad Ibn 'Umar al-Aslami informed us; he said: Usamah Ibn Zayd al-Laythi related to me on the authority of 'Amr Ibn Shu'ayb, he on the authority of his father, he on the authority of his ('Amr's) grand-father; (second chain) he (Ibn Sa'd) said: Musa Ibn Ya'qub al-Zam'i related to me on the authority of his father, he on the authority of his (Musa's) grandfather, he on the authority of Umm Salamah; (third chain) Musa said: Abu al-Aswad related to me on the authority of 'Urwah, he on the authority of 'Ayishah; (fourth chain) Muhammad Ibn 'Umar said: Ishaq Ibn Hazim related to me on the authority of Wahb Ibn Kaysan, he on the authority of Abu Murrah the mawla of 'Aqil, he on the authority of Umm Hani daughter of Abu Talib (fifth chain) he (Ibn Sa'd) said: 'Abd Allah Ibn Ja'far related to me on the authority of Zakariya Ibn 'Amr, he on the authority of Abu Mulaykah, he on

the authority of Ibn 'Abbas and others; their consolidated narratives are…(*Al-Tabaqat Al-Kabir* Volume I, English translation)

While the Bible relies on eyewitnesses who were with Jesus Christ, the hadith were compiled during the 8th and 9th centuries – more than 100 years after Muhammad died. The hadith manuscripts were not based on eyewitness accounts, but as Ibn Sa'd's description shows, they were derived from stories that had been passed from person to person for many years.

Because the New Testament accounts were based on eyewitness records, the Gospels and the book of Acts were recorded at very early dates. As noted by Strobel and others,[2] this prevented the development of legendary or mythological elements into the written records. This is a serious issue in our consideration of the Bible and the descriptions of Jesus Christ. We read in the Bible that Jesus Christ conducted many miracles, including the healing of the disabled, restoring life to dead people, calming a storm, and others. It also tells of Christ going to the cross to die as payment for our sins, His burial, and His bodily resurrection from the dead three days later. If the Bible books were written centuries later, then these miracles could have been "invented" over the years by followers of Christ. However, an early date of authorship would have prevented these types of legendary additions to the eyewitness accounts.

By studying the evidence, one finds that the gospel accounts were all written prior to 90 A.D., with Luke and Mark dating to 50-60 A.D (within 30 years of Christ's death). Since most scholars date the death of Christ to 30 A.D., these dates are within the lifetimes of many eyewitnesses of Jesus Christ's life and ministry. Had these writers included false or exaggerated accounts, then they could have been easily dismissed by non-Christian eyewitnesses. For comparison, Muhammad lived from 537 to 632 A.D., but his biography (the hadith) was not written or assembled until about 700-800 A.D. This was more than 100 years after his death and long after any eyewitnesses could have verified its details.

Thus, the basic doctrines or messages of Christianity were in place at a very early date. The early origins of Christian doctrines or messages can be shown from writings of the "church fathers." For example, Ignatius confirmed the orthodox Christian doctrines of the deity of Christ (Jesus Christ Himself is Creator and God), the humanity of Christ, and the crucifixion of Christ by Pontius Pilate.[3] Ignatius was himself executed for being a Christian, and just prior to his death, he wrote that Jesus Christ was raised from the dead, and those who believe in him would be raised, too. This letter was written prior to 117 A.D. Likewise, Clement of Rome wrote a letter to the Corinthian Christian church in about 96 A.D.[4] In his letter, he makes reference to the books (or letters) written by the Apostle Paul. He also mentions letters written to the Romans, Galatians, Ephesians, and the Phillipians. Moreover, he quotes from the book of Hebrews and it has references that appear to arise from three other New Testament books (Acts, James, and 1 Peter). Similar documents are known from other "church fathers" including, Polycarp, and Barnabas.[5] Not only do these manuscripts show an early date for the massages of the Bible, but importantly, none of these early documents make reference to Islam or use the term Muslim!

Evidence for the early dates of the Christian message also comes from the ancient creeds recited by followers of Christ. For example, the second century Rule of Faith states that Jesus Christ was the Son of God, crucified under Pontius Pilate and rose from the dead on the third day.[6] Scholars date this creed to mid-second century (i.e. 150 A.D.). Like the letters from the church fathers, this creed reveals that Christian doctrines were already being taught at very early dates. The evidence again suggests that the Bible was written at an early date, as the messages were provided from God. There is no indication that New Testament Scriptures have been subjected to a massive revision to extract or blot out Islamic theology.

Corroborating Accounts

As described in our studies of the crucifixion and resurrection, the four gospel accounts (Matthew, Mark, Luke, and John) are independent historical records. When two or more individuals provide eyewitness testimony - and their accounts are in agreement - this strongly suggests that the descriptions are accurate. In the gospel accounts of the New Testament, we have four written records that are in excellent agreement! We are not simply relying on one written account. This provides a great measure of assurance that they accurately recorded the messages of Jesus Christ and faithfully described the events of His life. Among the messages, events, and statements from Jesus Christ, the Bible contains corroborating accounts in many areas (Table 1). The listed areas of agreement are only a sampling of the events and statements from the gospel accounts. Further discussion may be found in Chapters 3 and 4.

Although some events from Christ's lifetime may only have one or two recorded accounts in the gospel books, this should not discredit the accuracy of the records. For example, John's gospel was the only one to mention the sinless life of Jesus Christ (John 8:46). However, this aspect of Christ's life is mentioned by several other New Testament writers and it is even suggested in Old Testament prophecies concerning the future Messiah. The Apostle Paul refers to Jesus Christ as one who "knew no sin" (2 Corinthians 5:21) and the writer of Hebrews says

Table 1. Subjects and events attributed to Jesus Christ and the agreement between historical accounts.

Area of Agreement	Authors	References
Virgin birth of Jesus Christ	Matthew, Luke	Matt 1:20, Luke 1:35
The prophet John came to Israel announcing the arrival of Christ	Matthew, Mark, Luke, John	Matt 3:16, Mark 1:9, Luke 3:6, John 1:34
Jesus Christ physically raised people alive from the dead	Matthew, Mark, Luke, John	Matt 9:25, Mark 5:41, Luke 8:54, John 11:43
Jesus Christ healed lame people	Matthew, Luke, John	Matt 15:31, Luke 7:22, John 5:7
Jesus Christ restored sight to the blind	Matthew, Mark, Luke, John	Matt 9:30, Mark 10:52, Luke 7:21, John 9:7
Jesus Christ is the Son of God	Matthew, Mark, Luke, John	Matt 14:33, Mark 1:1, Luke 22:70, John 1:34
Jesus Christ had compassion on sinners	Matthew, Mark, Luke, John	Matt 9:2, Mark 2:5, Luke 7:48, John 8:11
Jesus Christ was sent to save lost sinners	Matthew, Luke, John	Matt 1:21, Luke 19:10, John 12:46
Jesus Christ caused storms to cease	Matthew, Mark, Luke	Matt 8:26, Mark 4:39, Luke 8:24
Jesus Christ drove merchants from God's Temple	Matthew, Mark, John	Matt 21:12, Mark 11:15, John 2:15
Jesus Christ predicted that He would be killed but then rise from the dead	Matthew, Mark, Luke, John	Matt 16:21, Mark 9:31, Luke 9:22, John 2:19
Jesus Christ was betrayed by Judas, one of the 12 disciples	Matthew, Mark, Luke, John	Matt 26:14, Mark 14:10, Luke 22:48, John 18:3
Jesus Christ was brought before the Roman ruler name Pontius Pilate	Matthew, Mark, Luke, John	Matt 27:2, Mark 15:1, Luke 23:1, John 18:29
Jesus Christ was beaten and scourged	Matt, Mark, John	Matt 27:26, Mark 15:15, John 19:1
Pontius Pilate had Jesus crucified	Matthew, Mark, Luke, John	Matt 27:26, Mark 15:15, Luke 23:24, John 19:16
Jewish leaders taunted Christ as He hung upon the cross	Matthew, Mark, Luke	Matt 27:42, Mark 15:31, Luke 23:35
Jesus died and was buried	Matthew, Mark, Luke, John	Matt 27:60, Mark 15:46, Luke 23:53, John 19:42
Jesus Christ rose from the dead three days later	Matthew, Mark, Luke, John	Matt 28, Mark 16, Luke 24, John 20

Christ was "without sin" (Hebrews 4:15). The sinless character of Jesus Christ is also a message echoed by the Apostle Peter (1 Peter 1:19). The prophet Isaiah wrote in about 800 B.C., and in the 53rd chapter of his book, he writes that the Messiah would "do no violence" and have no "deceit in His mouth." This prophecy pointed centuries into the future at the sinless life of Jesus Christ. It corroborates the record of the gospel book of John. Although some events and messages may only appear once in the gospel records, they should still be considered reliable based on their consistency with other Bible texts. In the case of major Bible doctrines such as Christ dying for our sins and the resurrection of Christ, these appear in almost every New Testament book.

Archaeological and Historical Evidence

There are many archaeological findings that demonstrate the New Testament contains very accurate historical records. A complete survey of this topic is beyond the scope of this book but several excellent volumes have already been written on this subject.[7] When Biblical archaeology is actually studied, it becomes evident that widespread corruption of the Old and New Testament is impossible. There are far too many historically accurate details in the Scripture to suggest decay or corruption of its message. To briefly illustrate the historical accuracy of New Testament accounts, we will examine three important events: the birth of Jesus, the ministry of John the Baptist, and the arrest of Jesus leading to the crucifixion.

Archaeological and Historical Evidence: Birth of Jesus Christ

A complete account of the birth of Jesus Christ can be found in the first two chapters of the Gospel of Luke. The account describes how an angel visited Mary, the mother of Jesus. The angel told Mary that her baby would not be conceived from a man, but rather from the Holy Spirit of God. Thus, she would be the virgin with child, as prophesied by the ancient Jewish prophet Isaiah.[8] The account also describes how a Roman census required Mary (now pregnant) and her husband Joseph to register their names in Bethlehem. They arrived in Bethlehem and Jesus was born. The birth of Jesus Christ was announced by angels to the shepherds in the fields near Bethlehem.

With this overview of the birth of Jesus, some of the specific historical details can be examined. The first chapter of Luke begins with a statement describing John the Baptist's father, "There was in the days of Herod, the king of Judea...(Luke 1:5a)." Luke makes a reference to a king historians refer to as Herod the Great, who ruled on behalf of the Romans from 73 to 4 B.C. There are many scholarly works describing the reign of this particularly evil king – one who is known to have ruthlessly killed people. The Gospel of Matthew also describes how Herod was the ruler when Jesus was born to Joseph and Mary. Because Herod attempted to murder Jesus as an infant, God directed the parents to flee to Egypt:

> ...behold, an angel of the Lord appeared to Joseph in a dream, saying, "Arise, take the young Child and His mother, flee to Egypt, and stay there until I bring you word; for Herod will seek the young Child to destroy Him. When he arose, he took the young Child and His mother by night and departed for Egypt, and was there until the death of Herod... Matt. 2:13-15

Historical records indeed confirm that Herod was the ruler of Israel when Jesus Christ was born and his death can be dated (around 4 B.C) to the time when Jesus would still have been a young child. Archaeological discoveries include coins with Herod's inscriptions,[9] the finding of Herod's tomb,[10] and the thorough excavations of many of Herod's building projects.[11] Moreover, the writings of the historian Josephus are also in agreement with names and dates found in the New Testament. He dates the death of Herod at around 4 B.C., by making reference to an eclipse and the date of another ruler.[12] Thus, no serious historian questions the fact that Herod was king when Jesus was born. The evidence verifies the accuracy of the Biblical record.

In the second chapter of Luke, the physical birth of Jesus is described. Again we can find specific historical references that provide a measure of the Bible's accuracy and preservation. For example, the gospel of Luke reads:

> And it came to pass in those days that a decree went out from Caesar Augustus that all the world should be registered. This census first took place while Quirinius was governing Syria. So all went to be registered, everyone to his own city. (Luke 2:1-3)

As a result of this mandatory census, Joseph and Mary traveled the Bethlehem, which became the location of Jesus' birth. The historical references in this passage have been confirmed by archaeological findings. For example, archaeologists have discovered a "Quirinius coin" from Syria and Cilicia.[13] It dates from 11 B.C. to 4 B.C., indicating that there was someone named Quirinius ruling in this region during a time period in which Jesus Christ was born.

Moreover, a number of Roman census forms have been found by archaeologists, some of which date between 100 B.C. to 100 A.D. According to Price,[14] "both the Oxyrhynchus papyrus 255 (A.D. 48) and the British Museum papyrus 904 (A.D. 104) order compulsory returns to birthplaces for census-taking."

Not only does the Bible passage give the correct name for the regional ruler, but it also describes the unusual Roman method of taking census or registering citizens. The Romans required citizens to travel to their place of birth for the census. Since Joseph's family was from Bethlehem, Mary and Joseph returned to this town for the census. Thus, the passage from Luke's Gospel book is shown to have very precise historical references.

Earlier in the second chapter of Luke, the writer describes Joseph and Mary leaving the town of Nazareth for travel to Bethlehem. The town of Nazareth is where Jesus is said to have grown up. Some skeptics have argued that there was no evidence for the town of Nazareth during the lifetime of Jesus Christ, despite the record of Scripture. However, archaeologists have found a list describing the locations of priests that were resettled following the destruction of Jerusalem in 70 A.D.[15] According to the recovered document, one of the priests was assigned to the town of Nazareth. This indicates that the town of Nazareth was inhabited prior to this time.

Archaeological and Historical Evidence: Ministry of John the Baptist

In order to prepare the nation of Israel for the arrival of their long-awaited Messiah, God sent a prophet known as John the Baptist. He was to announce the coming of the Messiah and his ministry was even predicted by ancient Jewish prophets. The prophet Isaiah predicted John's arrival more than 800 years earlier. Isaiah described the future ministry of John as "the voice of one crying in the wilderness: 'Prepare the way of the LORD... The glory of the LORD shall be revealed, and all flesh shall see it together'...(Isaiah 40:3,5)."

Prior to his birth, John's parents were visited by an angel of the Lord. He was born shortly before Jesus. He began preaching and baptizing people in the Jordan River when he was about 30 years old. His message was simple – he was sent before the Messiah and the first century Jews were to prepare their hearts. When John did finally see Jesus, He proclaimed, "Behold! The Lamb of God who takes away the sin of the world!" and "this is Him on behalf of whom I said, 'after me comes a Man who has a higher rank than I, for He existed before me' (John 1:29-30)." John identified Jesus as the Messiah, and interestingly, he even makes a statement regarding the eternal nature of Jesus Christ.

In the Gospel of Luke, there is a detailed description of John the Baptist's ministry and it contains several historical references. It reads:

> Now in the fifteenth year of the reign of Tiberius Caesar, Pontius
> Pilate being governor of Judea, Herod being tetrarch of Galilee,
> his brother Philip tetrarch of Iturea and the region of Trachonitis,

and Lysanias tetrarch of Abilene, while Annas and Caiaphas were high priests, the word of God came to John the son of Zacharias in the wilderness. Luke 3:1-2

The reference to Tiberius Caesar is a historically accurate reference to the Roman Emperor who ruled during the time of John the Baptist. Historians date his rule from 14 to 37 A.D. Regarding Pontius Pilate, we have already seen the abundant archaeological and historical evidence regarding his rule at this time (see Chapter 2). This passage also mentions Herod, Lysanias, and Philip, as regional tetrarchs. In the Roman Empire, countries or provinces were sometimes divided into four divisions and each division was ruled by a tetrarch.[16] Thus, Luke's account is consistent with our knowledge of the methods by which the Romans governed.

Herod Antipas (a son of Herod the Great) tetrarch of Galilee was involved in the arrest and trial of Jesus, so he is discussed later. Regarding Lysanias the tetrarch of Abilene (a city near Damascus), archaeologists recently found an inscription dated from about 20 to 30 A.D. and it names him as the tetrarch in Abilene.[17] The inscription was found on the ruins of an ancient religious temple. Other confirmation of his rule as tetrarch includes a description by the first century historian Josephus.[18] Ancient coins have also been discovered bearing his name and title.[19] Likewise, the rule of Philip the tetrarch has been confirmed by historical records and archaeological discoveries. Josephus describes his rule in the historical book, *Antiquities*.[20] He is known to have founded and built the capital city of Caesarea Phillipi, located near the modern day Golan Heights. Coins have also been discovered with the inscription that states,[21] "of Philip the Tetrarch, Founder." Again, the records found in the New Testament are completely consistent with non-Biblical historical records, archaeological discoveries, and dated materials (i.e., coins). The accuracy of these historical references lead one to conclude that the accounts of John the Baptist are also reliable. This prophet appeared in Israel around 30 A.D., he testified that Jesus was the Messiah, and shortly after this, John the Baptist was executed by Herod Antipas.

Archaeological and Historical Evidence: the Arrest and Trials of Jesus Christ

According to the records in the book of Luke and elsewhere, Jesus was initially arrested by the Jewish Temple guard (a group of soldiers armed with clubs and swords). He was brought to a nighttime trial before the Jewish High Priest Caiaphas, his father-in-law Annas, and several leaders of Israel. During His arrest and trial, Jesus was beaten and abused. Although the chief priests brought forth several false witnesses, the High Priest eventually asked Jesus, are you "the Christ" and "are you then the Son of God?" To these questions, Jesus answered affirmative. These statements from Jesus prompted the High Priest and the council members to declare that Jesus should be put to death (see: Matt 26:66, Mark 14:64, Luke 22:71, John 18:31).

The Bible further describes how Jesus was sent to Pontius Pilate for another trail. This raises a natural question: if the Jewish leadership had already decided to condemn Jesus to death, then why would another trial be necessary? A Roman trial was needed because the Jewish leadership wanted an execution and only the Roman courts were permitted to levy this type of punishment. Moreover, chief priests and leaders wanted Jesus to die by crucifixion – a painful and humiliating punishment carried out by the Romans. Thus, Jesus was brought before Pilate for judgment. Almost immediately into the trial, Pilate recognized that Jesus was innocent of any wrong and he sought to release Jesus.

Pilate hoped to avoid sending Jesus to a Roman crucifixion, so he sent Jesus to be judged by the Roman ruler of Galilee, Herod Antipas. Herod had heard about Jesus – that He had conducted many miracles – but Herod decided not to judge Him and sent Jesus back to Pilate. With further pressure from the Jewish leadership, Pilate condemned Jesus to be crucified. Throughout the whole series of trials, Jesus was viciously whipped, beaten, and humiliated. A crown of thorns was pressed into His head. By the time he was nailed to the Roman cross, Jesus Christ was barely alive.

The accounts of the arrest and trials of Jesus contain several historical references and these have been confirmed by non-Biblical sources and archaeological findings. Four individuals were involved in the trials and each is well known to historians. The evidence for Pilate has been previously discussed. The High Priest during the time of Christ was an individual named, Caiaphas. He was the individual that orchestrated the arrest of Jesus and led one of His nighttime trials. During a recent building project in Jerusalem, a burial chamber was accidentally discovered and it contained 12 limestone ossuaries (a burial box used as a final resting place for an individual's bones/remains).[22] One of the boxes was ornately carved and it was inscribed with the name Caiaphas. In another discovery, the ossuary of Caiaphas's daughter was discovered.[23] It describes her as being the daughter of the priest. The first century historian Josephus also mentions Caiaphas in his accounts, describing the dates of his service as high priest, his duties, and the Roman leadership that appointed him to the office.[24] These historical records place Caiaphas in Jerusalem at the proper time for the trial of Jesus.

Similarly, the historical books by Josephus also document the priesthood of Annas. He dates Annas' high priesthood from 6 A.D. to 15 A.D. – after which he was removed from the priestly office by the Roman ruler Gratus.[25] The accounts of

Josephus also describe how Annas was a very influential and powerful Jew during the time of Jesus Christ. His sons and son-in-law (Caiaphas) all served as high priests. Of course, this gave Annas the opportunity to sit in judgment at the trials of Jesus.

As we have seen, Pilate found "no fault" in Jesus, so he hoped to release Him or defer judgment to someone else. The account in Luke reads,

> So Pilate said to the chief priests and the crowd, "I find no fault in this Man." But they were the more fierce, saying, "He stirs up the people, teaching throughout all Judea, beginning from Galilee to this place." When Pilate heard of Galilee, he asked if the Man were a Galilean. And as soon as he knew that He belonged to Herod's jurisdiction, he sent Him to Herod, who was also in Jerusalem at that time. Luke 23:3-7

This account is consistent with what is known about legal procedures in the early Roman Empire. Historians have found evidence for defendants being judged or tried by rulers from their home provinces or territories.[26] Thus, Pilate sent Jesus to Herod Antipas, because Herod was the ruler in Galilee and Jesus was said to be from Galilee. This is notable because the Bible correctly describes an unusual Roman legal procedure. Again, this type of historical accuracy would be impossible in an altered and corrupted Bible!

There have been several discoveries (non-Biblical manuscripts and other artifacts) that place Herod Antipas as ruler of Galilee for the judgment and crucifixion of the Jesus Christ. For example, Josephus describes the rule of Herod Antipas in the book *Antiquities*, including his reign over the region of Galilee.[27] Archaeologists have also found a few coins bearing dates and the name of Herod Antipas.[28] These coins are dated from 24, 33, 34, and 37 A.D. and they have the inscription "Herod the Tetrarch" on the coins. Both Josephus' accounts and the coins place Herod Antipas in the proper location and time frame to participate in the trials or judgments of Jesus Christ.

The New Testament Gospel books describe the birth, the ministry, the arrest, the trails, the crucifixion, the burial, and the triumphant resurrection of Jesus Christ. As we have seen, these accounts also contain very accurate historical references. Archaeological evidence has demonstrated the accuracy of the New Testament Scriptures. This evidence involves many elements, and in all of these aspects, the Bible has been shown to be genuine. Besides those items described above, this includes:

1. The names of rulers for locations outside of Israel.
2. The names of towns, cities, and other geographic details, outside of Israel.
3. The locations of first century Jewish synagogues outside of Israel.
4. The use of appropriate language and words for first century writers.
5. The use of appropriate writing style for the first century.
6. The use of appropriate names for people in the first century.

Indeed, Luke begins his books (Luke and Acts) with a clear declaration of his purpose, to give "an account of those things that have been fulfilled among us" based on the observations of "eyewitnesses." He also states that he "carefully investigated everything." Archaeology has demonstrated that Luke's writings to be first-rate historical records. With the agreement between Luke's writing and the findings from archaeology, two scholars noted,[29] "If Luke was so painstakingly accurate in his historical reporting, on what logical basis may we assume he was credulous or inaccurate in his reporting of matters that were far more important," such as the resurrection or the miracles of Jesus and his disciples? In other words, the skeptical Muslim is confronted with clear evidence for the preservation and truth contained in the New Testament books!

Non-Biblical Evidence

The accuracy of the New Testament record can also be seen by examining ancient non-Biblical manuscripts. There were several historical accounts written soon after the time of Christ and their records are generally in accord with the New Testament. For example, we have already seen that there are non-Biblical manuscripts and inscriptions verifying that Pontius Pilate was in the proper time and place to have presided over the trails and execution of Jesus Christ.

Other individuals can also be found both in the Biblical and non-Biblical historical records. The book of Acts describes how Herod Agrippa killed the Christian Apostle named James (Acts 12:2). In support of the account, this event is also described by the first century Jewish historian Josephus (*Antiquities*).[30]

Three gospel accounts describe how there was a "darkness" across the land on the day Jesus Christ hung upon the cross (Matthew 27:45, Mark 15:33, Luke 23:44). A description of a regional eclipse of the sun can also be found in the ancient literature corresponding to roughly the date of Jesus Christ's crucifixion. In about 52 A.D., a writer named Thallus described the history of the eastern Mediterranean. This account included a mid-day darkness around the time of the crucifixion of Jesus (30 A.D.).[31] Similarly, the Greek writer Phlegon wrote around 137 A.D. and he described "the greatest eclipse of the sun" which occurred at noon in the fourth year of the 202nd Olympiad, or 30 A.D.[32] Moreover, Phlegon described earthquakes that occurred at the same time – also an event described in the Bible.

Even in the Jewish *Talmud* (completed in 200 A.D.), there are passages that mention Jesus.[33] They do not acknowledge Jesus as Savior, of course, but they do make some claims that are indirectly supportive of the Biblical message. For example, the Talmud claims that he was a "false messiah who practiced magic." This old Jewish writing confirms that Jesus carried out miracles, although rather than attributing the works as signs from God, the writers believed that the works were the result of sorcery.

Conclusions

In general, there are multiple lines of evidence to show that the New Testament is an accurate description of the ministry and teachings of Jesus Christ. It has been shown that the gospel accounts were written at early dates, so they can be considered reliable eyewitness records of the events of that time. Moreover, we have accounts from different individuals and they are in agreement on both the details and the general aspects of their Scriptures. Finally, we have applied rigorous tests to examine the accuracy of historical records and preservation of the New Testament. When all of these points are considered, it becomes clear that large-scale revisions of God's revelations never took place. The Bible is completely accurate in its historical records. This idea was confirmed by Jesus Christ Himself when He said (Matt 24:35), "Heaven and earth will pass away, but My words will by no means pass away."

Indeed, the words of Jesus Christ have been faithfully preserved in the New Testament of the Bible. All of the old Bibles declare that Jesus Christ came for one purpose: to die for our sins upon the cross of Calvary and to be raised from the dead in glory, by God the Father. The consistent match between old copies of Scripture argues against the wide scale corruption of the New Testament of the Bible.

When the ancient copies of New Testament Scripture are actually studied, one finds an amazingly consistent message between copies. According to Hort, only one word in about one thousand has any substantial variation.[34] These are often just spelling variations, punctuation differences, or obvious "slips of the pen" during the copying. For example, one ancient manuscript may state "Christ Jesus" while another one may read "Jesus Christ." This led Bentley to conclude,[35] "the real text of the sacred writings is competently exact, nor is one article of faith or moral precept perverted or lost."

It must be emphasized that these scholars have a very large set of ancient manuscripts for these comparisons. As described by Strobel and McDowell, there are more surviving copies of the Bible than any other book from antiquity.[36] For the New Testament, this includes:

1. More than 5,000 ancient New Testaments and 90 papyrus fragments.
2. Portions of the four gospels and the book of Acts dating from 200-300 A.D.
3. Pauline epistles and Hebrews copies from about the year 200 A.D.
4. A papyrus document containing some of Revelation, dated from 200-300 A.D.
5. A papyrus dating from 100-150 A.D., containing five verses from the Gospel of John (since this was discovered in Egypt, far from the location of writing, it argues for a very early date for John's writing).
6. Greek manuscripts: uncial (all Greek caps), complete copies of the New Testament dating to 350 AD and 306 other old copies; minuscule (cursive) manuscripts dating from 800 A.D. onward, 2,856 copies.
7. Lectionaries (Bibles divided up to be read in church services), 2,403 ancient versions have been found.
8. 8,000 to 10,000 Latin Vulgate manuscripts.
9. 8,000 Ethiopic, Armenian, and Slavic manuscripts.

Rather than finding evidence for corruption and systematic revision of the Scriptures, the opposite is found. There has been a miraculous preservation of the Biblical texts and the messages of the prophets! Norman Geisler and William Nix conclude,[37] "The New Testament, then, has not only survived in more manuscripts than in any other book from antiquity, but it has survived in a purer form than any other great book – a form that is 99.5% pure." The archaeologist and scholar Price commented on the New Testament gospel accounts,[38] that they should "…be reckoned as carefully composed history rather than theological creations of a later Christian community."

What about the lack of Islamic teachings in the New Testament of the Bible? In the oldest manuscripts and manuscript fragments, there are no references or statements related to Islamic theology. Even within the large volume of material listed above, there is not a single reference to Allah. Nor do any of these ancient manuscripts refer to Adam, Abraham, or Jesus as Muslims! These doctrines and ideas only began to appear with the arrival of Islam in the seventh century. As noted earlier, the Quran quotes Jesus as saying, "...we bow to Allah as Muslims (5:111)." According to the record of the Bible, <u>Jesus never made this type of statement.</u>

The individual on the road from Mecca to Calvary must decide which is the reliable record – the Bible with its stunningly accurate historical records or the Islamic Scriptures (written seven centuries after Jesus walked the Earth). Was the New Testament corrupted or did Islamic writers invent and "make up" the supposed quotes from Jesus?

References:

(1)   E. F. Caner and H. E. Pruitt, *The Costly Call*, Kregel Publications, Grand Rapids, MI, 2005; pp. 17-23.

(2)   Lee Strobel, *The Case for Christ*, Zondervan, Grand Rapids, MI, 1998.

(3)   Strobel, p. 89. See also: David Hugh Farmer, "Ignatius of Antioch" in *The Oxford Dictionary of the Saints*, Oxford University Press, Oxford University Press, Oxford, UK, 1987.

(4)   Michael W. Holmes, *The Apostolic Fathers: Greek Texts and English Translations*, 3rd Ed., Baker Academic, Grand Rapids, MI, 2007; pp. 33-131.

(5)   Reference 4, pp. 272-333 and pp. 370-441.

(6)   Gerald Bray, *Creeds, Councils, and Christ*, Mentor – Christian Focus Publications, Scotland, UK, 2009.

(7)   James M. Holden, Norman Geisler, and Walter C. Kaiser, Jr. *The Popular Handbook of Archaeology and the Bible: Discoveries That Confirm the Reliability of Scripture*, Harvest House Publishers, Eugene, OR, 2013. Joseph P. Free and Howard F. Vos *Archaeology and Bible History*, Zondervan, Grand Rapids, MI, 1992. John McRay *Archaeology and the New Testament*, Baker Book House, Grand Rapids, MI, 1991.

(8)   Isaiah 7:14

(9)   Adam K. Marshak "The Dated Coins of Herod the Great: Towards a New Chronology" *Journal for the Study of Judaism*, 2006, (37), 212-240.

(10)   Steve Weizman "Archaeologists Find the Tomb of King Herod" *USA Today,* May 8, 2007.

(11)   Ehud Netzer, *Architecture of Herod, the Great Builder*, Baker Academic, Ada, MI, 2008.

(12)   Josephus, *Antiquities*, 17.6.4.

(13)   McRay, pp. 154, 385; Strobel, p. 101. It must however be noted that the interpretation of the "Quirinius" inscription is still a matter of debate among scholars.

(14)   Randall Price *The Stones Cry Out*, Harvest House Publishers, Eugene, OR, 1997; p. 299.

(15)   Strobel, p. 103. See also, M. Avi-Yonah "A List of Preistly Courses from Ceaesarea" *Israel Exploration Journal*, 1962, (12), pp. 137-139.

(16)   For a description of the Tetrarchy of Judea, see: H. H. Ben-Sasson, *A History of the Jewish People*, Harvard University Press, Cambridge, MA, 1976; pp. 246-248.

(17)   John Hogg, "On the City of Abila, and the District Called Abilene near Mount Lebanon, and on the Inscription at the Rover Lycus, in North of Syria." *Journal of the Royal Geographic Society of London*, 1850, (20), p. 43.

(18)   Josephus, *The Jewish War*, 2.12.8 and *Antiquities* 19.5,1.

(19)   David R. Sear, *Greek Coins and Their Values*, Vol. 2, Seaby Publishers, London, UK, 1979.

(20)   Josephus, *Antiquities*, 17.8-11

(21)   Ya'akov Meshorer *A Treasury of Jewish Coins: From the Persian Period to Bar Kokhba*, Amphora Books, Nyack, NY, 2001.

(22)   Michael Specter "Tomb May Hold Bones of Priest Who Judged Jesus," *The New York Times*, August 14, 1994. Available for download at: http://www.nytimes.com/1992/08/14/world/ tomb-may-hold-the-bones-of-priest-who-judged- jesus.html?pagewanted=all

(23)   Michelle Morris, "2,000-Year-Old Ossuary Authentic, Say Researchers" *Jerusalem Post*, June 29, 2011. Available for download at: http://www.jpost.com/Video-Articles/Video/2000-year-old-ossuary- authentic-say-researchers

(24)   Josephus, *Antiquities*, 18.2.2; 18.4.6.

(25)   Josephus, *Antiquities*, 20.9.1

(26)   A. N. Sherwin-White, *Roman Society and Roman Law in the New Testament*, Oxford University Press, Oxford, UK, 1963; pp. 28-31.

(27)   Josephus, *Antiquities*, 17 and 18

(28)   Wolf Wirgin and Siegfried Mandel, *The History of Coins and Symbols in Ancient Israel*, Exposition-University Book, Hicksville, NY, 1957.

(29)   John Ankerberg and John Weldon, *Ready With an Answer*, Harvest House, Eugene, OR, 1997; p. 272.

(30)   Josephus, *Antiquities*, 20.9.1

(31)   Robert E. Van Voorst, *Jesus Outside the New Testament: An Introduction to the Ancient Evidence*, Wm. B. Eerdmans Publishing, Grand Rapids, MI, 2000; pp. 20-21.

(32)   Gary R. Habermas, *The Historical Jesus: Ancient Evidence for the Life of Christ*, College Press Publishing Company, Inc., Joplin, MO, 1996; pp. 217-218.

(33)   *Talmud Sanhedrin* 107b, *Sotah* 47a.

(34)   B. F. Westcott and F. J. A. Hort, *The New Testament in the Original Greek*, Harper & Brothers, New York, NY, 1882; p. 22.

(35)   Charles Fremont Sitterly, "Text and Manuscripts of the New Testament" in the *International Standard Bible Encyclopedia Online,* downloaded September 3, 2013 from:
http://www.internationalstandardbible.com/T/text-and-manuscripts-of-the-new-testament.html

(36)   Josh McDowell, *The New Evidence That Demands a Verdict*, Thomas Nelson Publishers, 1999; pp. 33-34. Strobel, pp. 57-66.

(37)   Norman L. Geisler and William E. Nix, *A General Introduction to the Bible*, Moody Press, Chicago, IL, 1980; p. 367.

(38)   Randall Price, *The Stones Cry Out*, Harvest House Publishers, Eugene, OR, 1997; p 297.

Chapter 6

Old Testament: Corrupted Manuscript or Preserved Messages?

Praise the Lord! Blessed is the man who fears the LORD,
who delights in His commandments. Psalm 112:1

A young woman named Khadija also made the journey from Mecca to Calvary.[1] She made the trip by herself, as the rest of her family was firmly set in the Muslim faith. Her father was originally from Pakistan, but she was born in the United States. Both of her parents followed the Muslim faith. Although Khadija did not begin a formal religious education at a young age, she and her family travelled to Pakistan where an imam provided lessons and training in Islam. Throughout her youth, Khadija understood Islam to be the true faith and she would be responsible for learning its doctrines as a woman. As she grew up, she saw Islam as her great spiritual destiny:

> "...Islam shone out like a beacon of truth among Christianity, Judaism and other religions. It was filled with noble people. They were the most zealous believers, who prayed, fasted, and dressed modestly. It was obvious to me that these were the followers of the true God."

Upon reaching college age, she travelled to a university for studies. She sought to cultivate her Muslim faith, so she joined the campus Islamic Society. The Islamic Society distributed many types of reading materials and Khadija collected all the available literature regarding Islam. She read the materials with great interest.

As she made her way through the Islamic readings, she was left with a measure of doubt. She wondered about the reliability of the source material and many of the statements "were unfounded." This lead to a spiritual crisis for Khadija and it was compounded by deep depression that came over her. By her own account, her spiritual and emotion state "dragged me through frightening psychological depths."

It was at this time that a campus evangelist approached Khadija and invited her to attend a Bible study on campus. She had turned down similar invitations in the past, but she decided to attend the study on this occasion. Together they read passages from the Bible. Nevertheless, she understood very little regarding the teachings and soon she forgot about the messages.

Several months later, Khadija found herself in another state emotional upheaval. She experienced terrible panic attacks. She was extremely tense, even getting to the point of wanting to die. During one night of "mental torments and anguish" she "instinctively cried out to Jesus." She described the remarkable answer to her prayer:

> "What then happened to me was without doubt the most beautiful experience in all my life. My mind was cleared and freed completely from my disturbing and restless thoughts and replaced by a deep peace that I had not felt in many years."

Having experienced the peace of turning to Jesus, she began studying the Bible. The passages of Scripture came to life. She also realized that her unbelief and hardened heart had earlier prevented her from seeing the truth of Jesus Christ. Nevertheless, Khadija wanted to know the truth. She continually prayed to God for guidance, even to bring her back to the Islamic faith if indeed that was the way of truth.

Khadija considered the claims of Muslim apologists, such as Ahmed Deedat. But she stayed on the path from Mecca to Calvary. She wrestled with the questions regarding the deity of Jesus Christ and the incorruptible Word of God in the Bible. Through prayer and diligent study, God confirmed the truths found in the Bible. Khadija became ever more certain of the truth of Christianity. She also concluded,[1] "I can look at Islam now and say, with confidence, certainty and clarity that this is not a religion from the Almighty."

Like most Muslims on their journey from Mecca to Calvary, Khadija was confronted by the standard argument from Islamic teachers: the Bible has been corrupted. According to these individuals, the Bible is no longer a reliable source for God's revelation to mankind. They will admit that Moses, David, and Jesus Christ were all prophets sent from God, but the Muslim clerics deny that the Bible represents the actual teachings or messages from these prophets. Their claims usually continue with the idea that Abraham, Moses, and even Jesus Christ Himself, were really Muslims! In this chapter, these old ideas will be examined. We will look at the oldest part of the Bible itself to see if there is evidence for the type of large-scale corruption that is suggested by Muslim clerics. This chapter will examine the preservation of Old Testament.

Our investigation will begin by seeing what Jesus had to say about the Old Testament Scripture. Did He reprimand the Jews for altering their content? Did Jesus warn His followers about corrupted Scriptures and messages? Our study will also involve a search through the most ancient Biblical manuscripts and see if there is evidence for corruption and decay of the original messages from God. Along with this, we will see if any ancient manuscripts contain examples of Islamic theology or references to the Muslim religion. Finally, this part of the Bible contains many references to historical events and these can be used as internal checks for corruption in the Old Testament text. In this regard, we will examine to see if the historical records of the Bible are confirmed by archaeology and non-Biblical historical texts, or if the historical records of the Bible are shown to be in error. As noted previously, a Bible with accurate historical references is not likely to have been corrupted through the ages.

Preservation of the Old Testament: the testimony of Jesus and His disciples.
The Old Testament was written by more than 20 different Jewish prophets (including Moses, David, Isaiah, and others) over a period of about 900 years (1400 B.C. to 450 B.C.). The complete Old Testament was translated into the Greek language beginning in about 285 B.C., leading to the Septuagint (Greek) version of the Old Testament. Thus, the Jewish Scriptures were completed centuries before the arrival of Jesus Christ – who was born in about 6 B.C. The first four books of the Bible's New Testament (Matthew, Mark, Luke, and John) describe the life and ministry of Jesus Christ and they record many of the statements made by Christ. Based on Jesus' comments, there is no indication that the Old Testament Scriptures had been corrupted before His lifetime. Indeed, He makes frequent references to the Old Testament as authoritative revelation from God – citing or quoting from 24 of the 39 Old Testament books. Nowhere does Jesus Christ rebuke the Jews for removing references to Allah or Islam, but rather His references to the "Law and the prophets" always suggest that these Scriptures are in good order and completely truthful.
Consider the passage from the book of Luke, in which Jesus teaches in the synagogue at Nazareth (Luke 4:16-21):

> So He came to Nazareth, where He had been brought up. And as
> His custom was, He went into the synagogue on the Sabbath day,
> and stood up to read. And He was handed the book of the prophet
> Isaiah. And when He had opened the book, He found the place
> where it was written:
>
>> "The Spirit of the LORD is upon Me, because
>> He has anointed Me to preach the gospel to the
>> poor; He has sent Me to heal the brokenhearted,
>> to proclaim liberty to the captives and recovery

of sight to the blind, to set at liberty those who
are oppressed; to proclaim the acceptable year
of the LORD."

Then He closed the book, and gave it back to the attendant and sat
down. And the eyes of all who were in the synagogue were fixed
on Him. And He began to say to them, "Today this Scripture is
fulfilled in your hearing."

After reading this passage, Jesus does not say anything about the text or the
book of Isaiah being corrupted. Nor does He declare that Isaiah's manuscript
actually says "Allah," rather than LORD. Instead, His comment suggests the book
is truthful and authoritative. Jesus Christ also makes the claim that Isaiah's book
was speaking of Jesus' own life and ministry, as other portions of the New
Testament describe the ministry of Jesus to the poor, the broken hearted, the blind,
and the enslaved individuals.

In another example (Luke 10:25-29), a Jewish teacher asked Jesus, "What
shall I do to inherit eternal life?" Jesus answered by pointing the person to the Old
Testament Scriptures, saying to him, "What is written in the law? What is your
reading of it?" This reply indicates His trust in the preservation of the Scriptures
from Moses. Jesus used the same logic when He told a story about the salvation
and condemnation of sinners. Jesus quoted Abraham in Paradise, who says, "They
have Moses and the prophets; let them hear them (Luke 16:29)." Jesus confirms the
power of the Old Testament Scriptures to lead men to eternal life - and importantly -
He says nothing about the messages of the prophets being corrupted! He points to
the Old Testament Scriptures as a source of truth.

Through out His ministry, Jesus repeatedly cites the Old Testament Scripture
and He confirms its authority. For example, Jesus was angered by the merchants
having set up their businesses in the Jewish Temple and He confronts the Jewish
leaders (Matt 21:13). Jesus said to them (quoting Isaiah 56:7), "It is written, 'My
house shall be called a house of prayer'." The gospel accounts quote Jesus in at
least twelve statements saying, "it is written," as He cites the writings of the
prophets. In all of these discussions, Jesus never once said that the prophets'
messages had been altered or changed by Jewish scribes.

These statements by Jesus show that the Islamic position is unreasonable. If
Jesus knew that the Scriptures had been corrupted, then He certainly would not have
pointed to the writings of Moses. He would not have quoted them as the
authoritative Word of God. Islam acknowledges Jesus Christ to be a prophet, and
therefore, He would have known if the Old Testament messages were corrupted.

He would have certainly told His disciples about the errors and corruption in the Jewish Scripture (if they existed). But He did not ever suggest there were problems with the integrity of the Old Testament Jewish Scriptures. Indeed, the primary charge against the Jewish leadership and priesthood was, "you do not believe" the messages sent by God (see, John 5:47).

Besides the clear statements of Jesus Christ, there were nine righteous men who wrote books in the New Testament of the Bible (books written between about 45 A.D. and 95 A.D.). None of them described a corruption of Old Testament Scripture or a gross removal of doctrines from the Scriptures. This included several very well educated authors, such as the Apostle Paul and the medical doctor Luke.

Paul was considered one of the most educated men of his day. He was thoroughly trained in the study of Jewish Scriptures. What did he have to say about the Jews and their handling of the Scriptures? In Romans 3:2, he wrote that the Jews were blessed because they were given the "oracles of God" (oracle is the message from God). He condemns the Jews for not believing the message from God, but he says nothing about their corrupting or changing the text of Scripture. Paul also wrote (2 Timothy 3:15,16), "the Holy Scriptures, which are able to make you wise for salvation through faith in Jesus Christ" and he continued, "All Scripture is given by inspiration of God, and is profitable for doctrine…and instruction in righteousness." Even though Paul had left the Jewish religion to follow Jesus Christ, he said nothing negative about the Jews and their handling of Scripture through the ages. This first century scholar and Apostle repeatedly affirmed the integrity of the Old Testament Scriptures.

Likewise, Luke is regarded as a first-rate historian for his accounts in the book of Luke and the book of Acts. He says nothing about corruption of the "Law and the Prophets." Nowhere does he indicate that the Jews systematically removed references to "Allah" and Islam. Based on the statements from Jesus Christ and His Apostles, there is no indication that the Bible had been corrupted prior to their lifetimes. What about the Bible's complete lack of Islamic theology, references to Allah, and Muslims? We are forced to conclude that Old Testament authors such as Moses, David, Isaiah, and others, said nothing about Muslims or the religion of Islam!

Preservation of the Old Testament: proof from ancient copies.

The preservation of the Old Testament of the Bible was dramatically demonstrated by the discovery of the Dead Sea Scrolls.[2] These ancient documents were discovered by an Arab boy and found hidden in caves at Qumran near the Dead Sea. They included many papyrus manuscripts, but also some were written on leather parchment.

A complete copy of the Old Testament book of Isaiah was found among the Dead Sea scrolls. It has been dated to about 100 B.C. There are several lines of evidence archaeologists have used to date the ancient copy of Isaiah.[3] The Dead Sea scrolls were stored in pottery vessels and these pieces of pottery were found to be from the late Hellenic period (ca. 200 to 100 B.C.). Analysis of the Hebrew script also provided a date of authorship (writing forms, like languages, evolve over time). The Isaiah manuscript was compared to other Hebrew manuscripts, and based on the style of lettering, the date of authorship was estimated to be around 100 B.C. Before this discovery, the oldest copy of Isaiah's book was from 900 A.D. (Aleppo Codex). This provided Bible scholars an opportunity to evaluate the preservation of the Old Testament Scriptures.

With two books of Isaiah copied 1,000 years apart, large-scale corruption or revision would be easily recognized. Most remarkably, the contents of the ancient copy of Isaiah correspond exceedingly well with the copy from 900 A.D., as well as to our current Biblical versions of Isaiah. In the words of one scholar, there is "no major addition or omission" between the two versions.[4] This observation is devastating to the standard argument given by Muslim clerics - that the Bible has been corrupted through the ages and it is no longer reliable. If the Bible has been corrupted, then how could there be such a good correspondence between the ancient text and the modern text? Wouldn't we expect to see strange "new" doctrines in the modern text if the Bible were corrupted over the years? A second partial copy of the book of Isaiah was also discovered (in the same Dead Sea cave) with the complete copy of Isaiah. Its content also matches well with the complete Isaiah scroll. The complete Isaiah scroll – referred to as the Great Isaiah Scroll - can be viewed at the Israel Museum in Jerusalem.

Many other ancient documents were recovered among the Dead Sea Scrolls. All of these documents date to the same period of time as the Isaiah scrolls, although some are dated even earlier. These include more than 200 copies or copy fragments of Old Testament books - sections or complete copies of every Old Testament book (except the book of Esther) and even a fragment from the book of Samuel dated to 300 B.C. One cave alone yielded 40,000 manuscript fragments. This included commentaries on the Bible books and other writings, as well as 13 scrolls from Deuteronomy, 6 from Exodus, 5 from Genesis, 10 from Psalms, and 12 from Isaiah. Regarding the comparison of the Dead Sea scrolls with modern Old Testament books, Free and Vos state:

> ...during the period of copying the Old Testament by hand, there was a remarkable – can we say miraculous – degree of preservation of the text. What could be said of the Isaiah

manuscripts was approximately true of the rest of the scrolls as well.[5]

This treasure of old manuscripts provided scholars with verification that the Old Testament had been well preserved through the ages. The Scrolls have also enabled scholars to more accurately translate from the original language to modern languages, especially with the discovery of commentaries on the Bible books. Importantly, scholars have not found any Islamic doctrines on the thousands of ancient manuscript fragments!

Preservation of the Old Testament: evidence from archaeology
As noted previously, the preservation of the Old Testament Scriptures can also be shown through the science of archaeology. To appreciate the value or importance of an archaeological artifact, it is necessary to have reasonably good knowledge of ancient history and a familiarity with the Bible. This background knowledge allows one to compare the Biblical text with facts known from history. The Old Testament describes the history of the Jews and their nation Israel, as God prepared this people for one very important purpose: the avenue through which Jesus Christ would be born into this world. As the Savior of mankind, Jesus Christ fulfilled their ultimate destiny.

The Old Testament does of course describe events that predate the time of the patriarchs (Abraham, Isaac, and Jacob) and the nation of Israel. The book of Genesis describes the creation of our world by the hand of God. It also tells of a worldwide flood and the salvation of Noah and his family. In Genesis chapter 11, we read that God singles out a man named Abraham and the Lord promises to make him a "great nation." This is where we will begin our analysis of archaeological findings and our study of the preservation of the Old Testament Scriptures. From the time period of Abraham onward, virtually every historical period in the Bible has been studied through the science of archaeology. Moreover, each time period has provided archaeological discoveries that support the accuracy of the Old Testament accounts. Examples of these discoveries are described below for each Old Testament time period. A complete survey of Old Testament archeology is beyond the scope of this book, but the interested reader is directed to any one of the good books on this topic.[6]

Time period: the age of the patriarchs (ca. 2000 B.C. to 1800 B.C.)
The Bible describes how Abraham was called out by God to worship and serve Him, while Abraham's family and neighbors "served other gods." The Bible notes that Abraham lived in a Cannanite city called Haran. Archaeological excavations at

the ancient city of Haran have revealed that it was abandoned around 1800 B.C., or shortly after Abraham's family resided there.[7] It remained largely uninhabited for another thousand years. With this lengthy period of desolation, it suggests a historically accurate account of Abraham's life in the Biblical text. If the Bible (and the book of Genesis) had been corrupted over the centuries or it had been a forgery written in 500 B.C., then the author(s) would not place Abraham in Haran (a desolate city). The author(s) would have chosen one of the later, more powerful cites that emerged in this region. Moreover, the Bible gives names from the Patriarchal period: Serug, Nahor, and Terah (Abraham's great grandfather, grandfather, and father, respectively). Inscriptions on tablets reveal that these names were appropriate for this time frame (ca. 2000 B.C.) and they were used in this region of Syro-Mesopotamia.[8]

In the book of Genesis, there is an account describing Abraham's nephew Lot and the judgment and destruction of the cities of Sodom and Gomorrah. There are several elements of this account that has been supported by archaeological work. For example, critics have doubted the Bible's historical record, because it states that Lot chose to settle in the Jordan Valley. This area includes the region around the Dead Sea, perhaps one of the most inhospitable locations on Earth. In our day, the temperature can exceed 117°F (47°C) and its arid conditions do not support the growth of crops or livestock. However, archaeological exploration has found the remains of several towns in the Jordan Valley and Dead Sea region dating from the time period of 3000-2000 B.C.[9] Ancient historical accounts from the first century A.D. (Josephus) have also described the remains of cities near the southern end of the Dead Sea. Given the extent of habitation of this area during Abraham's time, some have speculated that the Jordan Valley area may have experienced a drastic change in its regional climate (sometime between Lot's day and our time). In fact, excavations and climatological surveys have indicated that the region of the Jordan Valley had been considerably wetter in the third millennium B.C.[10] This is in agreement with descriptions found in the Bible (i.e. the cities of the plain, including Sodom).

Regarding the destruction of Sodom and Gomorrah, the Bible describes how the Lord destroyed these towns with "brimstone and fire" which rained down "out of the Heavens" (Genesis 19:24). Near the region of Biblical Sodom, at a site called Bab edh-Dhra, excavations have uncovered layers of thick ash and evidence for structures that were burned from the roof downward into the building.[11] These findings have led some archaeologists to suggest that this is the site of "fire and brimstone" destruction in the city of Sodom. Similar deep ash deposits have been discovered at other ancient sites in the area, again suggesting that these are the "Cities of the Plain" described in the Biblical judgment and destruction. Indeed, archaeologists have discovered the ancient ruins of five cities on the southeast side of the Dead Sea, consistent with the Biblical account. These may very well be the "Cities of the Plain" described by Moses. The first century historian Josephus also recorded that the charred ruins of Sodom, Gomorrah, Admah, and Zeboiim, were still visible in his day.[12]

According to the Biblical record, Abraham was married to a woman named Sarah. She gave birth to a son named Isaac. When Sarah died in about 1900 B.C., Abraham sought to bury his wife in a tomb. As described in the Bible, Abraham purchased the Cave at Machpelah for her burial and he "weighed out" silver for the purchase. This burial place for Sarah is also the site where Abraham, Isaac, Rebecca, Jacob, and Leah, are buried - as recorded in the Old Testament. It is near present day Hebron. This record is confirmed by the presence of a 2,000-year old building marking the site.[13] The building is called the Tomb of the Patriarchs. It is also notable that Ishmael is not buried at this tomb with Abraham, Isaac, or Jacob. This stands as a testimony of the truthful record of Biblical Scriptures.

Interestingly, the Bible states that Abraham "weighed out" silver for the purchase. The coinage of precious metals was invented in about 700 B.C.,[14] many centuries after Abraham. Thus, it is expected that Abraham would have weighed out the silver. If these Old Testament accounts were corrupted hundreds, or even a thousand years after Moses, then historical details like this would most certainly be in error. The Jewish scribes would likely have written, Abraham counted out "100 silver coins" or something similar. Thus, the Biblical account is consistent with our knowledge of the development of money and exchange.

Time period: twelve tribes in Egypt and the Exodus under Moses (ca. 1800 B.C. to 1400 B.C)

The book of Genesis was written by Moses - the great Jewish prophet and leader. It describes how Jacob (Abraham's grandson) had twelve sons and God changed Jacob's name to Israel. The sons eventually became the twelve tribes of the house of Israel. This part of Biblical history begins when one of Jacob's sons (Joseph) is sold into Egyptian slavery. Because of their jealousy towards Joseph, his own brothers betrayed and sold him. Ancient papyrus documents found in Egypt state that slaves from Syria were highly sought by the Egyptians.[15] Thus, the non-Biblical records support the idea that a young man from Canaan or Syria could have been sold as a slave in Egypt.

The account in Genesis also describes how God miraculously raised Joseph up to one of the most powerful positions in Egypt. Skeptics have questioned whether it would have been possible for a foreigner, such as Joseph, to attain such a powerful position in Egypt. Egyptian archaeological work has found records of several foreign leaders among the powerful elite in ancient Egypt.[16] These findings again support the general, historical accuracy of the Bible's account.

A widespread famine forced Jacob's family – the tribes of Israel - to move to Egypt, a country with a large surplus of grain. With Joseph in a position of authority, and well regarded by the Pharaoh, his brothers and their families were initially welcomed into Egypt. According to the writing of Moses, the Jews prospered for nearly 200-300 years, but the Bible also describes how the nation of Egypt turned from a favorable attitude to a hostile attitude towards the Jews.

Again, the study of ancient Egyptian writings and artifacts supports the historical record of Genesis. It is known from non-Biblical historical records that a group of Asiatic people (the Hyksos) ruled Egypt between 1700 to 1570 B.C.[17] Historians are in general agreement that the Hyksos would have been inclined to treat the Jews favorable, as both groups were immigrants to Egypt. Following this period, native Egyptians seized control of the country and its power. The Pharaoh who first ruled during this period has been identified as Ahmose I (ruling from 1570 to 1545 B.C.).[18] The timing of this event coincides perfectly with the record in Genesis, where the ancient Jews soon found themselves in Egyptian slavery. Although the Egyptian records do not specifically mention the Jews or Hebrews, archaeologists have found records describing large numbers of foreign slaves from this period of time.[19]

The Bible further describes how the Pharaoh subjected the Jews to "hard labor of bricks and mortar." It further states that they were forced to build the "treasure cities" of Pithom and Rameses. Archaeologists have found both of these cities in the sands of Egypt.[20] In the book of Exodus, it is said that the Jewish laborers mixed straw with the mud when making bricks. Interestingly, ancient Egyptian papyrus documents also describe this process. A non-Biblical source, the Papyrus Anastasi, specifically mentions the need for straw in making bricks.[21] Even to this day, one can see ancient Egyptian ruins with some bricks having straw in their forms.

As described in the first few chapters of the book of Exodus, God raised up a man named Moses. He would be God's prophet, and eventually, he would lead the enslaved Jews to their freedom. In order to free the Jews from their bondage in Egypt, God sent plagues upon Egypt and used Moses to lead the people out. As God executed His judgments on Egypt, the Bible states that God "hardened" Pharaoh's heart. This Hebrew word can also be translated "heavy," suggesting that God made Pharaoh's heart "heavy." With the use of this term, it is clear that the Biblical writer must have intimately understood the religion and culture of ancient Egypt. Ancient Egyptian records indicate that many Egyptians believed in a religious system based on good deeds. Following an individual's death, their heart was supposedly placed in a balance and it was weighed out against the "feather of righteousness." If the person's heart weighed less than the feather, then they earned eternal reward. However if a heart was found more "heavy" than the feather, then this would lead to eternal doom. Thus, the biblical account is amazing in its historical accuracy. It uses a word that is perfectly appropriate for this time period in Egyptian history. It also reflected the eternal judgment and doom that awaited Pharaoh (and others who reject God's clear message).

The Bible also lists the plagues, or judgments, that came to Egypt when Pharaoh refused to allow the Jews to go free. Archaeological discoveries have revealed an interesting parallel between the plagues and the ancient Egyptian deities. The first plague involved the Nile River and this was one of their deities. The second plague involved frogs, another Egyptian "god." Another plague involved cows and this animal was also worshipped as a deity. These parallels are not accidental, but rather God and Moses were intent on demonstrating an important truth: the God of the Bible is the only true God. Moreover, the agreement between archaeology and the Bible account is significant. If the Bible were corrupted or historically inaccurate, then there would not be this agreement between the types of plagues and the ancient Egyptian deities.

As described in the book of Exodus, the Pharaoh eventually allowed the Jewish slaves to leave Egypt and return to the land of their fathers (Abraham, Isaac, and Jacob). This began an exodus, or departure, of the Hebrews out of Egypt. Following a miraculous crossing of the Red Sea, the Bible describes how Moses and the Jews came to Mount Sinai. It was here that Moses received the 10 Commandments inscribed on stone tablets. Although God attempted to bring the Jewish people into the land of Canaan, their rebellion and lack of faith led to a "wandering" in the Sinai desert for about 40 years.

The Bible gives a date for the Exodus and this corresponds perfectly with archaeological records. The specific years are listed in 1 Kings 6:1, where the exodus (of Jews) from Egypt was said to occur 480 years before the dedication of Solomon's Temple, during the 4th year of Solomon's reign as the King of Israel. Solomon's 4th year is thought to be 967-966 B.C., so the exodus occurred around 1440 B.C. After wandering in the Sinai desert for 40 years, the Jews began their movement into Canaan, including the conquest of Jericho in about 1400 B.C. Archaeological excavations at Jericho have dated the fall of this city at 1400 B.C. (see later discussion), in remarkable agreement with the Biblical record.

At the conclusion of the exodus period, Israel was ready to enter the land of Canaan. According to the writing of Moses, God gave the Israelites the land of Canaan:

But I have said to you, "You shall inherit their land, and I will give it to you to possess, a land flowing with milk and honey." I am the LORD your God, who has separated you from the peoples (Leviticus 20:24).

This time period involved the transfer of power and authority from Moses to Joshua. Moses died without entering into the promised land of Canaan.

Time period: Israel conquers the land of Canaan and the Judges period (ca. 1400 B.C. to 1000 B.C.)

Among the clay tablets and inscriptions dating to the time of Joshua (ca. 1400 B.C.), the Amarna Tablets are important evidence for the accuracy of the Biblical accounts.[22] These tablets were discovered in the northern Egyptian city of Amarna in the late 1800s. They are comprised mainly of correspondences between the neighboring powers and the Egyptian Pharaoh. The tablets confirm the general political picture in the land of Canaan and the Fertile Crescent, as described in the Bible: there was no dominant regional power at the time and that local kings ruled over a few cities. Interestingly, the ruler of Jerusalem (Abdi-Heba) wrote several letters to the Pharaoh and these letters make reference to the "Habiru." He also warns that these people were plundering the territory.[23] There are striking similarities between these letters and the accounts recorded in the Bible. This has led many to suggest the "Habiru" of the Amarna Tablets were the Hebrews of the Bible. It is also clear from the tablets that the ruler of Jerusalem was a loyal ally of the Egyptian king. This is also consistent with the Biblical record, which states that the Israelis had not yet driven the Canaanites from Jerusalem.

There have been Bible critics who claimed that the Joshua and the Jews did not conquer Canaan, as the Bible claims. However, archaeological findings have supported the general historical outline found in the Bible. Price outlines the evidence found for the military conquest of Canaan, presumably by Joshua and the Israelites.[24] Archaeological evidence has been discovered which dates the conquests and suggests military-type overthrow (as opposed to a "peaceful infiltration"). For example in the ruins of the ancient city of Hazor, there is evidence of a massive fire that destroyed the city. Besides a thick layer of ash, the remaining bricks show evidence of intense fire and vitrification (turned into glassy materials). This is in accord with the Old Testament passage (Joshua 11:13) which states:

But as for the cities that stood on their mounds, Israel burned none of them, except Hazor only, which Joshua burned.

The archaeological site has been identified by cuneiform inscriptions on clay tablets, recovered from the charred ruins. The inscription for "Hazor" has been positively identified.[25]

During their conquest of the land of Canaan, Joshua and the nation of Israel overtook the city of Jericho. This is described in one of the most well known passages of the Bible (Joshua chapter 6) and it has been strongly supported by archeological studies. The ancient city of Jericho was a fortified city, encircled by two massive walls. Being directed by the Lord Himself, Joshua began his assault in an unconventional manner. Rather than attacking the walls with battering rams or fire, he marched in circles around the city with the Jewish priests blowing trumpets and carrying the Ark of the Covenant (the central object of worship from the Jewish tabernacle). After 7 days of marching around Jericho, the people shouted to the Lord and the city walls collapsed. The Israeli army then attacked the city.

In accord with this account, archeological excavations around Jericho have found evidence for the *outward* collapse of the southern and western walls of the city.[26] Generally, a siege on a walled city caused the walls to breach *inward*, however Jericho's walls had collapsed *outward*. An excavation in the early twentieth century also found a section of the northern wall still standing and this section had homes (or the remains of homes) built against the wall.[27] This observation is remarkably similar to the account in the book of Joshua, where a woman named Rahab is said to have lived in a home on the exterior wall of the city. At the site of Jericho, archaeologists have also found grain storage in the ruins of this city.[28] This indicates that the city fell suddenly, as the citizens of Jericho did not have time to eat the grain or remove it during a retreat from the city. A date for Jericho's fall was estimated through the use of carbon dating (a method of dating based on the steady rate of radioactive carbon decay in an organic sample). A sample of charred wood from the Jericho "destruction layer" was analyzed by carbon dating and it was dated to 1410 B.C., with a range of error about ±40 years.[29] The archaeologist Garstang excavated Jericho in the 1930s.[30] Based on pottery evidence and other factors he concluded that the city was destroyed around 1400 B.C. These observations are in excellent agreement with the Biblical record. This is the same date that can be derived from the book of Joshua and 1 Kings in the Old Testament of the Bible.

The Bible then describes a period of time in which the Jews were ruled by leaders called "the judges." According to the Bible, these individuals were raised up by God to provide deliverance from some type of national crisis in Israel. The judges served as military leaders, prophets, and in other roles. This represents the time period between the conquest of the land of Canaan (by Joshua) and the start of the monarchy of Israel (Saul, David, and Solomon, as kings of Israel). Thus, the "judges" period is estimated to be from 1350 B.C. to 1050 B.C. This part of Israel's history is described in the Old Testament book titled, "Judges." A sizable number of archeological discoveries have also been found in support of this Biblical record. This includes:

1. Large number of settlements, towns, and cities that were founded in the land of Israel during this time period – consistent with the influx of a large migration of people into the land (i.e., the nation of Israel).[31]

2. Book of Judges describes the destruction of the Canaanite cities of Hazor, Debir, Gibeah, and Bethel. Excavations at these sites have found strong evidence for their destruction at about 1300 B.C., in accord with the dates found in the Bible.[32]

3. The city of Shiloh was occupied during the Judges period, but destroyed by the time of the Jewish prophet Jeremiah (600 B.C.; see, Jer. 7:12-14). Archaeological excavations at the ancient site of Shiloh indicated that the city was occupied from 1300 B.C. to 1100 B.C. - consistent with the historical records in the Bible.[33]

4. Hittite civilization is described in the Bible – excavations unearthed capital city of Hittites (near modern day Ankara, Turkey). Among the discoveries, a royal archive of inscribed records (clay tablets) was found, with more than 10,000 inscribed tablets being recovered.[34] These discoveries have provided overwhelming confirmation of the historical records found in the Bible.

5. In the book of Judges, there are many accounts of the Philistines and their attacks on the Jews. Archaeologists have found more than twenty-eight sites in Judea that can be connected to the ancient Philistines.[35]

Most remarkably, specific names in the Old Testament have even been found on non-Biblical sources. For example, the Canaanite leaders of Hebron are mentioned in Judges 1:10, two men named Ahiman and Talmai. These two names were also found inscribed in the Ras Shamra Tablets – clay tablets discovered in the remains of the bronze-age, eastern Mediterranean city of Urgarit.[36] As described below, several other examples of individuals' names have been found in non-Biblical sources from later periods in the Old Testament Scriptures. With these types of archaeological discoveries, we have good evidence for the preservation of these Old Testament Scriptures from the Judges period. As noted previously, corrupted Scriptures would not be expected to have such accurate historical records.

Around 1100 B.C., the Israelites began appealing to God for a king to lead their nation. This brought a close to the "Judges" period and began the monarchy of Israel, a time in which kings ruled the nation.

Time period: age of the monarchy, Kings Saul, David, and Solomon (ca. 1050 B.C. to 930 B.C.)

Israel's first king was named Saul and the Bible indicates that he was not a man of great spiritual strength or integrity. The Bible describes how Saul died by his own sword during a battle against the Philistines. The Philistine forces recovered his body, and according to the Bible (1 Sam 31), they hung his body from a wall of the city named Beth Shan. It also describes how Saul's armor was placed in the temple of Ashtaroth (a fertility goddess). Biblical dating would place these events at about 1000 B.C. Archaeologists have found the ancient site of Beth Shan and it was determined that the city was destroyed between about 1050 B.C. and 1000 B.C., in accord with the Biblical chronology.[37] At the site, an elaborate temple complex was also discovered and it was identified (by inscriptions, idols, and other artifacts) as the temple of Ashtaroth.[38] Thus, the Biblical record is well supported by these archeological findings.

Although there have been archaeological discoveries related to the reign of Israel's second and third kings, David and Solomon, it is a surprisingly small amount of material. This should not be reason to doubt the Biblical account, however. There may be several reasons why kings David and Solomon are not as well documented by sources outside the Bible. Firstly, the two most likely sources of archaeological artifacts, the ancient cities of Jerusalem and Hebron, are very difficult locations to carry out excavations. In our day, the cities lie in that volatile region that separates Muslims and Jews (Palestinians and Israelites). Although there are many sites to be explored in these two cities, political and religious forces prevent such archaeological work. Secondly, many of the writings during this period in Israel were likely done on papyrus. Unlike regions of Egypt where papyrus remained preserved for many centuries, the land of Canaan was fairly wet from seasonal rains. Consequently, papyrus documents from Jerusalem and nearby locations were not likely to have survived to this day. Although many papyrus writings have been discovered as part of the Dead Sea Scrolls, most of these date to around 100 B.C. to 100 A.D., long after the reign of David and Solomon. Nevertheless, archaeological work continues throughout the Middle East. Historical artifacts attesting to the reign of David and Solomon may very well be uncovered at anytime.

One such historical artifact was discovered in 1993, a piece of inscribed black basalt called the "Tel Dan Stele" or "House of David Stele." The inscription is part of a monument believed to have been produced by the Aramean king out of Damascus, named Hazael (who ruled from 842-800 B.C.).[39] The inscriptions state that he killed "Ahaziahu son Jehoram king of the House of David." The war between Hazael and Israel is described in the Bible (2 Kings 8:7-15). This archaeological finding is very significant because it places the term "House of David" in the proper time and context to support the Biblical accounts of David and his reign. Scholars have also noted that the inscriptions, or monument, were produced by one of Israel's most fierce enemies. Thus, there should be little tendency for Hazael to propagate a myth about a legendary hero of Israel, if indeed David were not an actual person.

According to the Bible, Israel's third king was Solomon (one of David's sons). It is during Solomon's reign that Israel held its position of greatest military and political power. Although some have questioned the accuracy of this claim, evidence indicates that the Bible's descriptions are historically accurate. For example, it is known that during Solomon's reign the other regional powers were in decline or had come to an end.[40] The Egyptians, the Hittites, and the Assyrians, were all an inconsequential threat to Solomon and his kingdom. As stated by Free and Vos, "There was a power vacuum in the Mediterranean world and the Near East," and consequently, this allowed Israel to rise in power.

Besides ruling over a mighty nation of Israel, Solomon is described in the Bible as having built the first Jewish Temple in Jerusalem. Given the significance of the Jewish Temple in both the Old and New Testaments, the entire next chapter is devoted to this topic.

Time period: the worship of false gods and a divided nation (ca. 931 B.C. to 722 B.C.)

The monarchy of Israel did not last long. Among other things, Solomon had many wives. Some of his wives came from nationalities such as, the Edomites, the Hittites, and the Moabites. These "foreign wives" compelled Solomon to worship false gods and this was a horrible sin against the covenant God had made. The Lord God spoke to Solomon and made this covenant, or agreement:

> Now if you walk before Me as your father David walked, in integrity of heart and in uprightness, to do according to all that I have commanded you, and if you keep My statutes and My judgments, then I will establish the throne of your kingdom over Israel forever, as I promised David your father, saying, 'You shall not fail to have a man on the throne of Israel.'

But if you or your sons at all turn from following Me, and do not keep
My commandments and My statutes which I have set before you, but
go and serve other gods and worship them, then I will cut off Israel
from the land which I have given them; and this house which I have
consecrated for My name I will cast out of My sight. Israel will be a
proverb and a byword among all peoples. (1 Kings 9:4-7)

In the second part of the covenant, the God of Heaven warned Solomon (and his
children) to avoid worshiping false gods. The passage also makes reference to "this
house," which is clearly a reference to the Jewish Temple built by Solomon.

Unfortunately, Solomon did not remain faithful to God, as described in the
book of 1 Kings:

For it was so, when Solomon was old, that his wives turned his heart
after other gods; and his heart was not loyal to the LORD his God, as
was the heart of his father David. (1 Kings 11:4)

As a result of this sin, God allowed Israel to be split into two nations: the northern
nation, composed of ten tribes and called Israel, and the southern nation, composed
of two tribes and called Judah. This was the beginning of the end. Soon the armies
from Assyria and Babylon would destroy the remains of the kingdom once ruled by
David and Solomon.

The Bible records the kings' names that ruled the northern kingdom (Israel)
and the southern kingdom (Judah). Again, this section of the Bible has been put to
the test by archaeological findings. The Assyrians were thorough at record keeping
and many of their clay tablets have been recovered from archaeological
excavations.[41] Since the Assyrians fought Israel and the battles are recorded on the
tablets, these non-Biblical sources provide independent verification of the historical
records in the Bible. In accord with the Bible, the Assyrian tablets make specific
references to the kings of Israel, for example king Ahab (ruled from 874-853
B.C.).[41] Other artifacts have been found bearing the names of these kings, such as a
seal with the Jeroboam's name (ruled from 931-910 B.C.).[41]

During the period around 850 B.C., the Moabites were subjugated by Israel (2
Kings, chapter 5). As described in the Bible, the king of Moab is named as
"Mesha" and it is said that he revolted against Israel. An important confirmation of
the Biblical account was found in the Moabite Stone, an engraved black stone
recovered in 1868 from an ancient site near present day Dhiban, Jordan.[42] The
stone was originally produced by the Moabites to memorialize the rebellion against

Israel. Several important Bible references are externally supported by inscriptions on the stone. First, the stone makes reference to the kings of Israel, including specific references to Omri (Israel's king from 880-874 B.C.) and one of Omri's sons (likely Jehoram). Reconstruction of line 31 is also thought to contain a specific reference to the "House of David." Secondly, the Bible makes reference to the false god worshipped by the Moabites, a deity named Kemosh or Chemosh (see, 1 Kings 11:33 and Numbers 21:29) and the Moabite stone also names their god as Chemosh. Finally, the stone also makes reference to the Hebrew name of God, YHWH (often rendered "Jehovah" in English Bibles). This inscription from ca. 840 B.C. represents the oldest known reference to Jehovah from outside the Hebrew Scriptures. The Moabite Stone provides outstanding confirmation of the historical elements found in the Biblical text.

Another large stone engraving of Assyrian origin, refereed to as the Black Obelisk of Shalmaneser, was discovered in 1846 near the ancient site of Nineveh.[43] This monument describes (via images and inscriptions) the conquests of several kingdoms by the Assyrians. It shows an image of a man bowing before the Assyrian king Shalmaneser III. The text on the Black Obelisk describes the tribute of Jehu, son of Omri, being paid to the Assyrian king. Omri reigned as king in Israel in about 870 B.C. (1 Kings 16). Again, this non-Biblical source is in general agreement with the names and dates that are found in the Bible.

From among the nations outside of Israel and Judah, many of their rulers are also listed in the Bible. These records are confirmed in many non-Biblical sources. For example, The Bible describes how the Syrian king named Ben-Hadad fought against Israel (ca. 850 B.C.). The Bible also describes how Ben-Hadad was murdered by an individual named Hazael, who then became ruler of Syria (2 Kings 8:7-15). Archaeologists have discovered inscriptions credited to Shalmaneser III (ruler of Assyria from 860-825 B.C.) which describes the rule of both Hazael and Ben-Hadad, as well as the assassination of this Ben-Hadad.[41] Similarly, clay tablets describing Assyrian history have confirmed the rule of Tiglath-Pileser III (Assyrian king from 745-727 B.C). This ruler is also mentioned in the Bible (1 Chronicles 5:26).[41] The Assyrian inscriptions are in agreement with the Old Testament record and place him in the correct Biblical time frame.

Other historical elements have also been confirmed. For example, the Bible records the sins of the Jewish people, especially in their desire to follow false gods instead of the God of their fathers (Abraham, Isaac, and Jacob). The book of 1 Kings describes how one of the queens of Israel introduced and popularized Baal worship (a Phoenician deity) into Israel. According to the Bible, this was said to have occurred during Ahab's rule and Baal worship became a widespread problem in the northern kingdom of Israel.

This has been confirmed by many archaeological findings. For example, it became popular for parents to name their children with names derived from this false god. Archaeologists have found inscriptions, records, and other artifacts, which have names derived from the name Baal, such as an inscribed ostraca (potsherd) recovered at Samaria. The Ostracon Number 2 describes payments of taxes and two of the individuals listed are named Abibaal and Meribaal.[44] These items have been dated by archaeologists to the time period in which the Jews began the worship of Baal.

Unfortunately, it was not only the northern kingdom that abandoned their relationship with the God of their fathers (Abraham, Isaac, and Jacob) and fell into the worship of false gods and idols. Soon after the northern kingdom fell into this sin, the southern kingdom of Judah followed in the apostasy. Archaeologists have discovered ample evidence for the accuracy of the Bible's account. For example, many of the sites of idolatry have been found in Israel and Judah and some have been conclusively dated to the first temple time period.[45] One of rulers from the southern kingdom, Josiah, made an effort to eradicate the worship of false gods. According the Bible (2 Chronicles 35:1-3), he instituted reforms throughout the nation of Judah. This included the destruction of the sites of idolatry and the institution of proper Temple worship of the true God (as prescribed in the books of Moses). Archaeologists have found evidence for this purge, with smashed idols, pottery, and worship implements, still under piles of stones!

Time period: defeat of the kingdoms and captivity for the Jews (ca. 722 B.C. to 538 B.C.)

One of Judah's most highly respected kings was the man named Hezekiah. He ruled Judah from 715 B.C to 686 B.C. and he is known as one of their "righteous" kings. As such, he worked hard to rid Jerusalem (and all of Judah) of the worship of false gods and idols. His reforms included helping to restore proper worship at Solomon's Temple in Jerusalem. As described in the Bible in 2 Chronicles 29:3, "...in the first year of his reign, in the first month, opened the doors of the house of the LORD, and repaired them." There are a number of archaeological discoveries related to Hezekiah that support the historical accuracy of the Biblical account. In order to understand the significance of the archeological findings, it is necessary to briefly consider the history of this time period.

Early in Hezekiah's rule, the northern kingdom of Israel fell to the Assyrians (2 Kings 18:9,10). Sargon II led these conquests and any Jews that survived were led away into slavery. The Assyrians then set their war machine against the southern nation of Judah. Under the rule of king Sennacherib (Sargon's son), the Assyrian army advanced through Judah, conquering every city in their path, and finally they approached Jerusalem (2 Kings 18:13; Isaiah 36:1). Hezekiah attempted to buy favor from the king of Assyria by offering a tribute or tax consisting of a large amount of silver and gold (2 Kings 18:14-16). However expecting an attack from Assyria, Hezekiah worked to build up the defenses of the city of Jerusalem (2 Chronicles 32:2-5). This included building up the walls around the city, constructing an underground tunnel to carry water into the city (i.e., an aqueduct), and building defensive towers. The Bible also notes that the Jews made countless arrows and spears as the attack seemed imminent. When the Assyrians finally did approach Jerusalem, their army consisted of about 200,000 men.

They encamped around Jerusalem and threatened to begin their siege (2 Chronicles 32:18; Isaiah 36:2), however according to the account in 2 Kings 19:35, the God of Israel came to their defense. Hezekiah and the prophet Isaiah had prayed to the God of their fathers for mercy and protection (2 Chronicles 32:20). As a result, the Lord sent an angel and 185,000 Assyrian soldiers were killed during one night (2 Chronicles 32:21; 2 Kings 19:35). The sight of his dead army evidently had a profound impact on Sennacherib and the remaining members of the army, as they fled back to Assyria and never again attempted to conquer Jerusalem (2 Kings 19:36). The Bible also states that Sennacherib himself was assassinated in his homeland of Assyria (2 Kings 19:37; Isaiah 37:7).

It should be noted that the Biblical accounts are recorded in three separate books (2 Kings, 2 Chronicles, and Isaiah), presumably written by three different authors. Whenever separate historical accounts, or eyewitness testimonies, are in agreement, it makes the stories even more trustworthy. Here three different ancient Bible books are in agreement regarding the overall account of Hezekiah's rule and God's defense of Jerusalem. Besides the Biblical records however, there are also archaeological discoveries that strongly support the historical accounts of the Bible. These include inscriptions and official records from the Assyrians themselves. Since the Assyrians would have no interest in verifying or supporting the Hebrew Scriptures, they can be taken as independent accounts. Most notable among the inscriptions are those found on the Taylor Prism, the Oriental Institute Prism, and the Nimrud Prism – official Assyrian historical records.[46] The inscriptions on the these Assyrian artifacts support several aspect of the Biblical account, including:

1.   Hezekiah was king of Judah during the reign of Sennacherib.
2.   The Assyrian army was about 200,000 men.
3.   The Assyrians attacked and defeated the fortified cities of Judah.
4.   In hopes of preventing an Assyrian attack on Jerusalem, Hezekiah paid gold and silver tribute or tax to Sennacherib.

Assyrian records in accord with Bible, continued:

5. The Assyrian army besieged Jerusalem and completely surrounded the fortified city.

6. The Assyrians were unable to capture the city and they returned to their own nation.

7. Sennacherib was murdered by his own son.

There have been several other types of discoveries that lend support to the historical accuracy of the Biblical record. For example, it is clear from the Biblical account that the Jews greatly feared the Assyrian army and Sennacherib. This was for good reason. Archaeologists have found of carved images in the ruins of the royal palace in ancient Nineveh (the capital of Assyria).[47] These images were meant to memorialize the conquests of the Assyrian army, often depicting their foes being tortured, mutilated, impaled, and killed. Their brutality was well known among the nations.

The Bible also describes how Hezekiah built an underground aqueduct, designed to bring water into the city of Jerusalem from a nearby spring. In 2 Chronicles 32:30, we read one of the Bible's descriptions: "Hezekiah also stopped the water outlet of Upper Gihon, and brought the water by tunnel to the west side of the City of David." The aqueduct was needed to provide the residents of the city with water during a lengthy siege. Known as Hezekiah's tunnel, it has been discovered by archaeologists and it can be seen in Jerusalem to this day.[48]

Just as the Bible describes how Hezekiah strengthened the fortifications, archaeologists have also uncovered the "broad wall" of his defenses.[49] The newly uncovered wall may be seen in Jerusalem and it measures more than 20 feet across. This immense wall was needed to withstand the battering rams of the Assyrian army. Although Hezekiah prepared Jerusalem as best as possible for the coming Assyrian siege, it was ultimately the mercy and power of the God of Israel that provided for their salvation. As Hezekiah rightly prayed regarding God's defense of Jerusalem, "Now therefore, O LORD our God, save us from his hand, that all the kingdoms of the earth may know that You are the LORD, You alone." (Isaiah 37:20). The mighty God answered his prayer, coming to Judah's defense, and wiping out the Assyrian army in a single night.

Unfortunately, the kings who followed Hezekiah were not as faithful to God and soon allowed idol worship throughout Judah. With Judah's idolatry, God's judgment fell upon the Jews. The Bible describes the invasion by the Babylonian army under Nebuchadnezzar in 597 B.C. (2 Kings 24:10-17). The accuracy of this Old Testament Scripture has been confirmed by archaeological findings. Most notably, many of the official records (inscribed clay tablets) of the Babylonian government have been found in ancient ruins.[50] Known as the Babylonian Chronicles, one record describes how the Babylonian king attacked the capital of Judah and took slaves back to Babylon. The record also provides a date for the attack and it is in agreement with Biblical chronology.

The Bible describes how the Babylonians burned Jerusalem to the ground after they conquered the city (Jeremiah 39:8). Archaeological excavations at a site called the "Israelite Tower" have shown the accuracy of the Bible's account, as a very thick layer of ash and burned material are found from this time period.[51] This location is also littered with iron arrowheads, remnants of that final battle in ancient Jerusalem. Again, archaeological findings confirm the historical accuracy of the Biblical accounts.

The Bible describes how the Babylonian ruler Nebuchadnezar swept into Judah and attacked Jerusalem (2 Kings 24 and 25). The king of Judah is listed as Jehoiachin and he surrendered to Nebuchadnezar. The Biblical account describes how he was taken captive to Babylon (along with other Hebrew prisoners) and imprisoned for almost 40 years. Following his imprisonment, he was released and given an allowance of food for his remaining days. Remarkably, these details from the Bible have been confirmed by records found on a clay tablet recovered from ancient Babylon. The inscriptions on a tablet notes Youkin (equivalent to Jehoiachin) king of Judah received allotments of barley, oil, and other food.[52] The Babylonian Chronicles also describe how Nebuchadnezar installed his own ruler, Zedekiah, to reign over Judah. This is in agreement with the account in the Bible (2 King 24:17).

As described previously, specific names listed in the Bible have been found on ancient artifacts. Besides the names of kings and rulers, the names of ordinary scribes have been discovered. This is powerful evidence for authenticity and accuracy of the Old Testament. One such artifact bears the name of the Judaean king's scribe, Gemaryahu or Gemariah (mentioned in Jeremiah 36:10-12 and 25-26). As a scribe, he would have been responsible for producing documents and keeping written records. These parchments were sealed with a piece of clay having the owner or author's seal on it. When Jerusalem was burned by the Babylonian army, the parchments were obviously destroyed by the fire, however the clay buttons, or bullae, were baked into a hardened ceramic. Several of these bullae have been discovered in Jerusalem and they have Gemaryahu's name preserved to this day.[53] Another group of bullae has been found with the name of Buruch, the scribe and assistant to the Jewish prophet Jeremiah (see, Jeremiah 36:26).

The Bible describes how God made a covenant with the nation of Israel and He warned them of the consequences of rejecting the laws given by Moses. As described in the book of Leviticus (26:14,17), God states,

> "But if you do not obey Me, and do not observe all these commandments...I will set My face against you, and you shall be defeated by your enemies. Those who hate you shall reign over you, and you shall flee when no one pursues you."

About 900 years later, this became a reality for most of the Hebrews as the army of Nebuchadnezar came in and conquered Jerusalem in 586 B.C. Based on the ruins discovered by archaeologists, it appears that Nebuchadnezar's destruction was severe and complete. His armies destroyed the cities in Judah and this was done so thoroughly that many were never re-built. He also carried many Jewish prisoners into Babylonian exile (as many as 25,000 prisoners from Jerusalem alone). This Babylonian exile of the Jewish people is considered a fulfillment of a prophecy that appeared 900 years earlier in the twenty-sixth chapter of Leviticus. In that passage, God and Moses warned Israel,

> "I will scatter you among the nations and draw out a sword after you; your land shall be desolate and your cities waste. Then the land shall enjoy its Sabbaths as long as it lies desolate and you are in your enemies' land; then the land shall rest and enjoy its Sabbaths." Lev. 26:33,34

The Bible's account is well supported by the official records of the Babylonians. For example in the Babylonian Chronicles, there is an explicit statement describing how Nebuchadnezar conquered Judah, received large tribute (gold and silver), and brought captives back to Babylon.[54] The specific record is referred to as the "Chronicles of the Chaldean Kings" and this clay tablet is presently housed in the British Museum.

Time period: the return of the Jews to their homeland (ca. 538 B.C.)
The Hebrews were in Babylonian captivity for 70 years. The God of their fathers had allowed their captivity because of gross sin against the Lord. According to the Biblical account, this sin violated long-standing covenants between the Jews and the God of Heaven. Consequently, they were conquered in battle and dragged into Babylonian slavery. Everything changed when Cyrus the Great invaded Babylon.

Upon conquering Babylon, the Persian leader Cyrus allowed the deported Jews to return to the land of Judea. He also permitted them to rebuild the Temple and he gave them the Temple artifacts, which had been taken by Nebuchadnezzar. These historical accounts can be found in the Bible in the book of Ezra and 2 Chronicles. They have been confirmed by a non-Biblical source, too. The Cyrus Cylinder was discovered in 1879 lying in the ancient ruins of Babylon.[55] Among the many inscriptions on the clay cylinder, one states that Cyrus "returned inhabitants" to their nations and even restored the gods into "their chapels." This statement is in accord with the Biblical account, where it is said that King Cyrus returned the items seized from the Jewish Temple in Jerusalem (Solomon's Temple):

> King Cyrus also brought out the articles of the house of the
> LORD, which Nebuchadnezzar had taken from Jerusalem and put
> in the temple of his gods (Ezra 1:7)

As described in the next chapter, Muslim clerics adamantly deny that the Jews ever had an ancient Temple in Jerusalem. This raises obvious questions here: if there was no Temple, then what Jewish "chapel" did Cyrus restore and from what "house of the LORD" did the articles (or treasures) come from?

The book of Ezra describes the return of Jews to the land of Judea. It was written in the Aramaic language. This has been a point of criticism for skeptics, as they have claimed the Aramaic to be a more recent language. Therefore, their argument is that Ezra could not have written the book during his lifetime (around 500 B.C.). However, archaeology again supports the Bible, as the discovery of papyrus documents in Egypt verify the use of Aramaic in Ezra's time. The Elephantine Papyri were discovered in the ancient ruins of a settlement in Egypt.[56] Hundreds of papyrus document were preserved in the dry soil and sand, in what was once a Jewish settlement. Some of the documents dated between 500-400 B.C. were written in Aramaic. This lends support to the authorship of Ezra in Aramaic - during his lifetime.

Besides giving a date to the Aramaic language, the Elephantine Papyri also contain other statements that are in accord with the Biblical record. For example, Nehemiah describes (Nem. 2:19) a man named Sanballat, a ruler in Samaria. He is specifically mentioned in one of the papyrus documents.[57] His sons Sanaballat II and Johanan are also mentioned in Nehemiah's Biblical text and in the Elephantine Papyri.

Elsewhere in the book of Nehemiah, there is a list of gifts provided by the Persians for the rebuilding of Jerusalem in about 450 B.C., as the capital city of

Judah still lay in ruins from Nebuchadazzar's conquest. Among the items listed in Neh. 7:70, it is said that 1,000 gold drachmas had been given. This has also been a point of criticism, as the charge has been made that drachmas were commonly used only after the conquest of Alexander the Great in about 330 B.C. The critics therefore claim that Nehemiah would have been unlikely to have drachma coins. However, archaeological excavations in the regions near Jerusalem have yielded drachma coins from the Persian level (between 530-330 B.C.) and well-preserved drachmas from 500 B.C. are known.[58]

The efforts to rebuild Jerusalem and the Temple were also supported by the Persian king Darius, who ruled from 522 to 486 B.C. As described in the sixth chapter of Ezra, king Darius examined the earlier decree from Cyrus and he endorsed its mission to rebuild the Jewish Temple. According to his own decree, he said "...let it be done diligently (Ezra 6:12b)." He backed up his decree by helping fund the construction of the Jewish Temple. The Bible indicates that the second Temple was dedicated in the 6th year of Darius' rule (515 B.C.). While Muslim clerics may object to the suggestion that a Jewish Temple could have been built in Jerusalem, this account is known to be accurate with respect to the names, dates, and locations of the regional political power (the Persians). The Bible correctly names Darius (and later his son) as the ruler in Persia. It is hard to explain how a historical account could be correct on major details, like the name of important rulers and kings, but then grossly in error on the issue of building a Temple. Moreover, it is known from recovered Persian documents that Darius (as well as Cyrus before him) exhibited tolerance and financially supported the different religious faiths throughout their territories.[59] This can be seen in his support of Greek and Egyptian religions, including the construction of temples for worship. These things strongly suggest an accurate Biblical record related to the Jewish Temple.

The Persian rule of Darius is known by many sources beside the Bible references. In the northwest portion of modern day Iran, there are a series of inscriptions and figures of men carved directly into the rock of the mountainside (located in Behistun, Iran).[60] Scholars have studied the inscription over the past two centuries and they were translated in the late 1800s. The dominant figure in the carvings (or bas-relief) was found to be the Persian ruler Darius the Great. Also mentioned in the inscriptions, one finds record of Xerxes (or Ahasuerus), the son of Darius. Both Darius and Xerxes are described in the Old Testament of the Bible, and indeed, they are important in the history of the Jewish people. As noted above, Darius is credited with supporting the Jewish efforts to rebuild the Temple in Jerusalem (Ezra 6:1-15), while Xerxes is described as taking a bride of Jewish descent (Esther). Besides the bas-relief and inscriptions in Behistun, Iran, the rule of Darius is described in many other ancient sources. This includes an extensive account by the Greek historian Herodotus, texts and inscriptions found in the ruins of Persepolis (the Persian capital city), and other sources.[61] These accounts are in excellent agreement with the Biblical time frame.

Time period: between the Old and New Testaments (440 B.C. to 40 A.D.)
Following the return of the Jews to their homeland and the construction of the second Temple, there were no other books of Scripture added to the Old Testament of the Bible (the Hebrew Scriptures). The closure of the Hebrew Canon of Scripture is verified in the writings of the first century historian, Josephus. In his book *Antiquities*, Josephus states that the Hebrew Scriptures were completed during the reign of Artaxerxes I, or roughly around the time of the Jewish prophet Ezra (ca. 440 B.C.).[62]

Since there were no more books added to the Hebrew Canon (Old Testament) after about 440 B.C., the next historical records in the Bible were authored in the first century A.D. by the followers of Jesus Christ. These books were part of the New Testament in the Bible. The previous chapter examined the preservation of the New Testament and the authenticity of its message.

Preservation of the Old Testament: overwhelming evidence!
In summary, there are three major lines of evidence to show that the Old Testament of the Bible has not been corrupted through the ages. Firstly, Jesus Christ and His Apostles confirmed the integrity of the Old Testament Scriptures. Jesus Himself quoted from the Old Testament books and He never spoke a word concerning the corruption of these books. <u>Jesus never accused the Jews of removing Islamic teaching or doctrines.</u>

Secondly, ancient Bible manuscripts and manuscript fragments have been recovered and they show little or no variance from our modern Old Testament books. If the Bible had been corrupted or altered over the centuries, then there would not be a good match between "old" and "new" copies of the Scriptures. <u>Islamic doctrines have never been found in these ancient copies of the Old Testament Scriptures.</u> This includes copies of Scripture dating back almost 2,200 years. Moreover, there is no evidence that Moses, David, Isaiah, or any of the Old Testament prophets were Muslims.

Thirdly, the historical records in the Old Testament books are astonishingly accurate. The accounts of ancient Israel and the surrounding nations have been verified by many archaeological findings. This is an important observation. If the ancient Jewish or Christian scribes had significantly altered the Old Testament books, then the historical records would have been distorted, too. However, this is not observed. Indeed, the eminent scholar W. F. Albright concluded, "archaeological and inscriptional data have established the historicity of innumerable passages and statements of the Old Testament," and "discovery after discovery has established the accuracy of innumerable details and has brought increased recognition of the Bible as a source of history."[13]

These multiple lines of evidence point to an obvious conclusion: the Old Testament has been preserved through the ages. As shown in Figure 1, there is no time frame in which the Jews could have altered the messages from their ancient prophets. Archaeology verifies the accuracy of the historical records, the Dead Sea Scrolls predate Jesus' time, and Jesus confirms the accuracy of the Old Testament. Since the Old Testament of Jesus' time is virtually identical to our Bible today, we can therefore conclude, Jesus and the first century Apostles have confirmed the accuracy and preservation of our present-day Old Testament!

Figure 1. Confirming the preservation of the Old Testament.

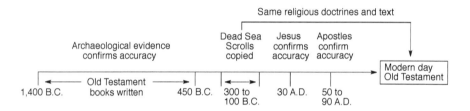

As for the Muslim claim that the Old Testament has been corrupted, there is absolutely no evidence for this accusation. God revealed messages through the ancient Jewish prophets, and evidently, God kept His hand on the Scriptures - preventing its corruption. This is abundantly clear from the Psalm of King David (written in 1000 B.C.):

> The words of the LORD are pure words, like silver tried in a furnace of earth, purified seven times. You shall keep them, O LORD, You shall preserve them from this generation forever. Psalm 12:6,7

References:

(1)   Based on a published testimony. Downloaded March 3, 2011 from::
       http://www.answering-islam.org/testimonies/khadija_uk.html

(2)   Geza Vermes, *The Complete Dead Sea Scrolls in English, 7th Ed.*,
       Penguin Classics, London, UK, 2011.

(3)   James C. VanderKam and Peter Flint *The Meaning of the Dead Sea
       Scrolls*, HarperSanFrancisco, New York, NY, 2002.

(4)   Millar Burrows, "The Contents and Significance of the Manuscripts."
       The Biblical Archaeologist, 1948, 60-61.

(5)   Joseph P. Free and Howard F. Vos, *Archaeology and Bible History*,
       Zondervan Publishing House, Grand Rapids, MI, 1992; p. 179.

(6)   Joseph M. Holden, Norman Geisler and Walter C. Kaiser Jr, *The
       Popular Handbook of Archaeology and the Bible: Discoveries That
       Confirm the Reliability of Scripture*, Harvest House Publishers,
       Eugene, OR, 2013, and references cited therein.

(7)   Randall Price, *The Stone Cry Out*, Harvest House Publishers, Eugene,
       OR, 1997; pp. 95-97.

(8)   Price, pp. 94-95.

(9)   Price, pp. 118-122. See also Free and Vos, p. 58.

(10)   James A. Sauer, "A Climatic And Archaeological View of the Early
       Biblical Traditions," *Scripture and Other Artifacts: Essays on the
       Bible and Archaeology in Honor of Philip J. King*, M. D. Coogan, J.
       C. Exum, and L. Stage, Eds., Westminster-John Knox Press,
       Louisville, KY, pp. 366-398.

(11)   Price, pp. 114-118.

(12)   Jospehus, *Wars of the Jews,* IV.8.4.

(13)   Free and Vos, p. 62.

(14)   Glyn Davies, *A History of Money: From Ancient Times to the Present
       Day*, University of Wales Press, Cardiff, UK, 2002.

(15)   Price, p. 133 and references cited therein.

(16)   Free and Vos, p. 71.

(17)   Donald B. Redford, *Egypt, Canaan, and Israel in Ancient Times*,
       Princeton University Press, Princeton, NJ, 1992.

(18)   Nicolas Grimal and Nicolas-Christophe Grimal, *A History of Ancient
       Egypt*, Wiley & Sons, New York, NY, 1994.

(19)   Free and Vos, p. 70 and Price, p. 133.

(20)   Free and Vos, p. 78.

(21)   Dieter Arnold, *The Encyclopaedia of Ancient Egyptian Architecture*,
       I.B.Tauris, London, UK 2002; p.40.

(22)   William L. Moran, *The Armana Letters*, John Hopkins University Press, Baltimore, MD, 1992.

(23)   Free and Vos, p. 116.

(24)   Price, Chapter 8.

(25)   Price, p. 148-149

(26)   John Garstang and J. B. E. Garstang, *The Story of Jericho*, Rev. ed., Marshall, Morgan, and Scott, London, UK, 1948; pp. 145-146.

(27)   Bryant G. Wood, *Biblical Archaeology Review*, 1990, 44-59. See also, Free and Vos, pp. 109-110.

(28)   Price, p. 152. See also, reference 27.

(29)   Price, p. 153.

(30)   Free and Vos, Chapter 10.

(31)   Price, pp. 144-145.

(32)   Free and Vos, Chapters 10, 11.

(33)   Donald G. Schley, *Shiloh: A Biblical City in Tradition and History*, Sheffield, UK, 2009.

(34)   Oliver R. Gurney, *The Hittites*, Penguin Books, London, UK, 1991.

(35)   Trude Dothan, *The Philistines and Their Material Culture*, Yale University Press, New Haven, CT, 1982.

(36)   Free and Vos, p. 119.

(37)   Free and Vos, pp. 128-129.

(38)   Alan Rowe, "Discovery of the Temple of Ashtaroth: Report of the Expedition to Palestine," *Museum Journal*, 1925, 16(4), 311.

(39)   Avraham Biran and Joseph Naveh, "An Aramaic Stele Fragment from Tel Dan," *Israel Exploration Journal*, 1993, 43(2/3), 81.

(40)   Free and Vos, p. 144.

(41)   Free and Vos, pp. 150-151.

(42)   Christopher A. Rollston, "Writing and Literacy in the World of Ancient Israel: Epigraphic Evidence from the Iron Age." *Archaeology and Biblical Studies,* no. 11, Society of Biblical Literature, Atlanta, GA, 2010; pp. 51-53.

(43)   P. Kyle McCarter, "Yaw, Son of Omri: A Philospohical Note on Israelite Chronology." *Bulletin of the American Schools of Oriental Research*, 1974, 216, 5-7.

(44)   Free and Vos, p. 155.

(45)   G. A. Barton, *Archaeology and the Bible* 7th ed., American Sunday School Union, Philadelphia, PA, 1937; pp.120-121.

(46)   Ira Maurice Price, *The Monuments and the Old Testament*, Philadelphia Judson Press, Philadelphia, PA, 1958.

(47)   Free and Vos, p. 170.

(48)   Amos Frumkin and Aryeh Shimron, "Tunnel Engineering in the Iron
         Age: Geoarchaeology of the Siloam Tunnel, Jerusalem," *Journal of
         Archaeological Science*, 2006, 33(2), 227-237.

(49)   Hershel Shanks, *Jerusalem: an Archaeological Biography*. Random
         House, New York, NY, 1995; p. 80.

(50)   Albert K. Grayson, *Assyrian and Babylonian Chronicles*, Eisenbrauns,
         Winona Lake, IN, 2000.

(51)   Andrew G. Vaughn and Ann E. Killebrew, *Jerusalem in Bible and
         Archaeology: the First Temple Period*, Society of Biblical Literature,
         Atlanta, GA, 2003.

(52)   Jack Finegan, *Light from the Ancient Past*, 2nd ed., Princeton
         University Press: Princeton, NJ, 1959; pp. 225-227.

(53)   Jane M. Cahill and David Tarler, "Excavations Directed by Yigael
         Shiloh at the City of David, 1978-1985" in *Ancient Jerusalem
         Revealed*, Hillel Geva, Ed., Israel Exploration Society: Jerusalem,
         Israel, 1994, pp. 39-40. Hershel Shanks, "Jeremiah's Scribe and
         Confidant Speaks from a Hoard of Clay Bullae," *Biblical Archaeology
         Review,* 1987, 13(5), 58-65.

(54)   D. J. Wiseman, *Chronicles of the Chaldean Kings (626-556 B.C.) in
         the British Museum*, Trustees of the British Museum: London, UK,
         1956. See also, Free and Vos, p. 194.

(55)   James B. Pritchard, *Ancient Near Eastern Texts Relating to the Old
         Testament*, 2nd, ed., Princeton University Press, Princeton, NJ, p. 316-
         7.

(56)   Free and Vos, p. 206.

(57)   Free and Vos, p. 211. See also, William F. Albright, *The Archaeology
         of Palestine and the Bible,* Gorgias Classic Archaeological Reprints 5,
         Gorgias Press, Piscataway, NJ, 2009.

(58)   Glyn Davies, *A History of Money: from Ancient Times to the Present
         Day,* 2nd ed., University of Wales Press, Cardiff, UK, 2002.

(59)   Peter R. Bedford, *Temple Restoration in Early Achaemenid Judah,*
         Koninklijke Brill NV, Leiden, The Netherlands, 2001, p. 144.

(60)   George G. Cameron, "Darius Carved History on Ageless Rock,"
         National Geographic Magazine, 1950, 98(6), 825-844.

(61)   Lindsay Allen, *The Persian Empire*, University of Chicago Press,
         Chicago, IL, 2005.

(62)   Free and Vos, p. 215. See also, Josephus, *Antiquities*, XX.11.2.

Chapter 7

The Jewish Temple

Wisdom abides in the mind of a man with understanding,
but it is not known in the hearts of fools. Proverbs 14:33

Farooq was born and raised in Pakistan.[1] His family was devoted to the Muslim faith, as they went to the mosque every Friday for prayers, fasted during Ramadan, and followed other Islamic customs. In his teenage years, Farooq was able to read and recite the Quran in Arabic. He also owned a study Quran translated by Abdullah Yusuf Ali and the Sahih Bukhari hadith collection.

Following his teenage years, Farooq wanted to attend a good university to study engineering. He took some classes at Engineering College in Karachi, Pakistan, but then he transferred to a college in the United States. Being a hard working and intelligent young man, he got into a very good university and worked towards his bachelor degree. Although he was involved with the local Islamic community, university studies soon dominated his schedule. He would eventually earn a masters degree, but he no longer practiced his faith.

A competitive and financially rewarding job awaited Farooq at the end of his college career. He was soon married and even had children. Life was simply too busy to worry about spiritual matters. He did little to maintain his Muslim faith. However, one day he was involved in a serious traffic accident. There were fatalities and Farooq was badly injured. Because of the severity of his injuries, he needed to take a medical leave from his job.

The accident prompted Farooq to think about life. What were his priorities? What was his purpose in life? What would be his legacy in this world? Where would he go when he died? Some of these questions lead him back to spiritual issues and his faith in Islam. He began to study the Quran and hadith for answers. He believed that the Quran was God's message to mankind, so he was confident that answers could be found in its pages. Shortly thereafter, some Christian friends told him that the only way to Heaven is through Jesus Christ and the Bible is the only source of God's message to mankind.

As a well-educated man, Farooq set forth and began a serious study of the two religious faiths. He now had a strong desire to learn the truth, follow this path, and even lead his family in this faith. As described in his personal testimony, he studied the lives of both Muhammad and Jesus, he read both the Quran and Bible, and he looked at the early histories of both religions. He even studied material written by atheists.

After these studies, he had more questions than ever. Regarding Christianity, he was confused about Jesus being God and the Christian doctrine of the trinity. He was unsure about the teachings about mankind's sin and the need for innocent blood to cover people's sin. He wondered if Jesus really died on the cross and rose from the dead. However, Islam had its own set of issues, too. He was concerned about the inerrancy of the Quran, especially given the notion of "abrogation" (a concept in which older revelations in the Quran get "cancelled out" or superseded by more recent revelations). An inerrant Quran (or revelation from God's prophet) should not need to be corrected at a later date, he thought. He was also bothered by the inconsistent messages, such as fornication being a sin but allowing men to have sex with women slaves. He also noticed that it was necessary to revise the Quran to standardize it and then all of the older manuscripts were burned. Why was this needed if the Quran was already a perfect revelation?

The weight against Islam was very great and Farooq was now unsure about this religious system. But he still did not know how to handle the problems he had with Christian doctrines or beliefs. He examined other faiths at this time, including Hinduism and Buddhism. These religions made even less sense. At this point, he prayed earnestly to the God of Abraham and he asked for guidance into the truth. He continued to pray, study, and meditate.

A short time later, the truth came over Farooq like a big ocean wave. He was praying and in his words,[1] "I sensed a burden lifted off me." The message that "Jesus is Lord" resonated through his mind and spirit, as the God of Heaven opened his eyes to the truth. He recalled the Biblical accounts of the arrest of Jesus and remembered that the Jews accused him of blasphemy and claiming to be God. Farooq now understood that Jesus was *and is* the God of Heaven. Statements in the Bible now became "crystal clear" and he saw the deity of Jesus Christ very much connected to the crucifixion. It was God's love for Farooq that lead Him to the cross on Calvary. He accepted Jesus Christ as his Savior, and most importantly, Farooq accepted the great gift from Heaven – full payment of his sin debt.

With his conversion to Christianity, his family and his Muslim friends tried to convince him to reconsider the decision. Since Farooq was firmly convinced of the truth of the Bible, his family gave up on him and considered him "an outcast." He continued to mature in his new Christian faith. God even helped him conquer long-standing problems with "pride, arrogance, anger, selfishness, and…other sinful traits." In Farooq's own words,[1] "He continues to change me from inside out to be more loving and kind to all."

Besides Farooq's salvation in Christ, there was another happy ending in his story. He was welcomed back into his family. His mother recognized the importance of keeping the family together, and despite their differences in religious beliefs, they have mutual respect for each other. More than twenty years have past since the Lord opened Farooq's eyes to the truth. He now says,[1] "I am sure of my faith in the Lord Jesus and continue to follow Him, even more (so) than at that day He chose to reveal Himself to me and called me to Him."

Like so many former Muslims, Farooq carefully considered the evidence in support of Christianity and the evidence in support of Islam. He prayed for God's guidance in his pursuit of spiritual truth. Nevertheless, men and women on the road from Mecca to Calvary must usually face a common claim from Islamic scholars: major parts of the Bible are incorrect, inaccurate, or outright lies. The previous chapters showed that there is overwhelming evidence for the death, burial, and resurrection of Jesus Christ. Moreover, the previous chapters also demonstrated ample evidence for the preservation of the Old and New Testament Scriptures. What about the Jewish Temple in Jerusalem? Muslim teachers also frequently claim that the Jews never had an ancient Jewish Temple in Jerusalem. Since this claim directly questions the accuracy of much of the New and Old Testament historical records, it will be specifically examined in this chapter.

The most vocal members of the "Temple denial" group are generally the leaders of the Palestinian Arabs. For example, Yassir Arafat was involved in the Camp David Summit and he claimed that the Jewish Temple never existed in Jerusalem.[2] This idea was repeated by a Palestinian minister, Nabil Sha'ath, who stated,[3] "Israel demands control of the Temple Mount based on its claim that its fictitious temple stood there." Dr. Ahmad Nawfal of the Shari'a Faculty of the University of Jordan, claimed,[4] "The Jews dug 40 meters into the ground, and found nothing. There is no indication that a temple existed there." As will be shown in this chapter, these gentlemen are all guilty of unscholarly trash talk.

Jewish Temple in Jerusalem

Among the differences between Christianity and Islam, one argument centers on a hill in the city of Jerusalem, a place called Mount Moriah or the Noble Sanctuary. Christians and Jews believe this was the site of the Jewish Temple. As such it is referred to as the Temple Mount. The Bible describes how Jesus Christ and his Apostles ministered, taught, and assembled, at the ancient Jewish Temple in Jerusalem, often referred to as Herod's Temple. As described above, Muslim leaders insist that the Jews never worshipped at Herod's Temple or a similar temple built by Solomon.

Discussions about the Jewish Temple, Jerusalem, and Mount Moriah, may quickly become heated, as this is one of the most sensitive issues between Jews and Muslims. As a Christian, this writer is far removed from that bitter debate, and quite happily, I have little interest in seeing another Jewish Temple built on Mount

Moriah. There seems to be a fear among Muslim clerics, that by agreeing with the historical evidence for a Jewish Temple, they are somehow supporting the Jewish claims on Mount Moriah. Some probably get worked up into a rage at this thought, because they imagine the beautiful Dome of the Rock being torn down and replaced by a Jewish Temple. This is certainly not being advocated here and the historical reality of the Jewish Temple (on Mount Moriah) should in no way jeopardize the Dome of the Rock and the Al-Aqsa Mosque. In our discussion in this chapter, we are primarily concerned with an impartial examination of evidence for an ancient Jewish Temple.

An obvious question then arises: is there any evidence for the ancient Jewish Temple located in Jerusalem? This is an important question. If the Muslim clerics are correct, then the Christian and Jewish Scriptures are truly corrupted and filled with errors. However if there was a Jewish Temple on Mount Moriah, then the Muslims teachers and Palestinian leaders are wrong. They either woefully ignorant or guilty of deception. Given the significance of this issue, it is not surprising that Muslim authorities in Jerusalem stubbornly resist the efforts of archaeologists to excavate around Mount Moriah. However, this raises an obvious question: <u>if Muslim authorities are so certain the Temple never stood on Mount Moriah, why then would they object to archaeologists digging at this site?</u>

For the benefit of providing a context, we will first consider what the Bible says about the ancient Jewish Temple. The Bible describes four periods related to Jewish worship at their Temple:

1. The Tabernacle period (1440 B.C. to 960 B.C.) - Following the exodus of Israel from Egyptian slavery, God instituted (through Moses) a system of animal sacrifice as a means of covering the sins of the people. For this purpose, Moses set up the Tabernacle as a site for animal sacrifice and the place where Israel could approach their God.[5] The Tabernacle is described in the Bible as being a series of tents. The most inward tent held the Ark of the Covenant.

2. Solomon's Temple (960 B.C. to 586 B.C.) - Following the Tabernacle period, the first Jewish Temple was built atop Mount Moriah by King Solomon. The Biblical account describes how Solomon's father, King David, purchased the hill and assembled supplies for construction of the Temple.[6] Experts in Biblical history and archaeology estimate that Solomon's Temple was completed in 960 B.C.[7] According to the Biblical record, Solomon's Temple operated for about 370 years, until it was destroyed by the Babylonian army in 586 B.C.[8] The Jewish people were

then carried away to captivity and slavery to serve the Babylonians, initially under King Nebuchadnezzar.

3. Second Temple (515 B.C to 19 B. C.) - The Jews were freed after 70 years of Babylonian captivity by the Persian leader, Cyrus the Great. He allowed the Jews to return to their homeland and rebuild their temple in Jerusalem.[9] It is known from Cyrus' own records that he released many foreign captives from Babylonian slavery and commissioned the restoration of the people's places of worship (see previous chapter).[10] Upon return to their land, the Jews built a second temple on Mount Moriah in Jerusalem. This temple provided a place for the Jews to offer sacrifices, but it was hardly the glorious temple that Solomon had built.

4. Herod's Temple (19 B.C. to 70 A.D.) - When the Romans invaded the land of Judea, they installed a man to govern who became known as Herod the Great. It was Herod the Great who built up the Jewish Temple and expanded the Temple complex to its appearance of splendor.[11] The Bible describes many instances in which Jesus and His disciples ministered or taught at this Temple. Jesus Christ predicted the destruction of Herod's Temple, when He stated,[12] "no stone would remain unturned." This prophecy was literally fulfilled when the Roman general Titus laid siege to Jerusalem and destroyed it in 70 A.D.[13]

Solomon's Temple

Archaeological findings from the Solomon's Temple are very rare. According to the Biblical record, the Temple was thoroughly destroyed by the Babylonians in the year 586 B.C.[8] The second Temple was built atop the remains of Solomon's Temple, and there have been many layers of building above that level. So any remains that might exist are buried very deep in Jerusalem, probably in locations that are inaccessible. There is the suggestion that some of the stones used in the "Western Wall" in Jerusalem may date from Solomon's construction, but no one knows for certain. Two artifacts have been recovered which do suggest a Temple. An ivory scepter head was discovered and it has been dated to about 800 B.C., concurrent with the likely time of Solomon's Temple.[14] The object is carved to look like a pomegranate and it is inscribed with the message, "Belonging to the hou[se of Y...] A holy thing of the priests." Archaeologists have suggested that it may have been used in the service of priests in the Jewish Temple, or house of God.

Another artifact is the "House of Yahweh Ostracon."[15] As described previously, an ostracon is a piece of broken pottery used as a means of written communication. This particular piece of pottery is likely a tax receipt for an individual and it ends with the statement, "...in the House of God." Archaeologists have dated the piece to 700 to 600 B.C., which places it at the time of Solomon's Temple, or House of God.

Herod's Temple

Being a more recent site, there is a great amount of evidence for Herod's Temple. For example, Herod's quarry was recently located.[16] This was the site where Herod's workers cut and excavated large stones for his building projects. Coins and pottery date the site to the time of Herod's rule (37 B.C. to 4 A.D.). Archaeologists have found blocks of stone cut to the dimensions of 9'x6'x6' (3x2x2 meters). This is the same size of stone found in the "Western Wall" on the Temple Mount in Jerusalem. Herodian masonry work is distinct and well known. Examples of this high quality stonework are found all around the Temple Mount. Likewise, archaeologists have found several underground cisterns (water reservoirs) dated to Herod's time. Their purpose was clearly to supply the Temple priests with waters for the duties.

Besides artifacts from Herod's Temple, there are several writings contemporary with the Temple that testified of its existence. Of course, the Bible describes the Temple in many portions of Scripture. The four gospel books (Mathew, Mark, Luke, and John) all mention or describe elements of Herod's Temple. Likewise, the historical book of Acts has many passages describing Herod's Temple. This represents eyewitness testimony from four different men describing the same landmark, Herod's Temple. Moreover, these men were all early Christians, and not followers of the Jewish religion. They would have had no vested interest in propagating a falsehood or lie about the existence of a Jewish Temple. Without a motive to spread a lie, their account can be taken for what it states - the truth.

Very thorough descriptions of Herod's Temple can also be found in the non-Biblical book titled, *Jewish Wars* by Flavius Josephus (written in 75 A.D.).[17] The Jewish *Mishnah*, a book describing Jewish customs and laws compiled in 200 A.D.,[18] described many of the customs of the Temple worship. The Roman historian Tacitus also described the fall of Jerusalem in *Histories* written in 109 A.D., where he states,[19] "The temple itself was in the nature of a citadel..." Even this non-Jew Tacitus testified of existence of the Jewish Temple in Jerusalem. The above writings all predate Muhammad by several centuries. If the Jewish Temple never existed, as Muslim teachers claim, then it is highly unlikely that these various sources would have written such comprehensive accounts of Jewish Temple worship. Indeed, no serious historian today doubts the existence of Herod's Temple. The Muslim clerics stand alone in their denial of this part of history.

Since the late 1960s, there have been several excavations around the Temple Mount. Archaeologists have found many object, artifacts, and structures that point directly towards the presence of Herod's Temple on Mount Moriah. Among these discoveries, a large stone balustrade (decorative, upper wall) was unearthed along the southwest corner of the Temple Mount.[20] It was found in the layer of stone and debris identified as the "Roman layer" which dates to about the first century B.C. On this piece of hewn stone, there is the Hebrew inscription that says, "To the Trumpeting Place." According to the description provided by Josephus (*Jewish War*, 5.582), the trumpeting place was a location in the Jewish Temple in which the priests blew a silver trumpet to announce times and events important to their worship. This stone artifact is presently on display at the Israel Museum in Jerusalem.

Not only is the stone inscription notable evidence for the Jewish Temple, but also because the inscription is in agreement with a first century, non-Biblical historical account (Josephus' writings). For archaeologists and historians, agreement between two ancient sources (i.e., an inscription on stone and a document) is very strong evidence for an event, person, or place. In this case, it is the existence of Herod's Temple. Nevertheless, individuals such as the "professor of religion," Dr. Ahmad Nawfal, will continue to falsely claim, "The Jews dug 40 meters into the ground, and found nothing." This is simply not true.

Visitors to Jerusalem may also view an immense set of stairs leading up towards the Temple Mount and the stone gates (double and triple gates). These stairs and gates are located along the southern wall of the Temple Mount and they are believed to be part of the main entrance for people into the ancient temple. This location at the temple complex is mentioned in the Bible where Jesus Christ came into and left the temple (which He referred to as His Father's house). In the book of Acts, there is also an account of Paul speaking to a crowd of Jews from these stairs that lead into the temple:

> "...Paul stood on the stairs and motioned with his hand to the people. And when there was a great silence, he spoke"...Acts 21:40

Since being excavated, the ancient stairway has provided further evidence for the historic reality of the ancient Jewish Temple. Moreover, the location of the stairway is consistent with first century accounts of the Temple.

Archaeologists have also excavated the area around the Temple Mount and uncovered the original streets from the time of Herod's Temple. The observations from this area are in perfect accord with the Bible's description of Herod Temple.

For example, three of the gospel accounts (Matthew, Mark, and Luke) describe a visit of Jesus Christ to the Jewish Temple. While Christ's disciples are marveling at the glorious buildings in Herod's Temple complex, Jesus describes a future destruction of the complex:

> And Jesus said to them, "Do you not see all these things? Assuredly, I say to you, not one stone shall be left here upon another, that shall not be thrown down." Matthew 24:2; see also Mark 13:2 and Luke 21:6

As archaeologists recently uncovered the dirt and debris from the long buried streets, they found immense, hewn stones that had been rolled down from the Temple Mount and came crashing down to the street level.[21] There are still massive indentations in the flagstone streets from the impacts of these stone blocks (which are typically 6 foot cubes). Thus, the prediction from Jesus became a reality when the Roman army destroyed the Temple Complex in 70 A.D. (and in later years).

The excavations at the street level also uncovered many alcoves intended for merchants. These shops around the Temple Mount indicate that there was a large amount of commerce at this site.[21] According to the Bible, these merchants and "money changers" overflowed into the sacred areas of the Temple Complex. All four gospel accounts describe how Jesus drove away these merchants from the sacred Temple of the Lord:

> Now the Passover of the Jews was at hand, and Jesus went up to Jerusalem. And He found in the temple those who sold oxen and sheep and doves, and the money changers doing business. When He had made a whip of cords, He drove them all out of the temple, with the sheep and the oxen, and poured out the changers' money and overturned the tables. And He said to those who sold doves, "Take these things away! Do not make My Father's house a house of merchandise!" John 2:13-16; see also Matthew 12:12-13, Mark 11:15-17, and Luke 19:45-47

When the Bible passages are compared with the uncovered artifacts and ancient sites around the Temple Mount, there is excellent agreement between the written text and the archaeological findings. This argues for a great measure of accuracy in the historical records of the Bible, including the records that describe a Jewish Temple in Jerusalem.

According to the record in the Bible, the Jewish Temple had an interior room called the "Holy of Holies." This was the unique location in the Temple in which the "Ark of the Covenant" was located.[22] During the normal functioning of the Jewish Temple, the Holy of Holies was entered one day each year by the Jewish High Priest. He entered on the Day of Atonement to offer an animal blood sacrifice to cover the sins of the Jewish people. The Old Testament of the Bible describes how God instructed Moses to build the Ark, a wooden box adorned with gold.[23] Moses was then instructed to place objects in the Ark, including the inscribed Ten Commandments. As described in the Bible,[24] the Ark of the Covenant was placed in the very center of the Holy of Holies, by command of God. Though the actual Ark of the Covenant has long since vanished from the hands of Israel, archaeologists have made a number of discoveries related to it and its location in the Holy of Holies. Perhaps one of the most interesting observations came from the very top of the Temple Mount. Archaeologist Leem Ritmeyer studied the stone surface on the mount (beneath the Dome of the Rock) and he observed a flat, rectangular depression carved into the stone surface. According to Ritmeyer,[25]

> "The dimensions of this level basin agree with those of the Ark of the Covenant, which were 1.5 x 2.5 cubits (2'7" x 4'4" or 79 cm x 131 cm), with the longitudinal axis coinciding with the Temple."

By analyzing the likely dimensions of the Temple and the Holy of Holies, Ritmeyer has shown that the location of the stone depression or basin would have been in the very center of the Holy of Holies. This is in accord with descriptions from both Josephus and the *Mishnah*.[26] Both ancient accounts stated that the Ark rested directly on a bedrock base. This bedrock base or depression can actually be seen in some photographs of the interior of the Dome of the Rock and visitors to the site (if one can get access to it) can see it with their own eyes.

In addition to artifacts around Jerusalem, the Arch of Titus is a large monument in Rome that commemorates the victory of Titus in Judea and, in particular, at Jerusalem.[27] On the monument, there are carved images of the Roman army carrying treasures from this conquest. Included in the carvings, there is a very prominent image of a seven-arm oil lamp stand being carried by the soldiers. When Jerusalem fell to the Roman siege in 70 A.D., Herod's Temple was destroyed. The wealth of gold (and other treasures) was plundered by Titus and the Roman army. Bible scholars believe that the seven-arm lamp stand depicted on the Arch of Titus is the same lamp described in the Bible (Exodus 27:20 and 1 Samuel 3:3). This is the lamp stand that stood in the ancient Jewish Temple.

Conclusions

In summary, there is an abundance of evidence in support of the Bible's description of the Jewish Temple in Jerusalem. The Bible has frequent and thorough references to the Jewish Temple – it is mentioned about 300 times in the Old and New Testaments. These references are in books of the Bible that, in previous chapters, have been shown to be historically accurate. An impartial examination of this evidence leads one to conclude that the Bible is correct in its description and record of the Jewish Temple in Jerusalem. This evidence also includes several non-Biblical historical accounts, recovered artifacts from the Temple itself, and the discovery of the very stones used in its construction.

Although Islamic scholars and Muslim political leaders may not like the fact that a Jewish Temple stood in Jerusalem, historical truth is not determined by a person's likes or dislikes. Rather, history is established by what actually happened in Jerusalem centuries ago. Since an overwhelming amount of evidence confirms the Biblical record, the honest Muslim should recognize the existence of an ancient Jewish Temple. To refuse this, it is either unscholarly or outright dishonest.

References

(1)   Based on a published testimony or account. Downloaded February 24, 2011 from the Internet at:
http://www.answering-islam.org/Testimonies/farooq.html

(2)   Dennis Ross, *The Missing Peace: The Inside Story of the Fight for Middle East Peace*, Farrar, Straus and Giroux, New York, NY, 2005, p. 694.

(3)   Yigal Carmon and Aluma Solnik, "Camp David and the Prospects for a Final Settlement, Part I: Israeli, Palestinian, and American Positions," August 4, 2000, *MEMRI*, Inquiry & Analysis Series Report No. 35, http://www.memri.org/report/en/print356.htm.

(4)   *MEMRI*, Special Dispatch, No. 1030, November 22, 2005, http://www.memri.org/report/en/0/0/0/0/0/251/1533.htm.

(5)   David Levy, *The Tabernacle: Shadows of the Messiah*, The Friends of Israel Gospel Ministry, Bellmawr, NJ, 2013.

(6)   2 Samuel 24:19-25

(7)   Jospehus, *Antiquities*, Book XIII, chapters 3-4.

(8)   Destruction of Solomon's Temple; Jospehus, *Antiquities*, Book X, 8.5.

(9)   2 Chronicles 36:22-23.

(10)   Mordechai Cogan, "The Cyrus Cylinder" in *The Context of Scripture. Vol. II: Monumental Inscriptions from the Biblical World*, Brill Academic, Leiden, The Netherlands, 2000.

(11)   Jospehus, *Antiquities*, Book XV, 11.1.

(12)   Luke 21:6

(13)   Randall Price, *Rose Guide to the Temple*, Rose Publishing, Torrance, CA, 2014, pp. 98-99.

(14)   Randall Price, *The Stones Cry Out*, Harvest House Publishers, Eugene, OR, 1997; p. 185.

(15)   Oded Borowski, *Daily Life in Biblical Times*, Society of Biblical Literature, Atlanta, GA, 2003.

(16)   Sean Gaffney, "Report: Herod's Temple quarry found," *USA Today*, September 24, 2007. Available for download at: http://usatoday30.usatoday.com/news/world/2007-09-24-1382898922_x.htm.

(17)   Josephus, *Jewish Wars* V, chapter 5.

(18)   *Mishnah*, Kodshim-Midos.

(19)   Caius Cornelius Tacitus, *The Histories*. Volumes I and II, HardPress Publishing, 2010

(20)   Ronny Reich, Gideon Avni, and Tamar Winter, *Jerusalem Milestones: A guide to the archaeological sites*, Israel Antiquities Authority, Jerusalem, Israel, 2009; p. 28.

(21)   Price, *The Stones Cry Out*, p. 196.

(22)   James Strong, *The Tabernacle of Israel*, Kregel Publications, Grand Rapids, MI, 1987; pp.79-86.

(23)   Randall Price, *Searching for the Arc of the Covenant*, Harvest House Publishing, Eugene, OR, 2005; pp. 14-16.

(24)   Price, *The Stones Cry Out*, pp. 211-216.

(25)   Leem Ritmeyer, *The Temple and the Rock*, Ritmeyer Archaeological Design, Harrogate, UK, 1996; pp. 24-25, 41.

(26)   Josephus, *War of the Jews*, V, 5.5. See also, Price, *The Stones Cry Out*, p. 211.

(27)   Fred S. Kleiner, *A History of Roman Art*, Wadsworth, Boston, MA, 2010; pp. 129-130.

Chapter 8

Prophecy: a Seal of Authenticity in the Bible

Return to the LORD your God, for He is gracious and compassionate,
slow to anger, and abounding in love Joel 2:12

The Caner brothers were living in Columbus, Ohio, when they first heard the truth of Jesus Christ. Their story is told in the Preface of their award-wining book, *Unveiling Islam*.[1] The three brothers (Ergun, Erdem, and Emir) were devout Muslims. They attended their local mosque regularly - which their father had helped establish. The brothers all followed the customs and requirements of Islam, including regular readings from the Quran and hadith, daily prayers, and celebrations of Ramadan. In commenting on their life as Muslims, however, they add,[1] "our devotion was not an act of love, but of fear. No Muslim has eternal security. Every Muslim fears the scales of justice, which weigh his good deeds against his bad deeds."

During their teenage years, Ergun had a good friend named Jerry who was a Christian. Jerry was the son of a Christian minister and he invited Ergun to attend a church service. Ergun had attended the Muslim mosque on many occasions, so he did not know what to expect at a Christian church service. The environment in this Baptist church was a surprise to Ergun. The people were warm and kind, and most importantly, he could sense a genuine love between the members of the church and this young Muslim visitor.

Ergun listened carefully to the message given at the Christian church. In particular, he heard messages describing salvation from sin and the cross work of Jesus Christ. He also heard about the Biblical concept of the trinity of God and the deity of Christ. It was through this message that Ergun immediately saw one of the errors of Islam. He knew the Islamic position on the nature of Jesus - that He was simply a great prophet from God. However, the Jewish authorities arrested and convicted Jesus of blasphemy. On several occasions (including at His trial before the Jewish authorities), Jesus made statements claiming to be God Himself. This meant that Jesus could not have been a prophet. No prophet speaking for God would actually claim to be the Almighty Lord, as Jesus Christ claimed!

With further study and guidance from the Lord, Ergun accepted the truth of the Bible. He saw that Jesus is our God and our Savior. He trusted in the work of Christ on the cross and Ergun's sins were forgiven. He was very excited to be free from the futile labors and ever present fear in the Islamic religion. He now had a new relationship with the God of Heaven. This was a relationship grounded in love

– God's love for Ergun. He shared the truth with his brother Erdem. Shortly there after, Erdem believed the message. He found out that Jesus Christ loved him and went to the cross to die for him. Now Ergun and Erdem could stand before the infinitely Holy God of Heaven. Their sins were forgiven and they were declared righteous based on the cross-work of Jesus Christ. About one year later, their brother Emir also learned of the Savior Jesus Christ and he was saved.

All three Caner brothers made the journey from Mecca to Calvary. Unfortunately, their father was not as open to the message. Not only did he reject the good news of the Christian message, but he also disowned his three sons who had become Christians. Although the Caner brothers loved their father dearly, they had to endure his rejection. While they had experienced the joy of having a living relationship with their God and Father in Heaven, the Caner brothers lost perhaps their most precious Earthly relationship - the one with their father. Thoughts of him still bring tears to their eyes.

Perhaps, a Muslim apologist might argue that the Caner brothers were simply naïve teenagers. They did not have the wisdom or the deep spiritual thoughts obviously present in their father. Not so. Both Ergun and Emir eventually earned Ph.D. degrees in theology and religious studies. Likewise Erdem became a successful businessman. Their Christian faiths have grown steadily through the years. They are highly sought after speakers, appearing on television, radio, and in many Christian churches. Their conversions to Christianity were definitely not the result of some impulsive teenage fad. Rather, these young men saw their need for a Savior. Regarding their decisions, they stated,[1] "we did not 'switch religions.' The blood of Jesus saved us."

The Caner brothers have continued their studies of the Bible, even confirming the origin of the Bible. As the God of Heaven revealed His messages through the writers of Scripture, He also incorporated features to help us identify the Bible as the true revelation from God. One such seal of authenticity is Biblical prophecy. Throughout the pages of the Old and New Testaments, the writers incorporated very specific predictions about future events. These are call prophecies. Since the Bible was written between 1,400 B.C. and 100 A.D., we are able to check for the accuracy of these predictions. As described in this chapter, the Bible has made accurate prophecies about major events of human history. The Jewish prophet Isaiah wrote an open declaration from the God of Heaven (Isaiah 49:6,7):

> Remember the former things of old, for I am God, and there is no
> other; I am God, and there is none like Me, declaring the end from
> the beginning, and from ancient times things that are not yet done,
> saying, 'My counsel shall stand, and I will do all My pleasure,'

The God of Abraham, Isaac, and Jacob, states that He alone is God and that He alone is able to declare "the end from the beginning." He demonstrated this in the pages of the Bible, as He made prophecies concerning future events in writing through His prophets.

This chapter will examine several aspects of Biblical prophecy. First, we will see how the Bible predicted the history of empires and nations. Centuries before the Persian and Roman empires, the Bible foretold of their rise to power. Secondly, we will see the miraculous predictions related to the history of Israel and the Jews. This includes prophecies concerning the formation of modern Israel in 1948. Thirdly, we examine the many specific prophecies related to the Savior Jesus Christ. These prophecies were fulfilled perfectly by Jesus Christ and Him alone. They were written in the Old Testament by ancient Jewish prophets between about 1,400 B.C. to 500 B.C. – many centuries before the arrival of Jesus Christ in 6 B.C. All of these prophecies represent a great seal of authenticity for the Bible. They offer evidence to the Muslim that the Bible is God's revelation to mankind and that its messages should be heard. Finally, we will also examine the Bible to see if similar prophecies were given related to Muhammad and the rise of Islam in 600 A.D.

Before examining the prophecies of the Bible, it is worthwhile to consider the most common objection and criticism of the miraculous character of Biblical prophecy. The Bible prophecies are so stunning in their accuracy that critics often claim the prophecies must have been inserted "after the fact." In other words, these critics claim that Christian and Jewish scribes looked back through history and intentionally added passages to the Bible - sections of Scripture that described past events. For example, Micah 5:2 reads, "But you, Bethlehem Ephrathah...out of you shall come forth to Me the One to be Ruler in Israel, whose goings forth are from of old, from everlasting." According to the skeptic's reasoning, the Old Testament accurately predicted the birth of Jesus Christ in the little town of Bethlehem in 6 B.C., because someone inserted the text after Jesus Christ was born. They might claim that a Christian monk added the verse to the Bible, for example, in 450 A.D. Yet, the Dead Sea Scrolls were copies of the Old Testament Scriptures dated from 300 to 100 B.C. These copies of the Old Testament books were made at least 100 years before the arrival of Jesus Christ. When the contents of the ancient scrolls are studied, one finds the same prophecies in the scrolls as in our modern Bibles. The Dead Sea scroll fragment - known as 4Q81 - contains Micah 5:1-2.[2] Our modern day copy of Micah reads exactly as the ancient copy from before the birth of Jesus! So there is no evidence for the prophecies having been added at a later date.

Sequence of empires foretold

One might also argue that prophecies and predictions could simply be reasonable conclusions made by ancient scholars of that day. Anyone can predict the downfall of a nation or city and this should not be considered evidence for Divine revelation in the Bible - so the critics would argue. However, a series of distant and remarkable prophecies were made concerning the rise of Gentile (non-Jewish) nations and empires. These prophecies were made by the ancient Jewish prophet Daniel. They could only have arisen from the Almighty God of Heaven as He looked ahead in time and declared "the end from the beginning."

Nebuchadnezzar's dream of empires

When Jerusalem was conquered by Nebuchadnezzar and the Babylonians in 597 B.C., the Jewish nation was brought into captivity or slavery in Babylon. During this time, the Babylonian king Nebuchadnezzar had a reoccurring nightmare and he sought to have a "wise man" interpret the terrifying dream. The Jewish prophet Daniel interpreted the dream and he also recorded the event in the Old Testament book that bears his name. The nature of Daniel's interpretation is made clear, as he stated to the king, "...there is a God in heaven who reveals secrets, and He has made known to King Nebuchadnezzar what will be in the latter days (Daniel 2:28)."

According to the account in the book of Daniel, the king had challenged Daniel to first describe the visions that appeared in Nebuchadnezzar's dream, and then he was to interpret the visions. Daniel correctly described the image: a giant and frightening image of a man – with a head of gold, its chest and arms of silver, its torso and thighs of brass, its legs of iron, and its feet of clay (ceramic) mixed with iron (Dan 2:32-33). Then, he describes how a "stone cut without human hands" crushes the figure, first by striking a blow to the feet. Finally, the stone becomes a "mountain that fills the entire earth." There is obviously the use of symbolism in this prophecy, however Daniel himself explains the symbolism.

He told king Nebuchadnezzar that the image represents kingdoms, or ruling powers, over this region of the world and each section of the image represents different empires or powers (Table 1). This was made clear by Daniels's statement to the king in verses Daniel 2:39-40,

> "But after you shall arise another kingdom inferior to yours; then another, a third kingdom of bronze, which shall rule over all the earth. And the fourth kingdom shall be as strong as iron, inasmuch as iron breaks in pieces and shatters everything; and like iron that crushes, that kingdom will break in pieces and crush all the others."

Historians date Nebuchadnezzar's rule from about 605–562 B.C., and therefore Daniel's book was written during this time or shortly thereafter. Bible scholars typically date its authorship around 540 B.C. and this provides a historical framework by which the prophecies can be examined. As Daniel explained to Nebuchadnezzar, the different sections of the image correspond to different political powers, with special significance being made to the materials. The metals in this

Table 1. Daniel's prophecies in 540 B.C. concerning future world powers.

Image	Empire or power	Dates of reign
Head of gold	Babylon and Nebuchadnezzar	600 BC
Chest and arms of silver	Medo-Persian Empire (eventually becoming the Achaemenid Empire)	550 BC-330 BC
Torso and thighs of brass	Alexander the Great and the Greek Empire	330 BC-150 BC
Legs of iron	Roman Empire	30 BC – 1450 AD
Feet of ceramics and iron	Union of strong and weak nations	Still future
Cut Stone made without hands	Return and reign of Jesus Christ	Still future

prophecy were meant to reflect the aspects of the future kingdoms. For example, the strength of the metals reflected the strength of military might in each kingdom. This is confirmed by the study of history, as the Roman military machine was the most fearsome and powerful. It succeeded in spreading the Roman Empire throughout Europe, Asia, and into Africa. This was the largest political power up until that time. Scholars have noted that the Roman Empire was divided into the eastern and western empires, symbolized by the two iron legs. Using a dream from the Babylonian ruler, the Jewish prophet Daniel correctly predicted three empires of the ancient world!

Daniel's prophecy may very well be describing modern times, too. As the sequence of empires continues, the final Gentile world power will consist of a union of nations symbolized by feet made with a mixture of iron and ceramic material. This mixture of materials is expected to be inherently weak because these two substances normally do not adhere to each other. Many Bible scholars suggest that this empire is presently starting to take shape in Europe, as strong nations are forming a union with much weaker nations. The European Union is composed of an unusual group of nations. Countries such as Germany have strong economic engines, while countries like Greece or Estonia have decidedly weaker economies. This type union is entirely consistent with Daniel's prophetic series of empires.

The interpretation of Nebuchadnezzar's dream includes a description of a "stone cut without human hands" crushing the feet. This is clearly a reference to the return of Jesus Christ at His second coming. For example, King David described (Psalm 2) how the God of Heaven declared that His Son would receive the "nations as His inheritance" and "dash them to pieces" like a piece pottery or ceramics. The passage finishes with good advice to the Muslim (Psalm 2:12), "Kiss the Son, lest He be angry, and you perish in the way…blessed are all those who put their trust in Him." When Jesus Christ returns in His second advent, He will come to Israel's defense with the armies of Heaven and He will crush the last Gentile empire. The dream also noted that the stone cut without human hands would grow into a mountain that would fill the earth. This is a description of the rule and reign of Jesus Christ as the future king of Israel. Regarding the reference to Jesus Christ as a "stone cut without human hands," other passages in the New Testament make reference to Jesus Christ as a stone (see, Acts 4:10-12).

Daniel's dream of rulers

Daniel himself also had a dream and it predicted the sequence of empires that would rule the region around Judea. Like Nebuchadnezzar's dream, it was filled with symbolism and imagery. As described in chapter 8 of the book of Daniel, a ram with two horns trampled the Earth but then a powerful goat destroyed the ram. The goat was said to have one large horn that was replaced by four smaller horns. Then there is a description of a new, small horn growing on the goat. A voice states that the small horn would "oppose the daily sacrifices; and he cast truth down to the ground (Daniel 8:12)" and that this event would last "two thousand three hundred days (Daniel 8:14)." The symbolism was interpreted by the angel Gabriel, explaining the dream to Daniel. Along with the dream of Nebuchadnezzar, it constitutes one of the most remarkable sets of prophecies in the Old Testament.

As explained by the angel Gabriel, the figures in the dream represent a series of empires that would conquer the region. Specific elements of the prophecy are presented in Table 2. It should again be emphasized that Bible scholars date Daniel's book to about 540 B.C., and his writings accurately predict the emergence of two world empires, the Medo-Persians and the Greeks. Even more remarkable, Daniel's prophecies describe the types of rulers in the empires. In one case, the prophecies even predict the number of days a ruler would curse or afflict Israel. The study of history shows that these Biblical prophecies were fulfilled perfectly. This argues strongly for the divine origin of these Old Testament Scriptures.

Table 2. Elements of Daniel's dream and prophecies (from 540 B.C.) concerning world events and their dates of fulfillment.

Passage of Scripture	Historical Event	Date(s) Fulfilled
...a ram which had two horns, and the two horns were high; but one was higher than the other, and the higher one came up last. Daniel 8:3b	Medo-Persian power arises; Persians become dominant power	549 B.C.
"The ram which you saw, having the two horns—they are the kings of Media and Persia." Daniel 8:20	Medo-Persians conquer Babylon	539 B.C.
"The large horn that is between its eyes is the first king." Daniel 8:21b	Alexander the Great emerges	336 B.C.
"And the male goat is the kingdom of Greece." Daniel 8:21a	Greek armies attack and conquer the Persians	330 B.C.
"As for the broken horn and the four that stood up in its place, four kingdoms shall arise out of that nation, but not with its power." Daniel 8:22	Alexander dies and the empire is divided between four military commanders	323 B.C.
And out of one of them came a little horn which grew exceedingly great toward the south, toward the east, and toward the Glorious Land. Daniel 8:9	Antiochus Epiphanes IV emerges	175 B.C.
And he said to me, "For two thousand three hundred days; then the sanctuary shall be cleansed." Daniel 8:14	Jews revolt from Syrian rule after about 6 years (2,300 days)	162 B.C.
...he shall be broken without human means. Daniel 8:25b	Antiochus Epiphanes IV dies from a disease	163 B.C.

The Muslim should consider if similar prophecies are given in the Quran. Did the Quran predict the Mongolian, British, and Ottoman empires? Did the Quran predict the rise of western civilization, or the emergence of the China, Russia, or the United States as world powers? These would be the equivalents of Daniel's prophecies. According to Islamic literature, Muhammad is said to have even spoken with the same angel as Daniel - the angel Gabriel. Neither God nor the angel Gabriel provided Muhammad with a comparable set accurate prophecies. Why? Perhaps it is because the Bible is God's true message to humanity.

Israel and the Jews

The Bible contains remarkable prophecies that predicted - centuries in advance - the course of history with the rise and fall of nations. These prophecies are compelling evidence that the God of Heaven is the ultimate author and inspiration for the Biblical Scriptures. The prophecies also argue for the preservation of the Scriptures, as corrupted texts would not contain accurate predictions regarding historical events. While the prophecies concerning Gentile (non-Jewish) nations are stunning in their accuracy, the prophecies concerning Israel and the Jews are even more amazing. The history of the Jews was placed in the Bible thousands of years in advance of its fulfillment and we are even seeing some of these prophecies being fulfilled in our day and age!

For example in about 1,400 B.C., Moses wrote about the future of his people. By the power of God, he had just led the Jews out of Egyptian slavery and they were about to enter into the land of Canaan. During this Exodus period, God and Moses produced the first five books of the Bible (Genesis, Exodus, Leviticus, Numbers, and Deuteronomy). As part of the covenant (or agreement) with God, the nation of Israel was to keep the commandments in the Law of Moses. Most importantly, they were to have no other gods in place of the God of Abraham, Isaac, and Jacob. They were to worship only the true God of Heaven.

However, the God of Heaven is all knowing, or as the scholars like to say, He is omniscient. God knew that the Jews would eventually begin worshiping the false gods of the region. God could even see into the future and He knew that the Jews would reject their Savior and give Jesus over to the Romans for crucifixion. God could also see 1,500 years ahead of Moses' day and know that the Jewish leaders would persecute the early Christian church. With this mountain of sins against them, God's judgment would fall upon the nation of Israel. Therefore, Moses accurately predicted (Deuteronomy 28:58,65) the sad future of the Jewish people:

"If you do not carefully observe all the words of this law that are written in this book, that you may fear this glorious and awesome name, THE LORD YOUR GOD...Then the LORD will scatter you among all peoples, from one end of the earth to the other, and there you shall serve other gods, which neither you nor your fathers have known—wood and stone. And among those nations you shall find no rest, nor shall the sole of your foot have a resting place; but there the LORD will give you a trembling heart, failing eyes, and anguish of soul."

As every historian knows, the Roman general Titus led a devastating siege against Jerusalem in 70 A.D. Shortly after the fall of Jerusalem, the Romans sent many of the Jews into slavery. Those that escaped with their lives fled to neighboring countries. The great world-wide dispersion of Jews continued through the centuries.

Elements of Moses' prophecy are remarkably accurate. Through the centuries, there have been many efforts or pogroms to kill the Jews. In recent history, the German Nazis targeted Jewish populations in Germany, Poland, and throughout Europe. Jews have suffered brutal persecution in almost every location in which they have settled, including throughout the Middle East during the expansion of Islam. This brings to mind the words of God and Moses, that the Jews would have a "trembling heart" and no "resting place."

Nevertheless, the Bible contains many prophecies concerning the future of Israel and the Jews. In God's providence, the Jewish people were preserved. This is one of the most amazing facts of history. A group of people was "scattered" among all the nations of the world about 2,000 years ago and yet they did not vanish from the scene. Many other groups of people have experienced similar fates and they have been assimilated into the nations. The Jews were persecuted in almost every nation into which they fled and yet they continued to exist! Their survival is even more remarkable when one considers that they have been murdered 100,000s at a time. God declared through many writers that the nation of Israel would be preserved, despite being scattered throughout the world (Table 3). Moses, David, Joel, and Paul recorded several prophecies clearly predicting the preservation of the Jews.

Besides these explicit passages of Scripture describing God's preservation of the Jews, there are also many references to God's agreements or covenants He made with the patriarchs of the Jews. As described throughout the Old Testament, God

Table 3. Prophecies concerning God's preservation and memory of the Jews.

Author	Passage	Year of writing	Prophecy
Moses	Lev. 26:44	1450 B.C.	Yet for all that, when they are in the land of their enemies, I will not cast them away, nor shall I abhor them, to utterly destroy them and break My covenant with them; for I am the LORD their God.
David	Psalm 94:14	1000 B.C.	For the LORD will not cast off His people, nor will He forsake His inheritance.
Joel	Joel 2:18	900 B.C.	Then the LORD will be zealous for His land, and pity His people.
Paul	Romans 11:2	57 A.D.	"God has not cast away His people whom He foreknew…"

made promises to Abraham, Isaac, Jacob, and David. For example Moses recorded God saying, "then I will remember My covenant with Jacob, and My covenant with Isaac and My covenant with Abraham I will remember; I will remember the land (Leviticus 26:42)." This prophecy refers to God reforming the nation of Israel with the surviving Jews. In order for these promises to be fulfilled, the Jews needed to be preserved as a people.

Although the prophecies concerning the Jews' preservation may be remarkable, their return to the land of Judea is one of the most extraordinary events of history. For a variety of reasons, this is a bitter issue for many Muslims. In order to consider Bible prophecy and history, it is necessary to step away from the conflict between the Arab Palestinians and the Jews of Israel. We will not address the issue of whether or not the Jews should have been allowed to occupy the land between Lebanon and Jordan. The simple fact remains: the modern nation of Israel became a reality in 1948. This was more than nineteen centuries after the Jews were scattered throughout the nations. Like other prophecies concerning the nation of Israel, the Bible accurately predicted this event. There are many, many prophecies related to the gathering of the Jews in the land. They have come from several different prophets during several different centuries. Some are given below (italics mine):

the LORD your God will bring you back from captivity, and have compassion on you, and *gather you again from all the nations* where the LORD your God has scattered you. (Deut 30:3, prophecy made by Moses in 1400 B.C.).

"I will bring back the captives of My people Israel; they shall build the waste cities and inhabit them; they shall plant vineyards and drink wine from them; they shall also make gardens and eat fruit from them. *I will plant them in their land,* and no longer shall they be pulled up from the land I have given them," says the LORD your God. (Amos 9:14-15, prophecy made in 800 B.C.)

It shall come to pass in that day that *the Lord shall* set His hand again the second time to *recover the remnant of His people* who are left...and will assemble the outcasts of Israel, and gather together the dispersed of Judah from the four corners of the earth. (Isaiah 11:11-12, prophecy made in 800 B.C.)

Thus says the Lord GOD: "*I will gather you from the peoples, assemble you from the countries where you have been scattered, and I will give you the land of Israel.*" (Ezekial 11:17, prophecy made in 600 B.C.)

Thus says the Lord GOD: "Surely I will take the children of Israel from among the nations, wherever they have gone, and will *gather them from every side and bring them into their own land*; (Ezekiel 37:21, prophecy made in 600 B.C.)

"The Gentiles shall know that the house of Israel went into captivity for their iniquity; because they were unfaithful to Me, therefore I hid My face from them. I gave them into the hand of their enemies, and they all fell by the sword. According to their uncleanness and according to their transgressions I have dealt with them, and hidden My face from them." Therefore thus says the Lord GOD: *"Now I will bring back the captives of Jacob,* and have mercy on the whole house of Israel; and I will be jealous for My holy name" (Ezekiel 39:23-25, prophecy made in 600 B.C.)

137

The above passages repeatedly describe how God would judge Israel and the Jews, scatter them across the world, and then bring them back to the land. Many other Old Testament passages describe this miraculous return of Jews to this land (see for example: Jer. 32:37; Isaiah 14:1 and 54:7; Ezekiel 34:13; Jer. 30:3). This land described in these passages was clearly the land of Canaan (i.e., Judah) and not some region in Europe, Russia, or the United States. According to the agreement with the patriarch Abraham, God was to place Abraham's offspring in the land of Canaan (see Genesis 17:8). The study of history and archaeology has also shown this to be the location of the ancient nation of Israel. Why do archaeologists in modern day Israel recover ancient artifacts having inscriptions in Hebrew? They do so because the Jews lived in the land for many, many centuries. However 2,000 years ago, God drove the Jews from the land of Israel. The Jews have returned to this same land. Thus, the prophecies of the Old Testament have been fulfilled.

The Old Testament book of Hosea provides one of the most interesting prophecies concerning Israel's future. Written in about 800 B.C. by the ancient Jewish prophet named Hosea, this book predates the invasion of Israel by the Assyrians and Babylonians by more than 100 years and it predates the worldwide dispersion of the Jews (by the Romans) by about 900 years. Remarkably, this passage of Scripture predicted the formation of modern Israel - almost 3,000 years in advance!

The book compares the nation of Israel to a prostitute, who instead of remaining faithful to a loving husband, she chooses to commit adultery with many other men. Israel's sad history includes their desires to serve false gods and deities, rather than worship the loving God of their fathers. The book of Hosea predicts that, "the children of Israel shall abide many days without king or prince, without sacrifice or sacred pillar, without ephod or teraphim (Hosea 3:4)." This passage specifically describes the end of the nation and its worship at the Temple. It is consistent with the scattering of the Jews in about 70 A.D. and the destruction of Herod's Temple in Jerusalem.

The chapter continues, however with the prophecy that "afterward the children of Israel shall return and seek the LORD their God...(Hosea 3:5)." Even more remarkable, Hosea gives a time period for this return to the land. At the end of chapter 5 and beginning of chapter 6, he wrote:

> "...I, even I, will tear them and go away; I will take them away, and no one shall rescue. I will return again to My place until they acknowledge their offense. Then they will seek My face; in their affliction they will earnestly seek Me." Come, and let us return to the LORD; for He has torn, but He will heal us; He has stricken,

but He will bind us up. After two days He will revive us; on the third day He will raise us up, that we may live in His sight. (Hosea 5:14b-6:2)

This passage of Scripture states that God would "tear them and go away" which is a reference to the judgment and scattering of Jews in 70 A.D. It also states how God would "return again to My place" which is a reference to the resurrection and ascension (to Heaven) of Jesus Christ. Then it says God will revive Israel after "two days" and raise them up "on the third day." Other parts of the Bible describe how Jesus Christ will rule Israel for 1,000 years upon His return. Thus, one day is equal to 1,000 years in this prophecy. How long has it been since Israel was a nation and Jews were in the land promised to Abraham? It has been about 2,000 years. *Hosea accurately predicted the time period of 2,000 years of dispersed and lost Israel!* Although the Jews are back in their historic homeland, it is the opinion of this author that the nation is yet to be fully "revived" by the Lord.[3] This day will represent the complete fulfillment of the prophecy.

Prophecies of Jesus Christ
His Birth

When Jesus was born in Bethlehem, a group of wise men came from the east in search of the newborn Savior.[4] They had seen a star in the sky, which was a sign of the birth of the Messiah. They entered Jerusalem and asked king Herod, "where is Him who is born King of the Jews?" Not being a man of faith, Herod had to ask his advisors for an answer. The advisors pointed to the Old Testament prophecy by Micah that said the Savior would be born in Bethlehem. So Herod sent the wise men to Bethlehem, where they found the young Jesus with Mary and Joseph.

This event was the start of a long series of miraculous events. The life, death, and resurrection of Jesus Christ were thoroughly described in the ancient Jewish Scriptures centuries before His arrival in Israel. The Jewish religious leaders often debated or challenged Jesus Christ during His three years of ministry in first century Israel. At one point, Jesus Christ responded to them with the truth, "You search the Scriptures, for in them you think you have eternal life; and these are they which testify of Me (John 5:39-40)." Jesus Christ claimed that the Old Testament "testified" of Him. Indeed, we shall see in this section many of the prophecies described Jesus Christ – prophecies like the one predicting His birth in Bethlehem. With the fulfillment of dozens of prophecies, this represents strong evidence that His ministry was Divinely ordained, and equally as important, that the Old Testament Scriptures are the true word of God.

Beside Micah's prophecy concerning the location of Christ's birth, Old Testament prophecies also described from which families the Savior would be born. Centuries before the birth of Jesus Christ, His lineage was described. For example, the Messiah and Savior was predicted to be **Abraham's Son**. The book of Genesis was written by Moses in about 1450 B.C. and it recorded an important event in the life of Abraham, "then the Angel of the LORD called to Abraham a second time out of heaven...In your seed all the nations of the earth shall be blessed... Gen. 22:15,19." In this passage, God promises that one of Abraham's descendants (*seed*, singular in Hebrew) would be a blessing to all nations and people.

Although the prophecy to Abraham might be misinterpreted as a prophecy regarding Muhammad (a son through the lineage of Ishmael), we see that God and Moses intended the prophecy to point centuries ahead to a **Son of Isaac**. Moses also wrote concerning Isaac, "then the LORD appeared to him and said...and in your seed (singular) all the nations of the earth shall be blessed (Gen 26:2,4)". In speaking to Isaac, this is clearly a reference to Jesus Christ, not Muhammad.

Isaac had two sons, one of whom was Jacob (later renamed Israel). Moses recorded another prophecy describing the Savior as the **Son of Jacob**. In a dream, Jacob sees a ladder reaching into to Heaven, "and behold, the LORD stood above it and said: 'I am the LORD God of Abraham your father and the God of Isaac...in you and in your seed (singular) all the families of the earth shall be blessed' (Genesis 28:14)." Through Moses, God is clearly stating that Jacob, otherwise known as Israel, will be a blessing to "all the families of the earth." How can this be? If you were to ask a Muslim in Syria or Iran or Egypt or Iraq, "Are the Jews and the nation of Israel a blessing to you?"

They would most emphatically say, "No!"

But God's revelation through the prophet Moses is clear. The nation of Israel and the Jewish people will forever be a blessing to the world. God did not qualify this prophecy with time limits or any other restrictions. If we return to the question, "how can this be?" then we should realize: it is because Israel gave us Jesus Christ, the Savior of mankind. Without Jesus Christ and His death on the cross, all mankind would be *lost in their sin*, destined to be *condemned* on the Judgment Day, and *doomed* to eternal punishment. Jesus Christ has brought salvation to all the people of the world, even to those standing in Mecca.

Moses continues his prophecies by describing the Messiah as a **Son of Judah**. As described in the book of Genesis, Jacob would eventually have twelve sons and these became the twelve tribes of the nation of Israel. One of the sons of Jacob was named Judah. Near the end of his life, Jacob described the futures for his twelve sons, and regarding Judah, he said, "the scepter shall not depart from Judah, nor a lawgiver from between his feet, until Shiloh comes; and to Him shall be the obedience of the people (Genesis 49:10)."

Admittedly, this prophecy is in veiled terms. It does not directly state that Judah will have a Son 1,500 years later - whose name is Jesus - and He will be Savior of all mankind. Nevertheless, it was through this verse that the ancient rabbis understood that the Messiah and King of Israel would come from the tribe or family of Judah. The term Shiloh is derived from a Hebrew word meaning tranquil, secure, and safe. It is also an individual with authority and power. Interestingly, some scholars translate the word Shiloh as three Hebrew words.[5] This translation renders the word "he whose it is" – a phrase which points to Jesus as King of Israel (the one who holds the scepter). In accord with this prophecy, Jesus Christ was born from the lineage of Judah.

Recall that Jesus Christ was born in Bethlehem. This was the ancestral home of King David. There were also prophecies that predicted the Messiah and Savior would be a **Son of David**. In about 1000 B.C., the prophet Samuel wrote concerning David, "Thus says the LORD of hosts... When your days are fulfilled and you rest with your fathers, I will set up your seed after you, who will come from your body, and I will establish his kingdom...And your house and your kingdom shall be established forever before you. Your throne shall be established forever (2 Sam. 7:12)." Based on this passage, first century Jewish leaders (the Pharisees) understood that the Messiah would be David's son. In Matthew's book, an exchange is recorded (Matt 41:21-22):

> While the Pharisees were gathered together, Jesus asked them, saying, "What do you think about the Christ? Whose Son is He?"
> They said to Him, "The Son of David."

While Christ was ministering to first century Israel, He was repeatedly referred to as the Son of David. In Matthew's gospel account alone, there are seven instances of this title being used for Christ. The title of Son of David describes two qualities of Jesus Christ - His family heritage and His claim to the throne of Israel.

Beginning with Moses, the writers of the Old Testament books made prophecies concerning the families to whom Israel's Messiah and Savior would be born. These ancient prophecies predicted that the Savior Jesus Christ would be a Son of Abraham, Isaac, Jacob (or Israel), Judah, and David. These prophecies were made no less than 800 years before the birth of Jesus Christ and He fulfilled each of these predictions. We know the lineage of Jesus from two accounts in the New Testament. The family heritage through Joseph - His adoptive father - is given in the book of Matthew. It begins with the statement, "the genealogy of Jesus Christ, the Son of David, the Son of Abraham." It continues with records describing Jesus Christ also as a Son of Isaac, Jacob, and Judah. As a former Roman tax collector, Matthew would have been skilled at record keeping and tracing genealogies.

Similarly, the lineage of Jesus Christ through Mary – His mother – is described in Luke's New Testament book. This historical record also describes Jesus Christ as the Son of David, Judah, Jacob, Isaac, and Abraham. The author Luke is known for his very accurate historical records (see Chapter 5), so there is no reason to doubt or question his record of Jesus Christ's genealogy or family history. Thus, we find that Jesus Christ fulfilled the Old Testament prophecies concerning the Messiah's expected family of origin.

Regarding the birth of Christ, the ancient Jewish prophets also made predictions that the Savior would be born from a virgin and He would be the unique Son of God. These were two further prophecies that were satisfied by Jesus Christ. About 800 years before the birth of Jesus, the prophet Isaiah wrote (Isaiah 7:14),

> "Therefore the Lord Himself will give you a sign: behold, the virgin shall conceive and bear a Son, and shall call His name Immanuel."

The account of Jesus Christ's birth can be found in Matthew's book (Matt. 1:18) and Luke's book (Luke 1:34-35). Both authors testify regarding the miraculous birth of Jesus Christ and that His mother was a virgin when He was born. The angel of the Lord explained this event to Mary (Luke 1:35), "the Holy Spirit will come upon you, and the power of the Highest will overshadow you; therefore, also, that Holy One who is to be born will be called the Son of God." Although Joseph and Mary were husband and wife, the Bible declares that Jesus Christ was conceived by a miracle from Heaven, rather than by sexual relations between Joseph and Mary. In fulfillment of Isaiah's prophecy, Mary was a virgin when Jesus was born.

Interestingly, Isaiah's passage declares that someone named Immanuel will be born, not someone named Jesus. The name Immanuel is translated from the Hebrew, "God is with us." Thus, the prophecy states that the Messiah would be born from a virgin, and it also states that this Son will be named "God is with us." One might argue that this is to be meant figuratively (i.e., that God is always with us), but with examination of other Bible passages, we find that this is a literal prediction. God is present in the person of Jesus Christ. This truth was stated very clearly by an Apostle named Thomas. Upon meeting Jesus Christ after His resurrection from the dead, Thomas exclaimed (John 20:28), "My Lord and My

God!" With these considerations, we see that Isaiah is referring to Jesus Christ as Immanuel.

The Old Testament also predicted that the Messiah would be the uniquely born Son of God – a title only given to Jesus Christ. One such prophecy stated, "The LORD has said to Me, "You are My Son, today I have begotten You (Psalm 2:7)." In this passage written by the prophet, King David, it looked centuries ahead to the day when Jesus Christ would be the only begotten, or uniquely born, Son of God. No other man can make this claim, nor will anyone else ever be able to make this claim. The Sonship of Jesus Christ was even declared by God Himself. Following the baptism of Jesus Christ in first-century Israel, God the Father proclaimed in a voice from Heaven, "This is My beloved Son, in whom I am well pleased (Matt 3:17)."

The title "Son of God" speaks to the deity of Jesus Christ. The deity of Jesus Christ is a tough doctrine for Muslims to grasp, as it was for many first century Jews. It is a difficult concept even for people this day. However this truth was taught by many of the prophets who came before and after Jesus Christ. A thorough treatment of the deity of Jesus Christ is found in Chapter 12.

His Ministry in Israel

Historians and Bible scholars estimate that Jesus Christ began His public ministry when He was about 30 years old.[6]   There are a number of specific prophecies which foretold of His ministry in first century Israel. For example, God sent a prophet named John the Baptist to ancient Israel and he had one purpose: John was to announce and present the Messiah to Israel.[7]   When he met Jesus Christ, John testified to all Israel that Jesus Christ was the Messiah from Heaven. Soon after, John the Baptist was executed by King Herod.

John's ministry should be a startling point for Muslims. If Muhammad was the most important prophet, then why didn't God send someone to announce the upcoming arrival of Muhammad? The ministry of John the Baptist is strong evidence for the Divine origin of the teachings and ministry of Jesus Christ. The account of John the Baptist is found in all four historical gospel books (Matthew 3; Mark 1; Luke 1 and 3; John 1) and his ministry is even described by the Jewish historian Josephus (in *Jewish Antiquities*, written in 94 A.D.).[8] As recorded in the gospel account (John 1:32, 34): And John bore witness, saying, "I saw the Spirit descending from heaven like a dove, and He remained upon Him…And I have seen and testified that this is the Son of God."

Regarding John the Baptist, his work was prophesied or predicted in the pages of the Old Testament. The prophet Isaiah wrote his Old Testament book about 800 years prior to the arrival of Jesus Christ and John the Baptist. In Isaiah's prophecies, he foretold of another prophet who would precede or come before the Messiah of Israel. Isaiah's prophecy concerning John the Baptist reads (Isaiah 40:3-5),

> The voice of one crying in the wilderness: "Prepare the way of the LORD; make straight in the desert a highway for our God. Every valley shall be exalted and every mountain and hill brought low; the crooked places shall be made straight and the rough places smooth; the glory of the LORD shall be revealed, and all flesh shall see it together; for the mouth of the LORD has spoken"

John the Baptist began "crying in the wilderness" around 30 A.D. Using water from the Jordan River, John baptized thousands of Jews and preached to them. The Jewish rulers of the day asked John, "Are you the Christ?" John replied (see John 1:23) that he was not the Christ, but rather, "I am 'The voice of one crying in the wilderness: 'Make straight the way of the LORD,' as the prophet Isaiah said." When Jesus Christ approached John, he identified Jesus as the Messiah and Savior.

When Christians and non-Christians read about the lifetime of Jesus, often the most striking aspect includes the descriptions of the miracles. Jesus and His chosen Apostles conducted many, many miraculous events. On more than one occasion, Jesus Christ restored the sight of blind individuals, He raised people from the dead (even one who had already been buried), and He commanded storms to cease. The Apostle John concluded his gospel book with the statement (John 21:25), "And there are also many other things that Jesus did, which if they were written one by one, I suppose that even the world itself could not contain the books that would be written." Indeed, the descriptions of the miraculous healing events note that "multitudes" or vast numbers of people came to Jesus and were healed of the medical problems.

The miraculous works of Jesus Christ were also prophesied or predicted by the writers of the Old Testament. For example, the prophet Isaiah wrote in 800 B.C.,

> Say to those who are fearful-hearted, "Be strong, do not fear! Behold, your God will come with vengeance, with the recompense of God; He will come and save you." Then the eyes of the blind shall be opened, and the ears of the deaf shall be unstopped. Then the lame shall leap like a deer, And the tongue of the mute sing...Isaiah 35:4-6a

Thus, Isaiah predicted that the Messiah would give sight to the blind, hearing to the deaf, mobility to those with paralysis, and the ability to speak to those who are mute. In the gospel records (Matthew, Mark, Luke, and John), there are eyewitness accounts of Jesus accomplishing these very types of miracles. These are outline in Table 4. The prophet Jeremiah also wrote about the miracles that would accompany Israel's then future Messiah. He wrote his book in about 700 B.C. - long before Jesus Christ came to Israel and healed many thousands of people. Jeremiah prophesied, "'Behold, I will bring it health and healing; I will heal them and reveal to them the abundance of peace and truth (Jer. 33:6)." Not only did Jesus bring "health and healing," but He brought "peace and truth." His teachings were absolute truth and Jesus Himself noted (John 14:3), "I am the way, the truth, and the life. No one comes to the Father except through Me."

Table 4. The fulfillment of prophecies related to healing by the promised Messiah.

Old Testament Scripture	Prophecy concerning Messiah	Fulfillment by Jesus Christ	New Testament Scripture
Isaiah 35:5	...the eyes of the blind shall be opened...	Now as Jesus passed by, He saw a man who was blind from birth... He anointed the eyes of the blind man with the clay... So he went and washed, and came back seeing.	John 9:1-12
Isaiah 35:6	...the lame shall leap like a deer...	...then He said to the paralytic, "Arise, take up your bed, and go to your house." And he arose and departed to his house.	Matt 9:6,7
Isaiah 35:6	...the tongue of the mute sing...	...they laid them down at Jesus' feet, and He healed them. So the multitude marveled when they saw the mute speaking...	Matt 15:30-31
Jeremiah 33:6	...I will bring it health and healing...	And the whole multitude sought to touch Him, for power went out from Him and healed them all.	Luke 6:19

The ancient prophets also described how the Gentiles would be included in the ministry and work of Jesus Christ the Savior. These were notable prophecies, because ancient Israel was distinctly separate from the other people and nations (the Gentiles). Thus, a prophetic message describing blessings to the Gentiles might not be warmly received by fellow Jews. Isaiah began the 42nd chapter of his book, "Behold! My Servant whom I uphold, My Elect One in whom My soul delights! I have put My Spirit upon Him; He will bring forth justice to the Gentiles." The context clearly refers to Israel's future Savior and Messiah, Jesus Christ. Later in Isaiah's 42nd chapter, God describes the Messiah, "...as a light to the Gentiles, to open blind eyes, to bring out prisoners from the prison." This prophecy has also been overwhelmingly fulfilled in Jesus Christ. When He died upon the cross, all of mankind's sins were punished. Salvation from sin can now be offered to all men, Jews and Gentiles.

As described in the gospel accounts, Jesus had a ministry in Israel for roughly three years (around 30 A.D.). During this time, He and his Apostles taught to various groups of Jews. Jesus ministered to individuals one-on-one and He preached to groups of several thousand at one time. At the end of His public ministry, He entered into Jerusalem for the last time (of course, He did return to Jerusalem following His resurrection), as He would soon be put to death on Mount Calvary.

This particular arrival of Jesus Christ in Jerusalem was the subject of several important prophecies. For example, the date of Jesus Christ's entry into Jerusalem had been placed in the Old Testament Scriptures by the prophet Daniel nearly 600 years earlier. Daniel wrote,

> Know therefore and understand, that from the going forth of the command to restore and build Jerusalem until Messiah the Prince, there shall be seven weeks and sixty-two weeks; the street shall be built again, and the wall, even in troublesome times. And after the sixty-two weeks Messiah shall be cut off, but not for Himself
> Daniel 9:25,26a

In this prophetic passage, each "week" is considered a seven-year period. The period of time begins with the decree from the Persian ruler Artaxerxes to restore and rebuild Jerusalem. Scholars date this decree at about 446 B.C. and Daniel's prophecy indicates that Messiah would enter Jerusalem sixty-nine weeks after this date.[9] This time period represents 483 years, however the Jewish calendar year was composed of 360 days (instead of our 365 days/year), so this number reduces to 476 years after the decree. Thus, Daniel prophesied that the Messiah and Savior would be formally presented to Israel in 30 A.D. (on our calendar). According to historical records in the New Testament, this was the year that Jesus Christ entered Jerusalem.

It is also notable that Daniel describes the Messiah being "cut off, but not for Himself." This is another prophecy pointing to the crucifixion of Jesus Christ on our behalf.

Again, the honest Muslim should begin to wonder why there were no similar prophecies concerning Muhammad. For example, the Almighty God of Heaven could have easily stated that the greatest prophet would conquer and enter into Median so many "weeks" into the future. However, no such prophecies are found in the ancient Old Testament Scriptures.

Besides the timing of Jesus Christ's arrival in Jerusalem, the event itself was described hundreds of years prior to the event. The Jewish prophet Zechariah wrote his book in 600 B.C. He describes how Israel's Messiah would present Himself at His arrival:

> Rejoice greatly, O daughter of Zion! Shout, O daughter of Jerusalem! Behold, your King is coming to you; He is just and having salvation, lowly and riding on a donkey, a colt, the foal of a donkey. (Zech. 9:9)

This Old Testament prophecy describes how Israel's King and Messiah would arrive riding into Jerusalem on a donkey. It implies that He would arrive as a humble Man - not arriving on a chariot with trumpets sounding and great feasts in His honor. These prophecies were indeed fulfilled by Christ in His arrival at Jerusalem. All four gospel accounts describe Jesus riding the colt or young donkey into the city. For example, Luke wrote (Luke 19:35), "And they threw their own clothes on the colt, and they set Jesus on him."

His Crucifixion and Resurrection

As described in earlier chapters, the rulers and religious leaders of Israel rejected their long awaited Messiah. In doing so, they delivered Jesus to the Roman ruler Pontius Pilate for crucifixion. Even the rejection of Jesus Christ by the Jews was foretold in the Old Testament Scriptures. King David predicted this event about 1,000 years before the Jews rejected Jesus Christ. Through the inspiration of God, David wrote (Psalm 118:22,23), "The stone which the builders rejected has become the chief cornerstone. This was the LORD's doing; It is marvelous in our eyes." This passage states that the "chief cornerstone" would be rejected by the builders - a reference to the future rejection of the Messiah Jesus Christ by the nation of Israel.

In the ancient world, the cornerstone was the most important part of a new building. It was laid at the foundation and it was the stone from which all of the measurements were made. It was the first and most important component in a new building. We find the prediction in Psalm 118 (and in Isaiah 28:16) that the rejected Cornerstone – Jesus Christ - becomes part of a great and Divinely ordained construction project. This great building is sometimes referred to as the church, or the body of Christ, and it represents all the individuals who have become Christians.

As described thoroughly in Chapter 3, the all-knowing God of Heaven made many prophecies or predictions regarding the crucifixion of Jesus Christ. These prophecies were made hundreds of years prior to His death. In Isaiah 53, there is a clear picture of crucifixion involving the Messiah or Savior of Israel. It should be noted that Isaiah predicted the Messiah's crucifixion centuries before it had become a common form of execution or death.

An even more remarkable prophecy - or "picture" of the Jesus' death - is found in the Jewish feast of the Passover (first held in about 1400 B.C.). As described in the Old Testament book of Exodus, God and Moses instructed the ancient Jews to keep the Passover feast. This feast was meant to honor and remember the night when God freed the Jews from Egyptian slavery.[10] As instructed by Moses, the Jews were to select a lamb for the Passover sacrifice on the 10th day of Nissan (the first month of the year in the Jewish calendar), the lamb was to be inspected for flaws or defects for three days, and then on the 14th day of Nissan the perfect Passover lamb was to be killed. In the context of prophecy, the Passover was a description – or pre-figuring - of the work of Jesus Christ. Indeed, Jesus Christ is the Passover lamb provided by God Himself.

First, God and Moses required that the lamb be perfect and a "male without defect." This corresponded to Jesus Christ having no sin. According to the records in the Gospel accounts (Luke 23:4), the Roman ruler Pilate declared, "I find no fault in this Man." Secondly, the Savior would not have any bones broken in His death. This is in accord with the command from Moses and God (Leviticus 9:12), that during the Passover sacrifice of the lamb, they should not "break one of its bones." This was fulfilled on the cross when the Roman soldiers decided not the break Jesus Christ's legs because He was already dead (see, John 9:13). This was specifically predicted in Psalm 34.

Even the timing of Christ's death matched the Passover commandments. On the day that the Passover lambs were to be chosen (10th Nissan), Jesus Christ entered the city of Jerusalem. On the day that the lambs were to be killed (14th Nissan), Jesus Christ was put to death. The Passover tradition was placed in the Old Testament to point centuries ahead to the Savior Jesus Christ. Just as the blood of the first Passover lamb protected the ancient Jews from the judgment and wrath of God,[11] the blood of Jesus Christ does the same for us in this day. This was summarized beautifully by the Apostle Peter (1 Peter 1:18,19; "redeemed" means purchased):

"... you were not redeemed with corruptible things, like silver or gold, from your aimless conduct received by tradition from your fathers, but with the precious blood of Christ, as of a lamb without blemish and without spot."

Interestingly, Jesus Christ was buried on the exact day that the Jews celebrated their "Feast of Unleavened Bread" and He rose from the dead on the exact day of the "Feast of First Fruits." These were not accidental events. Rather, the sovereign God of Heaven intentionally placed these feasts in the Jewish religion. They were to point ahead to the day when Jesus Christ would die on the cross, would get buried in the tomb, and would rise from the dead.

Many prophecies were fulfilled by Jesus Christ when He was crucified and buried (Table 5). As the single most important event of history, God thoroughly described it in the Old Testament prophecies. These ancient prophecies described very specific details, such as the price of Jesus' betrayal (30 pieces of silver) and the Roman soldiers gambling for His clothing. These details have been verified by the eyewitness accounts found in the New Testament gospel books. It is important to note that God made no predictions or prophecies that support the Islamic notion that Jesus Christ would escape crucifixion or that someone else would die on the cross.

The Old Testament prophets also predicted the resurrection of the Messiah, although at the time they did not understand its significance. As described in Chapter 4, there were several prophecies to indicate that Jesus Christ would be resurrected from the dead. First and foremost, there are the two parallel descriptions of Israel's Messiah, the suffering Servant and the glorious King. We now know that these prophecies are describing the same individual – Jesus Christ. In His role as suffering servant, He took our sins (yours and mine) and bore the Divine judgment, wrath, and punishment for those sins. This brought Jesus Christ to the cross where He died for us. With the resurrection three days later, Jesus Christ was risen by God the Father and seated at the "right hand of God."

He now waits for the appointed time for His triumphant return to Earth to judge the nations. At that point, He will return as Israel's glorious King. *The Old Testament prophecies concerning the glorious King of Israel are actually describing the rule and reign of the resurrected Jesus Christ.* It should be emphasized that these prophecies cover the full breadth of Old Testament

Table 5. Old Testament prophecies concerning the crucifixion of Jesus Christ.

Prophecy	Element	Date of prophecy	Fulfillment of prophecy
Zech. 11:12	Betrayed for 30 silver pieces	520 B.C.	Judas was paid 30 pieces of silver for betrayal; Matt. 26:15
Zech 12:10; Pslam 22:16	Body pierced	520 B.C. and 1000 B.C.	Nailed to cross; side pierced; John 19:34 and 20:27
Isaiah 53:10	An offering for sin	800 B.C.	Body of Jesus offered; see, Heb. 10:10
Psalm 69:21	Offered gall and vinegar for drink	1000 B.C.	Prior to being crucified, He was offered gall; Matt. 27:34
Isaiah 53:9	Death near wicked men	800 B.C.	Crucified between two thieves; Matt. 27:28
Isaiah 53:9	Death with rich man	800 B.C.	Buried in rich man's tomb; Mark. 15:46
Psalm 22:18	Garments divided	1000 B.C.	Soldiers gambled for Christ's clothes; John 19:23,24
Isaiah 53:3	Despised and rejected of men	800 B.C.	Jewish leaders did not believe in Him; John 7:5,48
Psalm 22:7,8	Taunted while on cross	1000 B.C.	Jewish leaders and other people insulted and taunted Christ; Matt. 27:39
Psalm 34:21	Bones not broken	1000 B.C.	No bones broken; John 19:33
Amos 8:9	Darkness to cover land	800 B.C.	Sun was darkened when Christ died; Matt. 27:45
Psalm 22:1	Forsaken by God the Father	1000 B.C.	At His death, Christ cried out to the Father - as forsaken; Matt. 27:46

revelation. It is more than one or two passages of Scripture. Rather, it involves many different authors. These prophets wrote over a period of about 1,000 years and their dozens of prophecies are fulfilled perfectly in Jesus Christ.

Moreover, there are specific prophecies that described the physical resurrection of Jesus Christ. As discussed in Chapter 4, King David wrote most of the books of Pslams around 1000 B.C., and Pslam 16:10 states, "…nor will You allow Your Holy One to see corruption." This is understood to be a prophecy concerning the physical resurrection of Jesus Christ. The term corruption is in reference to the decay of His slain body. This prophecy was fulfilled three days after the crucifixion of Jesus, when God the Father raised Him from the dead. According to the accounts in the New Testament, the resurrected Jesus Christ then appeared to His followers in a glorified body, a body that had not seen decay or corruption in the tomb. Similar prophecies may be found in Psalm 30:3 and Psalm 41:10.

Old Testament prophecies even described how Jesus Christ would be raised to sit in a position of great honor and authority in Heaven. Following the resurrection, God the Father raised Him and set Jesus Christ on Heaven's throne. King David also wrote of this event in the Old Testament book of Psalms: A Psalm of David. THE LORD said to my Lord, "Sit at My right hand, until I make Your enemies Your footstool (Psalm 110:1)"

This passage uses two different Hebrew words for God, essentially saying that God the Father invites God the Son to sit "at My right hand" or in the position of authority until the enemies are conquered. This outcome is clear from the testimony of the Apostle Paul, who wrote in the New Testament (highlights mine):

> …may the God of our Lord Jesus Christ, the Father of glory, give to you the spirit of wisdom and revelation in the knowledge of Him... according to the working of His mighty power which He worked in Christ when He raised Him from the dead and seated Him at His right hand in the heavenly places, far above all principality and power and might and dominion, and every name that is named, not only in this age but also in that which is to come (Ephesians 1:17, 19b-21).

Indeed, several other New Testament passages verify the exalted position of the resurrected Jesus Christ. This truth is presented several times in the book of Hebrews. For example in reference to Jesus Christ, the first chapter states: "…when He had by Himself purged our sins, sat down at the right hand of the Majesty on high (Hebrews 1:3b)." Peter's testimony at Pentecost stated:

"This Jesus God has raised up, of which we are all witnesses. Therefore being exalted to the right hand of God...(Acts 2:33)"

Thus, Old Testament prophecies suggested that the Messiah would be called to sit in an exalted position in Heaven. This was fulfilled by Jesus Christ at His resurrection.

Prophecies concerning Islam

For more than thirteen centuries, Muslim clerics have been searching the Bible for prophecies concerning the arrival of Muhammad. Perhaps they have seen the overwhelming numbers of prophecies concerning Jesus Christ, so they assume that similar prophecies must describe Muhammad. Apologists for Islam do make the claim that some passages in the Bible predict Muhammad's arrival in the distant future. However with examination of the supposed prophecies, it becomes clear that Muhammad is not the subject of specific Bible prophecies.

There are two Scriptures often cited by Muslim apologists as prophecies concerning the arrival of Muhammad in 570 A.D. The first of these passages was written in about 1,450 B.C. by Moses and it reads (as a direct quote from the Lord to Moses),

"I will raise up for them a Prophet like you from among their brethren, and will put My words in His mouth, and He shall speak to them all that I command Him. And it shall be that whoever will not hear My words, which He speaks in My name, I will require it of him." Deut. 18:19

Muslim clerics like to claim this verse for Muhammad because of its description of a future Prophet who will speak for God. However, this passage of Scripture has an important context that is almost always ignored by Muslim apologists. In the preceding verses, Moses says (Deut. 18:15,16),

"The LORD your God will raise up for you a Prophet like me from your midst, from your brethren. Him you shall hear, according to all you desired of the LORD your God in Horeb in the day of the assembly, saying, 'Let me not hear again the voice of the LORD my God, nor let me see this great fire anymore, lest I die."

152

Firstly, the passage clearly states that the Prophet will be raised up "from your brethren." Since Moses and God were speaking to the nation of Israel, this means the Prophet would be Jewish. This observation lead the Muslim scholar, Hamran Ambrie (see Chapter 2), to conclude the prophecy actually points ahead to the arrival of Jesus Christ, not an Arabian man named Muhammad!

Secondly, this passage makes reference to an event at Mount Horeb (or Mount Sinai) and the desire for the Jews to have an intercessor between God and man. The Hebrews had just been led out of Egyptian slavery by Moses and they were brought to Mount Sinai. It was here that God presented Moses and the Jews with the two stone tablets inscribed with the Ten Commandments. The top of Mount Sinai was enveloped in a cloud and fire - lightning flashed and thunder roared. The glory of God came upon the mountain, completely terrorizing the Jews in the camps below. This was the proper response for sinful mankind in their meeting with the almighty and righteous God of Heaven. Moses described the event in the passage, Deuteronomy 5:23-27. The Jewish elders asked Moses to be the mediator, intercessor, or "middle man," who would speak to God and receive messages from Him. So the prediction of a Prophet like Moses specifically described a person of Jewish lineage, who would act as an intercessor between God and man.

The promised mediator was fulfilled in the arrival of Jesus Christ, not in the person of Muhammad. This fact was clearly presented by the Apostles Peter and Paul in the first century A.D. For example Paul wrote (1 Tim. 2:5,6a), "for there is one God and one Mediator between God and men, the Man Christ Jesus, who gave Himself a ransom for all." This truth has never been revoked or altered. The great eternal mediator is Jesus Christ. With His death on the cross, He alone is able to provide us with forgiveness of sin and make us presentable before a holy and righteous God. His shed blood was the ransom or payment for all of our sins. This makes Jesus Christ the proper mediator between God and men.

Peter also declared to the men of first century Israel (Acts 3:22, 26), "Moses truly said to the fathers, 'The LORD your God will raise up for you a Prophet like me from your brethren. Him you shall hear in all things, whatever He says to you. And it shall be that every soul who will not hear that Prophet shall be utterly destroyed." Peter's description of "a Prophet" like Moses is followed by a reference to Jesus Christ. He does not suggest that a man from Arabia would fulfill this prophecy six centuries later. It was an accomplished fact in 50 A.D. Even to this day, those who refuse to hear the voice of Jesus Christ - the Prophet - will perish in their sins. This warning was stated by Jesus Christ Himself when He said (Matt. 10:33), "whoever denies Me before men, him I will also deny before My Father who is in heaven."

The second major prophecy claimed by Muslims derives from a promise by Jesus Christ to His disciples. In this passage, Jesus Christ promises His followers that they would receive the Holy Spirit of God. This is not a reference to a human being, but rather it is a reference to God Himself in the person of the Holy Spirit. The Apostle John records this statement from Jesus:

> And I will pray the Father, and He will give you another Helper, that He may abide with you forever the Spirit of truth, whom the world cannot receive, because it neither sees Him nor knows Him...(John 14:16,17a)

Muslim apologists claim that this is a prophecy concerning the future arrival of Muhammad. With closer examination of this passage, one finds that it cannot refer to Muhammad.

This statement was made during the "Last Supper," shortly before Jesus would be crucified. He was preparing His disciples for the traumatic days ahead, when He would be put to death and the followers of Christ would be persecuted. As such, He assures the disciples that God would remain with them. He specifically states that the Holy Spirit would "abide" with them "forever." He also said the Holy Spirit would help them recall the teachings of Jesus (a necessary process for the writing of New Testament books),

> But the Helper, the Holy Spirit, whom the Father will send in My name, He will teach you all things, and bring to your remembrance all things that I said to you (John 14:26).

The clear context describes how the "Helper" was to comfort and aid the disciples after the death of Christ, when He returned to be with God the Father. The Greek word used by Jesus - παράκλητος, parakletos – is often translated comforter. This raises an obvious question: how could these first century Christians possibly be helped, aided, or comforted by a man born in Arabia more than five centuries later? The plain statement of Jesus must be referring to an immediate blessing for these men in the first century. It is complete nonsense to suggest that Jesus could be making reference to Muhammad in this discussion with His disciples! The Helper is in fact the Holy Spirit of God.

Unfortunately for the Muslim, one finds that there are no specific Bible prophecies concerning the future arrival of Muhammad. The follower of Islam is forced to explain why so many prophecies were written concerning Jesus Christ, but none were made regarding their prophet Muhammad. It should also be disturbing to

Muslims that their scholars try to take passages of the Bible and apply them to Muhammad, when these Bible passages are clearly referring to God. In the case of Deuteronomy 18, Moses is describing the arrival of the Son of God. In the case of John 18, Jesus is describing the arrival of God the Holy Spirit.

In a general sense, the rise of Islam was prophesied in the Bible. The writers of the New Testament did predict that mankind would follow religious messages that denied the message of the cross and the Lordship of Christ. In this regard, the Apostle Paul described (2 Tim 3:5) how men would have a "form of religion but denying its power." Likewise the Apostle Peter predicted,

> "...there will be false teachers among you, who will secretly bring in destructive heresies, even denying the Lord who bought them, and bring on themselves swift destruction. And many will follow their destructive ways (2 Peter 2:1-2a)"

These are certainly not prophecies to which Muslim scholars will point. Nevertheless, they do seem to describe Islam. The passage is a warning of "false teachers" among the early Christians, however its larger scope includes Islam. In Peter's warning, he describes teachers who will be "denying the Lord that bought them." This is the teaching of Islam. Biblical Christianity teaches how Jesus died on the cross for our sins. He took the penalty for our sins when He was crucified on the cross. Jesus Christ paid the great sin debt for us and He bought us with His sacrifice on the cross. Islam denies that Jesus died on the cross and paid a sin debt for us. Thus, the teachings of Islam certainly "deny the Lord that bought them." With about one billion followers of Islam, Peter accurately predicted that "many will follow their destructive ways."

Other Bible prophecies seem to look centuries ahead to the violence carried out by the followers of Islam. In the past 100 years, there has been a marked increase in the number of murders done in the name of Islam, particularly within the old, established Christian communities in Muslim countries. Jesus Christ Himself predicted this offense against His followers. He warned early Christians (John 16:2), "...the time is coming that whoever kills you will think that he offers God service. And these things they will do to you because they have not known the Father nor Me."

While the initial fulfillment of this prophecy came in first century Israel with the persecution of Hebrew Christians, the legacy of murder is carried out to this day primarily by Muslim violence against Christians. Although it is beyond the scope of this text to call to memory all of deadly assaults over the past century,[11] a sample is provided below:

1. Indonesia (2000 to 2002): an estimated 10,000 Christians were violently murdered for refusing to convert to Islam.[12]

2. Pakistan (2013): two Muslim jihadists entered a Sunday church service in Peshawar, detonated bombs, and 81 Christians were killed.[13]

3. Sudan (1991 to 2001): up to 2 million Christians and animists were slaughtered in a civil war that was generally characterized as the Islamic forces of northern Sudan pounding the mostly Christian regions of southern Sudan.[14]

4. Nigeria (2000-present): hundreds of Christians have been brutally murdered in Muslim-instigated riots. In the Plateau state (March, 2010), 500 people were shot and hacked to death (many of whom were women and children) during nighttime attacks on Christian villages.[15]

5. Turkey (1914 to 1918): in the final days of the Ottoman Empire, there was a massive persecution of the Armenian Christian population - enforced by the Islamic Turkish authorities. Between 1,000,000 and 1,500,000 people were killed in this slaughter.[16]

6. Iraq (2013-present): the group known as the Islamic State of Iraq and Syria (ISIS) has murdered hundreds of Christians throughout Iraq. This grotesque slaughter included the beheading of children in Mosul and displaying their severed heads in parks.[17]

During the recent attacks on Christians in Nigeria, at least one survivor said that the Muslim attackers chanted "Allah Akbar" as they killed the villagers.[18] The prophetic words of Jesus Christ ring true. These Muslim thugs believe that they are doing God's will as they murder Christians.

Are these violent men carrying out God's work and fulfilling His desires? This question was answered in another prophecy by Jesus Christ. He described the setting on Judgment Day, wherein He is sitting on the throne of Judgment,

> Many will say to Me in that day, 'Lord, Lord, have we not prophesied in Your name, cast out demons in Your name, and done many wonders in Your name?' And then I will declare to them, 'I never knew you; depart from Me, you who practice lawlessness!' (Matt 7:22,23)

This passage of Scripture (as well as several others) notes that many men will appeal to the Lord Jesus Christ as He sits in Judgment of their souls. Their eternal destiny hangs in the balance, as they claim to be followers of God. Yet, this vast group of religious people is condemned to eternal punishment. This truth is also made abundantly clear by the writings of the Apostle Paul,

> ...the Lord Jesus will be revealed from heaven with His mighty angels, in flaming fire taking vengeance on those who do not know God, and on those who do not obey the gospel of our Lord Jesus Christ. These shall be punished with everlasting destruction from the presence of the Lord and from the glory of His power (2 Thessalonians 1:7-9)

This section of Scripture is specifically addressing the persecution of Christians at the hands of "those who do not obey the gospel of our Lord Jesus Christ." As such, this clearly applies to the violent and brutal soldiers of Islam. While they may chant "Allah Akbar" as they murder Christians in Africa, the Middle East, and Asia, the Lord Jesus Christ promises to avenge the violence against His church. Moreover, He makes it abundantly clear that these men are not following the will of God.

Conclusions

In summary, the Bible was written between about 1,400 B.C. and 100 A.D. and it contains many prophecies concerning the future events. This includes the futures of nations, the destiny of the Jewish people, and many prophecies concerning the arrival of Israel's Messiah and Savior of mankind, Jesus Christ. These prophecies are remarkable in their accuracy, even predicting future events with specific time periods. We have even seen some of these predictions in our own day with the formation of the European Union and modern Israel (2000 years after the destruction of ancient Israel). Moreover, a thorough and objective study of the Bible does not reveal any prophecies concerning the arrival a major prophet from Arabia, the man known as Muhammad. There are Bible prophecies that describe major world religions that would arise in the centuries ahead, but these religions are always condemned in the pages of Scripture. The Bible clearly teaches that the followers of these religions will face condemnation at the Judgment Day, because they have rejected God's Savior and His offer of free salvation to sinners. Among the Biblical prophecies concern Islam, these are the most significant ones.

Finally, an objective person must ask: where are the prophecies of the Quran? The God of the Bible described the history of nations centuries in advanced, He described future political and military leaders, and He even described details regarding the life, death, and resurrection of His Son Jesus Christ. Did the Quran predict the long-standing Ottoman Empire or the worldwide rule of the British? Can the Muslim apologist show prophecies in Quran describing the great dynasties in China or the Mongolian Empire? Did the Quran predict the reign of Saladin, the wise Sultan of Egypt and Syria? The answer is no. Only the God of the Bible had accurately declared the future. God rightly says (Isaiah 46:9), "there is none like Me."

References:

(1)   Ergun Caner and Emir Fethi Caner, *Unveiling Islam*, Kregel Publications, Grand Rapids, MI, 2009.

(2)   See, http://www.biblequery.org/mic.htm; "Emanuel: studies in Hebrew Bible, Septuagint, and Dead Sea scrolls in honor of Emanuel Tov" by Emanuel Tov, Shalom M. Paul, Eva Ben-David; Brill: Leiden, The Netherlands; 2003, p. 247.

(3)   Obviously, we cannot know for certain if modern Israel is the final fulfillment of these prophecies. The nation could fall to a civil war or hostile enemy attacks, but then reform as a nation in the future.

(4)   Matthew 2:1-12

(5)   R. D. Culver, *Systematic Theology: Biblical and Historical*, Mentor Books, Denver, CO, 2005.

(6)   Luke 3:23

(7)   John the Baptist was not the same individual referred to John the Apostle, the individual who produced the Gospel of John, the letters of John, and the book of Revelation.

(8)   Josephus, *Antiquities of the Jews*, 5:2

(9)   *The Triumphal Entry*, downloaded 6/2/2014, http://www.khouse.org/enews_article/2007/1190/print/

(10)   The first Passover involved protection from the judgment and wrath of God. In order to protect the first-born children from God's wrath, the Jews were instructed to paint lambs blood on the doorposts of their home. When the Lord saw the blood, he spared the inhabitants from judgment and wrath. See, Genesis, chapter 12.

(11)   For a comprehensive account of the brutal persecution of Christians by Muslims, see: Raymond Ibrahim, *Crucified Again*, Regnery Publishing, Washington, D.C., 2012.

(12)   Serge Trifkovic, "Islamism's Other Victims: The Tragedy of East Timor." *Frontpage Magazine,* November 25, 2002. See: http://archive.frontpagemag.com/readArticle.aspx?ARTID=20986 Downloaded June, 4, 2014.

(13) Anugrah Kumar, "81 Christians Killed in Pakistan's 'Deadliest-Ever-Church-Attack.'" *The Christian Post*, September 23, 2013. See: http://www.christianpost.com/news/81-christians-killed-in-pakistans-deadliest-ever-church-attack-105111/ Downloaded February 13, 2014.

(14) Sabit A. Alley, "A Brief Overview on: War and genocide in Sudan." As presented at *The 19ᵗʰ Annual Holocaust and genocide Program: Learning Through Experience*, Raritan Valley College, New Jersey, 2001. See also: http://webarchieve.org/web/20051221045218/http:///www.iabolish.com/to day.features/sudan/overview1.htm.

(15) "Christians brutally massacred in Plateau state." *The Voice of the Martyrs.* See: http://www.persecution.net/ng-2010-03-11.htm Downloaded May 2, 2014.

(16) a. Ara Safarian (ed.), *The Treatment of Armenians in the Ottoman Empire, 1915–1916: Documents Presented to Viscount Grey of Falloden by Viscount Bryce, James Bryce and Arnold Toynbee, Uncensored Edition.* Gomidas Institute, Princeton, NJ, 2000. b. John Kifner, "Armenian Genocide of 1915: An Overview," *The New York Times*. Retrieved 22 March 2014, see: http://www.nytimes.com/ref/timestopics/topics_armeniangenocide.html

(17) Leonardo Blair, "ISIS 'Systematically Beheading Children' in Iraq; They Are 'Killing Every Christian They See,' Says Chaldean Leader," *Christian Post*, August 10, 2014. See: http://www.christianpost.com/news/isis-systematically-beheading-children-in-iraq-they-are-killing-every-christian-they-see-says-chaldean-leader-124594/. Downloaded August 21, 2014.

(18) a. Robert J. Morgan, "The World's War on Christianity," *The Huffington Post*, March 16, 2014. See: http://ww.huffingtonpost.com/robert-j-morgan/the-worlds-war-on-christianpersecutiuon_b_4590933.html Downloaded March 22, 2014. b. Christian Purefoy, "11 dead in fresh Muslim-Christian violence in Nigeria." *CNN World*, March 17, 2010. See: http://www.cnn.com/2010/WORLD/africa/03/17/nigeria.violence/ Downloaded June 5, 2014.

Chapter 9

Evidence for Truth: Progressive Revelation

When my father and my mother forsake me,
then the LORD will take care of me. Psalm 27:10

Nabeel Qureshi was born in the United States to parents who were from Pakistan.[1] His journey from Mecca to Calvary is described in the outstanding book entitled, *Seeking Allah, Finding Jesus*.[2] Nabeel's parents were devoted Muslims. Through his mother's instruction, he learned Arabic and read the entire Arabic Quran by the age of five. As he grew older, he not only loved Islam but he also understood the faith. In a conversation with his father, Nabeel concluded,[2] "Allah will weigh our good deeds and our bad, if our goods deeds are greater than our bad deeds, Allah will give us paradise."

Following the example set by his parents, he did not simply "believe anything blindly." Rather he studied and knew the basis of his faith in Islam, even learning Islamic apologetics. At a highly intellectual level, Nabeel was capable of defending his Muslim religion. In college, he developed a friendship with David, a young man who was Nabeel's teammate on the university forensics team. On one occasion, he saw David reading a Bible. This surprised him. While Nabeel had read his Quran almost every day of his life, most Christians he knew rarely - if ever - studied their Bibles or Scriptures. He immediately began questioning David about his faith. As an individual trained in Islamic apologetics, he was on the attack, "Was the Bible corrupted? Did Jesus ever really claim to be God?"

Unknown Nabeel, David was not a casual Bible student, but rather he was a serious Bible student who also had studied Christian apologetics. The debate was on. David systematically answered Nabeel's questions. Initially, the answers were so convincing that Nabeel thought, he must be "making all of this up." So he investigated the matter himself. When Nabeel examined the facts regarding the preservations of Biblical Scriptures, he concluded:[1]

> "The result of my investigation was that there is no evidential reason to believe that the modern editions of the New Testament are in any way substantially different from the original autographs themselves."

Likewise, Nabeel carefully considered David's response to the challenge about a claim of deity by Jesus. David pointed to passages in the Old Testament, such as

Daniel 7:14,15, in which Jesus was called by the same title (Son of Man) that is given to the Almighty God. He also pointed to several New Testament passages where Jesus was called "I AM" – the same name God supplied when Moses asked, "what is Your name?" Following his analysis, Nabeel decided (emphasis his):[1]

> "After actually reading parts of the New Testament itself instead of merely reading Muslim books on the topic, I came to agree with David's claim: *both the New Testament in general and Christ Himself claimed that Jesus is God.*"

Even with these studies, Nabeel still wrestled with some weighty questions. He understood the concept of sin and judgment, and he believed the concept of personal responsibility for one's own sins. As taught both in the Quran and Bible, each individual is held accountable for their own sins and must face God's judgment for that sin. This he believed. Nevertheless, Islamic teachings held that no one else could take away his sin. He remembered the passage:

> And be on your guard against a day when one soul shall not avail another in the least, neither shall intercession on its behalf be accepted, nor shall any compensation be taken from it, nor shall they be helped. (Quran 2:48)

This seemed to be at odds with the basic Christian doctrine that Jesus Christ died for his sins. How could God allow His Son to accept other men's sins? It did not seem fair or logical that God would punish the innocent One for the deeds of sinners and unrighteous men or women! With further studies, Nabeel saw the great truth: God has infinite love for people. God's love for Nabeel is without measure or ending. It was God's love for the hopelessly lost sinner that moved Him to send His beloved Son to the cross. He thought about the words of Jesus Himself, as recorded by the Apostle John:

> For God so loved the world that he gave his one and only Son, that whoever believes in him shall not perish but have eternal life. (John 3:16)

When he considered the love of God shown in Jesus Christ, he was profoundly impacted – touching in his very soul. He had previously thought the crucifixion of Jesus and the message of Christianity was a "sick and twisted" story, but he soon concluded that it was in fact the "the greatest love story in history." He saw that

Jesus carried his sins to the cross and Jesus suffered to save Nabeel from judgment and punishment.

There were still many doubts and difficulties for Nabeel, so he earnestly prayed to God for guidance. During this time, he fervently studied Islamic doctrines, but he began to find disturbing issues. For example, Muhammad's very first biography, *Sirat Rasul Allah* by Ibn Ishaq via Ibn Hisham, contains a plain statement about Muhammad's life story being altered by the author, so it would not be offensive or distressing to people.[2] In other words, the hadith did not contain accurate historical accounts. In Sahih al-Bukhari, he also found the passage at hadith 1.24, where Muhammad is quoted as saying, "fight people until they become Muslim or until he killed them and took their property." This seemed at odds with the Quran's plain statement, "there is no compulsion in religion." Nabeel also took notice of Muhammad's slaughter of the Qurayza Jews - described both in the hadith and sirah. Many other examples of brutal violence were found in the early Islamic literature and he could feel the "pressure building" as he questioned his faith. Even his solid trust in the Quran began to erode, as he noted:[2]

> "I added up all the pieces in my mind: multiple recitations of the same verse, missing verses, missing surahs, disputes over the canon, controlled destructions of all variants. How could we defend the Quran as being perfectly preserved?"

Despite seeing these problems with Islam, Nabeel continued to resist the call from his Savior. He considered "the cost of embracing the cross." He knew what happened when individuals travel from Mecca to Calvary. At the very least, a conversion to Christianity can bring great shame to a Muslim family and dishonor within their community. In the worst cases, converts to Christianity are killed as apostates. Nabeel consulted with many imams with his question and struggles, but he could not find adequate answers.

Finally during a time of despair, Nabeel sought counsel from the Bible. After reading the Quran, he felt that it was little comfort for his particular situation, so he began reading a copy of the Christian Scriptures. His reading brought great comfort to his mind and soul. Nabeel's journey from Mecca to Calvary was completed during that sleepless night. He lay awake, considering the words of Jesus Christ Himself:

Whoever acknowledges me before men, I will also acknowledge him before my Father in heaven. But whoever disowns me before men, I will disown him before my Father in heaven (Matt 10:32-33).

On this occasion, Nabeel surrendered to Jesus Christ, praying to the Almighty God of Heaven,[1] "I submit. I submit that Jesus Christ is Lord of Heaven and Earth, and that He came to this world to die for my sins. I am a sinner, and I need Him for redemption. Christ, I accept You into my life."

Like many individuals who have left Islam for Christianity, Nabeel's family did not receive the news with happiness or rejoicing. Although the Bible proclaims that there is rejoicing in Heaven over the salvation of one sinner, there was sorrowful mourning from his parents. Both his mother and father cried when they heard of Nabeel's conversion. Of course, this brought pain to Nabeel's heart, but he again found comfort in the truth of the Bible. He read the words of Jesus,

Jesus said to them, "Truly I tell you...everyone who has left houses or brothers or sisters or father or mother or wife or children or fields for My sake will receive a hundred times as much and will inherit eternal life." Matthew 19:28-29

In the years since his conversion, Nabeel's Christian faith has grown and it has become evermore satisfying. The Lord has strengthened him for the tasks set before him. He has the strong desire to share the good news of Jesus Christ with his family and friends. Indeed, his message to those in Mecca and looking towards Calvary,[1] "I invite you to search for Him and lay your current life on the line as I did. He is there, and He is waiting for you to come to Him so that He can walk with you...My prayers are with you."

Nabeel was a man who did not "believe anything blindly." He considered the evidence for Christianity and its truth. As we saw in the previous chapter on prophecy, the Bible contains countless predictions of future events and this represents powerful evidence for God's hand being involved in the writing of Biblical Scripture. Prophecy is evidence for spiritual truth in the pages of the Bible. This type of evidence is convincing even to someone who refuses to "believe anything blindly."

In this chapter, we will examine a particular aspect of the Bible called "progressive revelation." This term describes how messages from God were revealed through His prophets and developed over the centuries and it represents powerful evidence for the spiritual truth of the Biblical message. Several aspects will be examined. Firstly, we will consider how God wrote the Bible using multiple human authors. As described below, the Bible was written by 40 men and over a period of about 1,500 years. Secondly, the miracle of prophecy will be considered. As described previously, God's revelation included many specific predictions of future events. These were gradually revealed through the centuries and they are part of God's progressive revelation. Finally, the types and foreshadows of the Old Testament Scriptures will be described. Theologians refer to this as "typology" in Scripture. This is an amazing part of the Bible in which God placed events, people, and institutions in the ancient past and in the Scriptures. These Old Testament foreshadows and types all point centuries ahead to the arrival of the Savior Jesus Christ. Written in the ancient Scripture of the Bible, these "pictures" described the death, burial, and resurrection of Jesus Christ. God's sovereignty and divine control even provided us with types and foreshadows related to our salvation and for His mercy towards sinners.

Multiple Human Authors

A most remarkable aspect of the Bible is its coherent message and quality. The whole Bible fits together perfectly. Unlike the Quran, the Bible contains 1,500 years of "progressive revelation," a term describing how nearly 40 men were inspired by God to write books that became the Canon of Scripture. The progressive revelation of the Bible contains literally thousands of elements, and in itself, this is a miracle that verifies the Bible to be the true revelation of God. What are the chances that 40 men from varying backgrounds could write a coherent manuscript on a controversial topic such as theology and spiritual truth? It is impossible. Without the guiding hand of the Almighty God, these men would have numerous contradictions and wildly varying beliefs.

As explained in one of the New Testament books written by Peter, we are told that God "inspired" or "superintended" the writing of the Bible by the work of the Holy Spirit.[3] The writers of the Bible included men with backgrounds as diverse as fishermen, tax collectors, kings, soldiers, shepherds and farmers, medical doctors, and others. Some were well educated and others had little formal education. Yet, the Bible unrolls like a beautiful Persian rug with intricate weavings and detailed images. Progressive revelation has involved a work of God through the centuries: a careful, deliberate, and gradual delivery of a life-giving message to mankind.

Of course, Muslim clerics are quick to answer that the Quran continues the progressive revelation of the Bible and that it is the ultimate and final message from God. This is commonly taught throughout the Islamic world. It usually involves further statements about Jesus Christ himself being a Muslim, and sometimes asserts that the Bible and Quran have complimentary messages. With these ideas, Muslims then claim that their religion is far superior then the Christian faith. Unfortunately, even a casual inspection of the Quran and Bible show that they do not have complimentary messages. Nor does the Islamic message fit with any of the previous divine revelations that had been so carefully laid out on scrolls of parchment by the God of Heaven. This topic will be more thoroughly examined in the next chapter

To fully appreciate the progressive revelation of the Bible, it is useful to examine the individual authors of the books and their approximate dates of writing (Tables 1 and 2). It should be noted that all of the books of the Bible were complete by about 90 A.D., although some scholars have even earlier dates for New Testament books. The entire Bible was fully accepted by the church by 100-200 A.D., hundreds of years before the arrival of Muhammad. It is beyond the scope of this text to fully develop the history of the Canon of Scripture, however the interested reader is referred to one of several excellent reviews on this topic.[4]

As described briefly in Chapter 2, the Bible itself has been organized into several major sections and these sections correspond roughly to the type of revelations inspired by God. Most importantly, the overall theme of the Bible is God redeeming mankind from sin and death; it is the story of our great God and Savior Jesus Christ. The entire Old Testament represents the **preparation** for the arrival of Christ. There are several types of inspired books in the Old Testament. These include:

The Law: Genesis, Exodus, Leviticus, Numbers, Deuteronomy.
History: Joshua, Judges, Ruth, 1st and 2nd Samuel, 1st and 2nd Kings, 1st and 2nd Chronicals, Ezra, Nehemiah, Ester.
Wisdom: Job, Psalms, Proverbs, Ecclesiastes, Song of Solomon.
Prophecy: Isaiah, Jeremiah, Lamentations, Ezekiel, Daniel, Hoseam Joel, Amos, Obadaiah, Jonah, Micah, Nahum, Habakkuk, Zephaniah, Haggai, Zechariah, Malachi.

In the New Testament, the four Gospels (Matthew, Mark, Luke, and John) and the book of Acts describe the **arrival** or "manifestation" of Jesus Christ. These books are historical, eyewitness accounts of the events related to the Savior. They describe His arrival in human form and His resurrection. Largely through the books of the Apostle Paul, the spiritual implications are **explained**, that is to say, we learn about the results of Christ's work on the cross. From these New Testament books, we learn about salvation through Christ, how He died for our sins, how God loves

Table 1. Books of the Bible as appearing in the Old Testament, with human authors and approximate dates of authorship.

Book	Author	Date	Book	Author	Date
Genesis	Moses	1430 B.C.	Psalms	David and others	1000 B.C and later
Exodus	Moses	1430 B.C.	Proverbs	Solomon and others	960 B.C. and later
Leviticus	Moses	1430 B.C.	Ecclesiastes	Solomon	960 B.C.
Numbers	Moses	1430 B.C.	Song of Solomon	Solomon	960 B.C.
Deuteronomy	Moses	1430 B.C.	Isaiah	Isaiah	800 B.C.
Joshua	Joshua	1400 B.C.	Jeremiah	Jeremiah	650 B.C.
Judges	Unknown	1100 B.C.	Lamentations	Jeremiah	600 B.C
Ruth	Unknown	1000 B.C.	Ezekiel	Ezekiel	600 B.C.
1st Samuel	Unknown	1000 B.C.	Daniel	Daniel	540 B.C.
2nd Samuel	Unknown	1000 B.C.	Hosea	Hosea	800 B.C.
1st Kings	Unknown	600 B.C.	Joel	Joel	900 B.C.
2nd Kings	Unknown	600 B.C.	Amos	Amos	800 B.C
1st Chronicles	Unknown	500 B.C.	Obadiah	Obadiah	600 B.C.
2nd Chronicles	Unknown	500 B.C.	Jonah	Jonah	800 B.C.
Ezra	Ezra	500 B.C.	Micah	Micah	800 B.C
Nehemiah	Nehemiah	500 B.C.	Naham	Naham	700 B.C.
Esther	Unknown	500 B.C.	Habakkuk	Habakkuk	700 B.C.
Job	Unknown	Unknown	Zechariah	Zechariah	500 B.C.
			Malachi	Malachi	450 B.C.

Table 2. Books of the Bible as appearing in the New Testament, with human authors and approximate dates of authorship.

Book	Author	Date	Book	Author	Date
Matthew	Matthew	50 A.D.	1st Timothy	Paul	64 A.D.
Mark	Mark	68 A.D.	2nd Timothy	Paul	67 A.D.
Luke	Luke	60 A.D.	Titus	Paul	65 A.D.
John	John	85 A.D.	Philemon	Paul	60 A.D.
Acts	Luke	60 A.D.	Hebrews	Unknown	68 A.D.
Romans	Paul	57 A.D..	James	James	45 A.D.
1st Corinthians	Paul	56 A.D.	1st Peter	Peter	65 A.D.
2nd Corinthians	Paul	57 A.D.	2nd Peter	Peter	66 A.D.
Galatians	Paul	50 A.D.	1st John	John	90 A.D.
Ephesians	Paul	60 A.D.	2nd John	John	90 A.D.
Philippians	Paul	60 A.D	3rd John	John	90 A.D.
Colossians	Paul	60 A.D.	Jude	Jude	68 A.D.
1st Thessalonians	Paul	51 A.D.	Revelation	John	90 A.D.
2nd Thessalonians	Paul	51 A.D.			

us, how He offers eternal life to us, how we can be given new life, and so on. Finally, the Lord completes His message to man with the book of Revelation, a section of text that **describes the end of the age** or consummation. It is here that we find Jesus Christ judging the saved and the lost. It is here that the eternal judgments, with rewards and condemnations, are fully described. The book of Revelation expands on some of the prophecies and topics found in the Old Testament Scriptures (i.e. in the book of Daniel). Thus, the Bible was gradually revealed by God's prophets between about 1,500 B.C. and 90 A.D. The purpose and plan of God has been to seek and save lost mankind. This was accomplished through Jesus Christ. The Bible describes salvation in Jesus Christ - from beginning to end.

Prophecy

As God revealed His message through 1,500 years of Scripture, He included many prophecies concerning important events. An overwhelming number of prophecies described the arrival and ministry of Jesus Christ. Indeed, we saw in the previous chapter that many prophecies described His crucifixion and resurrection and these were foretold centuries before Jesus was even born! The prophetic element of Scripture is an important part of the progressive revelation.

Through the centuries, God's predictions or prophecies became more and more well developed. He revealed increasing amounts of detail regarding His plans for saving mankind from their lost and hopeless state. For example, Moses described a conversation involving God in the Garden of Eden (Genesis 3:15). Almighty God is quoted and said that a child or offspring of Eve would "crush" Satan's head. But God also says that the serpent or Satan would "wound" this offspring's heel. Although the conversation dates to a period of time shortly after creation, Moses recorded this in about 1,400 B.C. It is considered the first prophecy related to Jesus Christ. Both predictions were fulfilled at the crucifixion – Satan was mortally wounded and Jesus Christ had a nail driven through His foot or heel.

The prophecies related to Jesus Christ became more complete with progressive revelations. As described in the previous chapter, the Jewish prophets would eventually describe many aspects of the birth, life, ministry, death and resurrection of Jesus Christ. While Moses simply recorded that the Messiah's heel would be wounded, King David described it in more detail (Psalm 22) - that His hands and feet would be pierced. Isaiah further predicted (Isaiah 53) that He would carry the "sins of many" and He would be "wounded for our transgressions." Thus, Moses, King David, and the Prophet Isaiah made their respective prophecies 1400, 1000, and 800 years prior the cross of Jesus Chirst. Over the centuries dozens of other Messianic prophecies were added to the Canon of Scripture. This progressive revelation has the true character of a miracle and it is strong evidence for the work of God Almighty. Only the sovereign God of Heaven could have provided a clear and consistent series of predictions over a period of 1400 years as mankind awaited the Savior Jesus Christ. Moreover, the miracle of prophecy – especially gradually developed – is further evidence for spiritual truth in the Biblical message. Biblical prophecy was specifically discussed in Chapter 8.

Old Testament Types and Foreshadows

What does this mean – God placed types and foreshadows in the Old Testament? What are they and how are they evidence for God's production of the Bible? As described above, a type or a foreshadow is something or someone which provides a "picture" of God's future plans. These foreshadows were historical events placed in ancient time as proof for the Divine plan of salvation in Jesus Christ. It is only through God's hand that these miraculous foreshadows could have occurred and been placed in the Bible.

Christian theologian C. I. Schofield noted that there are four illustration types or foreshadowing types to be found in Scripture regarding Jesus Christ. There are people, events, things, and institutions, which provide for us a glimpse and understanding of God's work in Christ. These are also a major part of God's progressive revelation found in the Bible. Examples of these types and foreshadows will be given below.

Types and foreshadows: mankind's need for salvation

The Law and Commandments are a prominent example of the foreshadowing and progressive revelation found in the Bible. As described above, the Law was given to the Jews by God through the writings of Moses. A summary of the Law was written in the 10 Commandments. These include commandments, such as: you should not murder, lie, covet, steal, or worship gods other than the true God of Heaven. The full version of The Law of Moses actually had 613 commandments written in the pages of the Old Testament. Following the exodus of the Jews from Egypt, the ancient nation of Israel was expected to keep all of the commandments in the Law.

Why did God establish the Law of Moses? This question is answered very plainly by the Apostle Paul in the New Testament (Romans 3:20b): "…by the law is the knowledge of sin." Well-meaning men and women often believe that by adhering to the Law's ancient rules and regulations, it will make them justified before God. Indeed, if you ask a person, "Why should God let you into Heaven," the common response is often, "I am a good person." Sometimes people even respond by saying that they keep the 10 Commandments. Of course, Islam has many of the same commands, or requirements placed upon individuals, including prohibitions of many sinful activities. Muslims are required by commandments to fast regularly, make a pilgrimage to Mecca, abstain from certain foods and drinks, wear certain clothes, and strictly follow all of the rules laid out in the Quran and hadith.

However with Law of Moses found in the Bible, an honest person comes to the same conclusion as the individual named Job. That is to say, "how can man be righteous before God (Job 9:2)?" The Bible teaches that the Law of Moses was absolutely perfect and just. It commanded men to be faithful to their wives, to be honest in business dealings, to be kind to other people, to avoid getting drunk, and above all to honor God with a sincere life of praise and worship to Him. It demanded that men should not steal, murder, or worship false deities. On the surface, these commandments of the Law seem to be good advice and they also appear to be a reasonable way to please God. This would be true, if mankind could actually keep the Commandments and the Law.

As children of Adam however, we are all sinful creatures. No one is able to keep the Commandments and fulfill the demands of the Law. Moreover, as the

Apostle James recorded, "whoever shall keep the whole law, and yet stumble in one point, he is guilty of all (James 2:10)." God Himself states in several places that it is our tendency to sin which creates a problem with the righteous commandments found in the Law of Moses. For example, Moses wrote (Deuteronomy 27:26a), "Cursed is the one who does not confirm all the words of this law."

So why did God give us a set of righteous commandments (in the Old Testament) that no one is able to fully keep? This returns to the great miracle of the God's progressive revelation found in the Bible. The Law of Moses had one purpose: the Law was to demonstrate to men and women that they needed a Savior. The Law demands perfection and we all fail. The Law also stated that sinners would be punished. As God declared through Ezekiel, "Behold, all souls are Mine; the soul of the father as well as the soul of the son is Mine; the soul who sins shall die (Ezekiel 18:4)."

When asked about the most important commandment to keep, Jesus quoted a passage from Moses and stated, "You shall love the LORD your God with all your heart, with all your soul, and with all your mind (Matt. 22:27)." When has anyone done this...can you claim to have kept this commandment during every moment of your life? The honest person must admit, no. Similarly, the Apostle Paul (see the book of Romans) admits his own failings of keeping the Law when he came to the commandment, "you shall not covet." Since we all seem to have the tendency to desire things - especially things that we do not possess - this commandment condemns every last human being. Ultimately, these commandments point to our need for forgiveness, mercy, and redemption from sin. Thus, the Law of Moses was meant to lead you and I to the cross, the place where a sinner can find forgiveness, mercy, and redemption in Jesus Christ. Indeed, the Law makes no one suitable to stand at the Judgment Day. It is only through Christ's work on the cross that we can be made presentable at the judgment. As the Apostle Paul wrote in Galatians 3:24, "Therefore the law was our tutor to bring us to Christ, that we might be justified by faith." The Law of Moses was a great foreshadow and a remarkable example of progressive revelation in the Scriptures. This was addressed when Christ tells His disciples (Mark 5:17), "Do not think that I came to destroy the Law or the Prophets. I did not come to destroy but to fulfill."

Types and foreshadows: pointing to the cross

A major part of the Old Testament describes the sacrifices that God required from men and women in ancient times. This foreshadow pointed directly to the cross of Jesus Christ. Since the very beginning, the problem of sin and judgment hung over our heads. The books of Moses describe how God instituted the sacrificial systems for mankind. That is to say, animals were killed as sacrifices for

170

our sin. First, the sacrificial system was individual and seemingly informal, but with the arrival of the Law of Moses and the construction of the Tabernacle (the location where sacrifices would be offered), the process became a more formal ritual. As we read in the book of Leviticus (Lev. 17:11), God declared that, "For the life of the flesh is in the blood, and I have given it to you upon the altar to make atonement for your soul..." The message is further explained by God in the New Testament book of Hebrews (9:22), where we read, "and according to the law almost all things are purified with blood, and without shedding of blood there is no remission."

The terms "atonement" and "remission" refer to God passing over sins and accepting payment for the debt or penalty coming from these sins. In other words, the Old Testament animal sacrifices were to cover people's sins before the righteous God of Heaven. These sacrifices involved taking an innocent animal, symbolically placing an individual/family/nation's sin on the creature, and killing the animal at the alter of the Temple. Millions of animals were slain. However, God declared that it is impossible to take away sin with the blood of bulls and goats, but rather it was only through the sacrifice of God's perfect and sinless Son that our sins could be removed. This is described in the great tenth chapter of Hebrews (Heb. 10:4-5),

> For it is not possible that the blood of bulls and goats could take away sins. Therefore, when He came into the world, He said: "Sacrifice and offering You did not desire, but a body You have prepared for Me."

We now know that these sacrifices were meant to be a foreshadowing, or illustration, of the future sacrifice of Jesus Christ. A "body" was prepared and this was the human body of Jesus Christ. While God is said to have honored some of the Old Testament sacrifices, they were only meant to be a picture of a future work of atonement or reconciliation to God – the death of Jesus Christ on the cross.

As described in the previous chapter, a very powerful foreshadow or type is presented by Moses in the account of the Passover in Egypt (see Exodus, chapter 12). The idea of sin, judgment, and death was clearly seen in this event. Without the blood of the young sheep (lamb) painted on the doorpost of the home, the firstborn of the home died that night. This was a dramatic foreshadowing of Christ's blood covering our sin and protecting us from God's wrath. Just as the blood of the Passover lamb protected the first-born in Egypt on the night of the Passover, so we are also "passed over" in the judgment of sin by God. This concept was taught by Jesus Christ Himself and it was further explained in the New Testament Scriptures:

John 3:36   Jesus: "He who believes in the Son has everlasting life; and he who does not believe the Son shall not see life, but the wrath of God abides on him."

Romans 5:9   "Much more then, having now been justified by His blood, we shall be saved from wrath through Him."

With respect to sacrifices, another important example of foreshadowing involved the call from God to Abraham and the sacrifice of his son, Isaac. There are several aspects of this event that point directly to Jesus Christ, His future work on the cross, and His resurrection from the dead. It should be noted, however, that Islamic teaching differs here in major parts of the story. Whereas the Biblical account describes Abraham offering Isaac as the sacrifice, Islamic scholars claim it was Ishmael who was offered. The Old Testament account of this event was originally written by Moses in about 1,400 B.C. The same account is also found in the Greek translation of the Old Testament (the *Septuagint*) and the Dead Sea Scrolls, which respectively date to about 285 B.C. and 100 B.C. Thus, the original Old Testament account of this event predates the Quran and Islamic teachings by more than twenty centuries. Moreover among the surviving Old Testament manuscripts that predate the Quran, none of these ancient manuscripts describe Ishmael as the sacrifice. The historical accuracy of the Old Testament has already been described (Chapter 6). Therefore, it seems reasonable to expect accuracy and truth in the Biblical account of Abraham's sacrifice.

After the birth of Isaac, this son of Abraham grew up. One day the Lord spoke to Abraham and commanded him to proceed to a specific mountain in the region of Jerusalem and offer Isaac as a sacrifice upon an altar. As Abraham and Isaac approached the mountain, Abraham told his servants to stop there and wait for Abraham and Isaac to return from the mountain. A little later, Isaac was bound with rope and laid atop the wood. Abraham was ready to plunge a knife into the young man, Isaac. However, an angel halted Abraham before he killed Isaac. God provided a ram for the sacrifice and the angel directed Abraham to the animal that was caught in a bush or thicket. Abraham and Isaac then offered the ram as the sacrifice. In the Genesis account of this event, there are several notable aspects:

1.   When Isaac asked his father why they did not bring an animal for the sacrifice, Abraham responded by saying, "...My son, God will provide for Himself the lamb for a burnt offering (Genesis 22:8)." This is a beautiful foreshadowing of God sending His Son as a sacrifice for you and I. Just as the ram was killed

in place of Isaac, Jesus Christ, the Lamb of God, was put to death and suffered in our place.

2.   It appears from this account that Abraham was fully intent on killing Isaac, as the Lord had commanded him. However, Abraham also told his servants that "...we will come back to you (Genesis 22:5)." Abraham believed that Isaac would walk back down the mountain *with* him. Thus, Abraham understood that Isaac must somehow live, as the blessings of the Lord were to be through Isaac. This suggests a bodily resurrection of Abraham's son Isaac. A resurrection from the dead pointed ahead to our future resurrection as saved men and women.

In this Old Testament event, God directed Abraham to carry out an unthinkable task: slay his dear and precious son, Isaac. Why would the Almighty God ask a man to do such a thing? Through this event, we learn about the sovereignty of God in providing a sacrifice for the offering. It was never God's intention that Isaac should be killed by his father, Abraham. Rather, this event pointed ahead to the day when God would provide His own Son as an offering for our sins. The event also reveals some interesting things about Abraham and Isaac, including Abraham's tremendous faith or trust in the God of Heaven. This idea is brought out in New Testament Scripture where we read, "By faith Abraham, when he was tested, offered up Isaac... concluding that God was able to raise him up, even from the dead...(Hebrews 11:17,19)."

In this regard, the story speaks to all of the men and fathers in the centuries to come. Fathers have the comfort of knowing that God loves their sons and daughters and He has provided a sacrifice for them, too. Jesus Christ is their substitute. We know from the New Testament Scriptures that God has redeemed (i.e., purchased) our children "with the precious blood of Christ, as of a lamb without blemish and without spot (1 Peter 1:19)."

Type and foreshadow: pointing to the resurrection of Jesus Christ

Besides foreshadows involving events and institutions, God also used people in this type of progressive revelation. There are several individuals found in the Old Testament books whose lives clearly foreshadow Jesus Christ. These men and women lived centuries before the arrival of Christ and their stories were recorded in Jewish Scriptures many centuries prior to the arrival of Jesus Christ. In several cases, these individuals foreshadowed perhaps the most important event in human history – the resurrection Jesus Christ from the dead.

One of the examples of resurrection foreshadowing involves the experience of Jonah, the ancient Jewish prophet. As Jesus Christ told the Jewish leaders before

His death and resurrection, "For as Jonah was three days and three nights in the belly of the great fish, so will the Son of Man be three days and three nights in the heart of the Earth (Matt 12:39-40)." From this and other statements (see for example, John 2:19), Jesus Christ made it clear that He would rise bodily from the dead after His death. Jonah's experience provided a picture or foreshadow of this.

In the sovereignty of God, Jonah experienced being eaten by a whale or giant fish, and then he was spit up, alive, three days later (see the book of Jonah). After being "resurrected" from the whale, Jonah then traveled to the Gentile (non-Jewish) city of Nineveh and preached a message of judgment to the people. Amazingly, the Bible describes how the people of Nineveh changed their ways, sought God's mercy, and received forgiveness.

In accord with this foreshadow, Jesus Christ was raised from dead three days after His death. But the picture does not end there. Beside the physical resurrections of their bodies, the account of Jonah also shows parallels in the spiritual effects that resulted from their resurrections. Just as the ancient people of Nineveh sought God's mercy as a result of Jonah's message, so also the Gentile nations seek God's blessings through Christ. On the basis of the resurrection of Jesus Christ, many Gentiles have accepted His mercy, love, and forgiveness – including those making the journey from Mecca to Calvary.

Previously, it was shown how the Old Testament prophecies described two roles for Israel's Messiah and Savior. One set of prophecies described the "suffering servant" while a second set of prophecies described the glorious king. We now understand these prophecies to be describing the suffering and death of Jesus Christ on the cross – fulfilling His role as the suffering servant. And we can see that the resurrected Jesus Christ will be the promised king of glory. This series of events were also the subject of a remarkable instance of Old Testament foreshadowing.

As described by Moses in the book of Genesis (chapter 35), Abraham had a grandson named Jacob. Jacob would eventually become known as Israel and his twelve sons were to be the twelve tribes (or families) of the nation of Israel. Jacob's youngest son was named Benjamin. When Benjamin was born, Jacob's wife experienced a very difficult childbirth, so much so, that she died shortly after Benjamin's birth. As she was dying, Rachel said the boy's name would be Ben-Oni, which in Hebrew means "son of my suffering." However, Jacob instead decided the boy's name should be Benjamin, which in Hebrew means "son of my right hand or strength."

This event is considered to be a foreshadowing of the two roles of Jesus Christ. As the "son of my suffering," Jesus Christ went to the cross, but as "son of my strength," Jesus Christ will rule the world as Israel's king. As such, it also implies the need for the bodily resurrection of Christ from the dead.

Types and foreshadows: our salvation in Jesus Christ

When an individual completes the journey from Mecca to Calvary, he or she becomes a Christian. This event involves their salvation from sin and condemnation – being rescued from spiritual death and eternal punishment in the Lake of Fire. Moreover, God gives the individual many, many blessings in Jesus Christ. This includes a new spirit, eternal life, a restored relationship with God, adoption into the family of God, forgiveness of sin, power over sin, and other blessings (see Chapter 13). Importantly, Christian salvation involves the simple belief or trust in the good news of Jesus Christ – that He died for our sins. The truth of this Biblical message is also confirmed by examples of foreshadowing during Old Testament times.

Among the Old Testament events that provide a picture of the salvation found in Jesus Christ, Moses described an event that is a beautiful foreshadow of the cross of Christ and our salvation from sin. This event involved the bronze serpent. As the nation of Israel moved out of Egypt and wandered through the Sinai desert, the Lord miraculously provided for them. They were sent a type of food (called manna in the Bible) that fell from Heaven at nighttime and kept the Israelites fed during their journeys. At one point during their wanderings, many of the people became discouraged, complained about the Lord's provisions, and were even longing to return to slavery in Egypt. Despite the miraculous provision of manna, these folks were saying "our soul loathes this worthless bread (Numbers 21:5)."

As a consequence of their sinful attitude, the people of Israel were punished by the Lord. We read in Numbers 21:6 that some kind of venomous snake was set upon Israel: "So the LORD sent fiery serpents among the people, and they bit the people; and many of the people of Israel died." It should be noted that Israel had already agreed to follow the commandments of the Lord while at the foot of Mount Sinai, (Exodus 19:8). The law was a system of conditional blessing and curses. If Israel kept the Law and was faithful to the Lord, then they would be blessed. However if Israel disobeyed the Law and dishonored God, then they would receive judgment and a punishment or curse. In this case, they had shown bitterness to their God, and even worse, they had refused to believe His promises to Israel. Thus, the snakes went after the people in judgment and punishment.

Following the snake attacks, the people of Israel recognized that they had sinned against the Lord. They appealed to Moses for him to pray on their behalf and asked for forgiveness from God. We read in Numbers 21:7: therefore the people came to Moses, and said, "We have sinned, for we have spoken against the

LORD and against you; pray to the LORD that He take away the serpents from us."
So Moses prayed for the people. At this point, God instructs Moses to do an
unusual task. He was to place a bronze serpent (or a metal sculpture of a snake) on
a pole in the camp of Israel. Then God told Moses, "…it shall be that everyone who
is bitten, when he looks at it, shall live." If a person had a potentially fatal snake
bite, then he or she could be miraculously healed by simply looking at the bronze
serpent.

This is an amazing foreshadow, or picture, of the cross of Christ. More than
1,400 years after the bronze serpent was raised up in the desert, Jesus Christ was
nailed to a Roman cross, raised up on the wooden cross, and died as payment for
our sin. Like the ancient Jews of the exodus, we have all been inflicted with a
deadly wound - one which arises out of sin. Our sin will result in condemnation and
death for every person. However, we have a means of salvation. Like the ancient
Jew, we can "look and live." Our life-giving salvation arises by looking towards the
cross, where God has promised to forgive our sins, restore our relationship with
Him, give us a new birth and life, and pour out many other blessings.

The Christian salvation experience occurs through a trust in the work of Jesus
Christ on the cross, and it is completely separated from any "good works" in us. In
a similar respect, the healing of the snake-bitten Jews was based simply on God's
mercy and the individual Jew's "trust" in God's message ("look and live"). If a
snake-bitten Jew refused to believe God's message and refused to look towards the
bronze serpent, then he died from the snake-bite. Likewise, if men and women
refuse to believe the message of the cross, then they will remain guilty and
condemned from sin. As Jesus Himself warned in John 8:24, these people will "die
in their sins."

Over the centuries, God has supported this idea repeatedly in the progressive
revelation of the Bible. For example, King David wrote in Psalm 34:22, "The
LORD redeems the soul of His servants, and none of those who trust in Him shall
be condemned." In our day, we can also experience salvation from sin and new life
if we follow the timeless command, "look and live." Rather than looking towards a
bronze serpent on a staff however, we are to look towards the Savior nailed to a
wooden cross.

A woman named Rahab is also a good example of Biblical foreshadowing
related to our salvation. Following the death of Moses, the nation of Israel crossed
over the Jordan River to occupy the land of Canaan. According to the Old
Testament account described in the book of Joshua, the Israelites first conquest
involved an area of land that included the city of Jericho. The divinely appointed
leader of Israel was now an individual named Joshua and he sent two men into
Jericho on a reconnaissance mission. Generally, this kind of mission involved

gathering information on a city's military strengths and defenses. The two men entered Jericho, but their identities were soon discovered. The king of Jericho sought to capture the men, and most certainly, he would have killed them upon their arrest. However, a woman named Rahab took in the men and helped them escape. It is in this woman that we find a great foreshadowing of the salvation found in Christ.

In the story of Rahab, this woman provided a hiding place for the two Israelites while the men of Jericho sought to capture them. When it was safe to do so, she lowered the men out of a window of her home (which was located on the exterior wall of the city). Before freeing the men however, she appealed to them for mercy and safety from the impending attack by the nation of Israel. She understood that God had "delivered the land of Canaan into their hands," but she asked that her family be spared from the slaughter. Rahab was instructed to tie a scarlet or red ribbon from her window, so when the onslaught took place, everyone in the home would be spared. This salvation is remarkably similar to the Passover judgment that took place in Egypt. Both of these salvation events provide a foreshadow or point forward to this day when anyone "in Christ" will be saved from the wrath and judgment of God.

It is worth noting that the Biblical account describes Rahab as a prostitute or harlot. She is often referred to as "Rahab the Harlot." Generally speaking, most people would consider this profession (prostitution) to be an immoral line of work. Despite this immoral background, she was the one whom God chose to spare in the entire city (in addition to her family). Thus, the salvation of Rahab is closely related the New Testament salvation found in Jesus Christ. As we find in Ephesians 2:8-9, "By grace (undeserved kindness) you are saved by faith, and it is not of yourself, it is the gift of God, so there is no boasting." Salvation is the result of Jesus Christ's work on the cross and it is not the result of our own good works. Indeed, a horrible sinner like a prostitute is sometimes the most likely person to realize their need for mercy and salvation from the Lord. It is also clear from New Testament Scriptures that God rejects our good works, and instead God demands that we approach Him on the basis of faith. Faith in the Bible always means trust or belief in God's revelation to mankind. Rahab understood and believed in God's power to inflict judgment and destroy Jericho. This faith led to her salvation.

Types and foreshadows: lives that point to Jesus Christ

For centuries, Christians have observed the remarkable similarities between the life of Joseph and the life of Jesus Christ. This is considered one of the beautiful foreshadows of Christ found in the Old Testament. Not only does this event further verify that the Bible is the authentic book from God, but Joseph's life also reveals something about the power of the God. The God of the Bible is unique in His ability to see into the future and to control the outcome of human events. As we read in Genesis 41:32, "the thing is established by God, and God will shortly bring it to pass." Thus, God used the life of Joseph to mirror the future life of Christ, especially in his role as Savior for God's people.

Joseph's story is described in the book of Genesis. Here we find that Joseph was one of Jacob's twelve sons. Among the parallels between Joseph and Jesus Christ, we find several notable aspects (see Table 1). His eleven brothers rejected Joseph and sold him into Egyptian slavery. However, God raised Joseph up to a leading position in Egypt. He was then able to save his brothers and their families from certain death by providing food for them during a severe drought. Like Jesus

Table 1. Parallels or foreshadows of Jesus Christ in life of Joseph.

Joseph	Jesus Christ
Favorite son of his father. Genesis 37:3	God's beloved Son and His only begotten. Matt. 3:17, Mark 1:11, Luke 3:22,
Betrayed by his own brothers and kinsmen. Genesis 37:27	Betrayed by his fellow Jews and kinsmen. Acts 7:52
Sold into slavery for pieces of silver. Genesis 37:28	Betrayed for 30 pieces of silver, the price of a slave. Matt. 26:15, Mark 14:11, Luke 22:5
Cast into a prison, a symbol of death. Genesis 39:20	Crucified and buried. Matt. 27, Luke 23, Mark 15, John 19
Cast into prison despite having done nothing wrong. Genesis 40:15	Put to death on the cross, despite having done nothing wrong or sinful. Luke 23:14; John 18:38; John 8:46
Raised out of the prison via a miraculous work of God: a symbol of resurrection Genesis 37:28	Raised bodily from the dead to a glorified position in Heaven via a miraculous work of God. Matt 28, Luke 24, Mark 16, John 20, Romans 1:4
Becomes ruler over Gentiles. Genesis 41:40-41	Adored and worshiped by Christian believers, most of whom are Gentiles. Romans 9:25
Saves his people from certain death by providing food for them during drought. Genesis 42:2	Saves God's people from their sin and their own spiritual death. Romans 5:17-21
Accepted by his own brothers (in Egypt). Genesis 45	Accepted as Savior by the Jewish people (in the future). Romans 11:11-12, Romans 11:25-27, Joel 2

Christ, Joseph was rejected by his brothers, but in this rejection he was able to provide life-giving salvation. Even the resurrection of Jesus Christ can be seen in the life of Joseph. After being betrayed by his brothers, Joseph was sold into slavery in Egypt. Joseph was thrown into an Egyptian prison based on a false accusation of wrongdoing. A miraculous series of events led to Joseph being brought out of prison and he was made a ruler of that mighty nation. In this case, Joseph's release from prison is considered to be symbolic of the resurrection of Christ. It is also notable that Joseph was given the authority to rule Egypt after his "resurrection" from the depths of prison. In a similar respect, Jesus Christ will be given the authority to rule over Gentile nations upon His return. This was made possible by His resurrection.

Like the historical account of Joseph, there are also great similarities between the life of Moses and that of Jesus Christ. As described previously, it was Jesus Christ who fulfilled the prophecy by Moses, "The LORD your God will raise up for you a Prophet like me from your midst, from your brethren. Him you shall hear (Deut. 18:15)."

The life of Moses began in Egypt during the period of time in which the twelve tribes of Israel were in forced slavery. By divine providence, Moses was adopted into the family of the Pharaoh. He fled Egypt as an adult, but returned years later after being empowered by God to free the Jewish people. Among the parallels between Moses and Jesus Christ, we find several notable aspects (Table 2). A skeptical person might argue that these aspects of Moses' life were not foreshadows of the coming Messiah Jesus Christ, but rather they were "coincidental" aspects of each man's life. Or perhaps these were similarities created by Christian churchmen and they were not deliberately placed in Scripture by the Almighty God of Heaven. A careful study of the Old and New Testament Scriptures however reveals that these similarities are no accident nor are they deliberate fabrications by the Christian church. These foreshadows or types found in Moses was the direct result of the providence of God.

The identification of Jesus as the foreshadow found in Moses was clearly taught by the first-century Christian Apostles. For example, the Apostle Peter declared to a gathering of Jews (Acts 3:22-26), "And it shall be that every soul who will not hear that Prophet shall be utterly destroyed from among the people" and "…God, having raised up His Servant Jesus, sent Him to bless you, in turning away every one of you from your iniquities." Peter's speech identifies Jesus Christ as the Prophet who was to be "like" Moses. God states plainly through the Apostle John, "For the law was given through Moses, but grace and truth came through Jesus Christ (John 1:17)."

Table 2. Parallels or foreshadows of Jesus Christ in life of Moses.

Moses	Jesus Christ
Rejected by the Jews in his first advent, but accepted by the Jews in his second advent. Exodus 2:14, then Exodus 4:31	Rejected by the Jews in his first advent, but accepted by the Jews in his second advent (still in the future). Acts 7:52, then Romans 11:11-12, Romans 11:25-27, Joel 2
Rescued his people from the bondage and servitude of slavery. Exodus 15:13, Deut. 7:7-8	Rescued God's people from the bondage and servitude of sin. Romans 6:17-23
Did miracles by the power of God, demonstrating to Pharaoh the will of the Almighty God. Exodus 4:8.	Did miracles by the power of God, demonstrating to all people that He was sent from the Almighty God. Acts 2:22, Hebrews 2:1-4
Raised the nation of Israel out of the Red Sea to a new life as a free people. Exodus chapter 14	Raises Christian believers to a new life as those born again. Romans 6:4-6.
Established the old covenant with Israel based on the Law of Moses. Exodus 19:5	Established the new covenant with Israel and all nations based on His work of the cross. Lev. 31:31-32, Heb. 9:11-15, Heb. 13:20-21

Conclusions

For the Muslim, the progressive revelation of the Bible raises some very difficult questions. If Jesus Christ is dismissed as a lesser prophet than Muhammad, then why is Christ the subject of so much foreshadowing in the Old Testament Scriptures of the Bible? Were all of these things simply the result of coincidence or chance? Or were these things carefully laid out by an Almighty and Sovereign God who wanted to point the way to the Savior for a lost, sinful, and hopeless world? Could God have used foreshadows and types as "proof" for the spiritual truth of the Bible's message?

We have seen that the Bible is a unique collection of individual books authored by about 40 different men over a period of 1,500 years. The message is consistent and gradually unfolding – God carries out a plan for mankind's salvation. The Bible has all the hallmarks of true Divine revelation, including fulfilled prophecies and accurate historical facts. Added to this, Biblical foreshadows and types could only have occurred through the work of an all powerful, Sovereign God. The ancient Jewish religion, with its systems of sacrifice and worship, all pointed to a coming Savior, the man Jesus Christ. Several individuals are also seen to be vivid

Old Testament pictures of the coming Messiah. Other events were clear pictures of the Divine work to be accomplished by Jesus Christ, especially in His death on the cross and subsequent resurrection. With all of these considerations, one can have great confidence in this: the Bible is God's truthful revelation to mankind.

References

(1)   http://www.answering-islam.org/Authors/Qureshi/testimony.htm. Downloaded March 7, 2011.

(2)   Nabeel Quresh, *Seeking Allah, Finding Jesus*, Zondervan, Grand Rapids, MI, 2014.

(3)   2 Peter 1:20,21

(4)   Josh McDowell, *The New Evidence That Demands a Verdict*, Thomas Nelson Publishers, Nashville, TN, 1999; pp. 17-32 and references cited therein.

(5)   Isaiah 64:6

Chapter 10

Progressive Revelation: when did it end?

Every word of God is pure,
He is a shield to those who put their trust in Him.
Do not add to His words, lest He rebuke you, and you are found a liar.
Proverbs 30:5,6

Nederah is a woman of Iranian background.[1] She was born into a royal Shi'ah Muslim family. Her father was executed by the Iranian government, but Nederah's mother was able to raise her and there was a clear expectation that she whould follow the religious requirements of Islam. As a youth, she observed the Islamic prayers, fasted, and regularly studied the Quran.

She married at the age of sixteen and her husband was a wealthy man. Soon after being married, she asked her husband to hire a mullah, or tutor, for advanced studies in the teachings of the Quran. She studied diligently for 10 years. Despite her studies of Islamic theology, she could sense a lack of peace within her soul. She had been a good wife and mother, and she did her best to meet the requirements of the Islamic religion, but she did not feel well acquainted with God nor did she "personally" know Him.

This prompted Nederah to seek an important goal. She thought that a pilgrimage to Mecca would bring spiritual life to her Islamic faith. She asked her husband for the opportunity to make the trip to Mecca. He agreed and made the arrangements for Nederah. She obtained her passport and purchased the special clothing for the pilgrimage.

She travelled with other pilgrims under the supervision of a specially appointed mullah. She observed all the sacred rites for the pilgrimage to Mecca. She was filled with joy and contentment from the journey to Mecca. However, her return trip to Iran was not at all inspiring to her faith. During the return flight, she visited the restroom, and in doing so, she needed to remove her face and body coverings. She put on an ankle-length coat (manto) and a head-scarf in its place. When she returned to her seat, the mullah confronted her. He said,[1]

> "What have you done hajieh (a female pilgrim)? Why are you wearing a scarf and manto? Are you aware that I can see your hair showing from under your scarf? Don't you know that with this violation you are going straight to Hell?"

This confrontation had a profound impact on Nederah. She had feelings of despair - as she did her best to draw near to God, only to be seemingly thrust towards Hell by God and his mullah.

Shortly after her trip to Mecca, Nederah and her family moved to the United States. She developed a friendship with a woman who was a Christian of Armenian background. Having been dissatisfied by the Islamic faith, she decided to attend a Christian church service with her Armenian friend. The pastor of the church was able to provide a copy of the New Testament written in Persian. This was a copy of the Gospel of Jesus Christ, or *Injil*.

She read through the New Testament and recognized it as the message of truth, declaring,[1] "I knew I had found the Living, True and Eternal God. He was not the person I had been told about all my life." At this point, she decided to leave Islam and she became a Christian. She was then saved from all sin and given eternal life in Christ. Although Nederah experienced the "true peace and joy" found in a relationship with Jesus Christ, her life had many hardships in the following years. The Iranian government executed some of her relatives. On a trip to Iran, her husband was arrested and badly beaten in Iranian prison. All of their family's possessions were confiscated in their home country of Iran. Nevertheless, she can look back and see how God "has sustained my family and me through the difficulties of life." Moreover, she knows that, "salvation is my greatest wealth."

When Nederah examined the messages in the Bible, she recognized it as spiritual truth. As described in the previous chapters, there is abundant evidence that the Bible is indeed the product of God's inspiration. In God's plan for revelation, He included several elements that offer "proof" for the individual. This includes remarkable prophecies of future events and the stunning development of the His message through progressive revelation. Further evidence includes many notable miracles accomplished by the prophets of the Bible (see Chapter 11). In this chapter, we will consider the critical question – were Muhammad's teachings the final piece of God's magnificent progressive revelation?

Progressive revelation: what was the final word?

When the progressive revelation of the Bible is considered, it is important to notice that certain spiritual truths or concepts are consistently developed throughout the book. Biblical teachings are presented at the very beginning - even in the books by Moses - and then God expands and develops these ideas in later revelations through the writers of Scripture. The God of Heaven even placed foreshadows, types, and prophecies, in the Bible to demonstrate this development. As shown later in this chapter, the basic spiritual truths remained constant throughout 1,500 years of God's communication to mankind. However even a casual inspection of Islamic teaching reveals that a monumental change in theology has taken place. The Quran contains completely a different message. Although Islamic teachers would argue that the Quran and hadith are in fact the final messages to mankind, there are several lines of evidence and reasoning through which this is shown to be wrong.

Closure of the Canon of Scripture

When God accomplished His plan of salvation for mankind, He inspired His prophets and Apostles to write the New Testament Bible books. These revelations were very clearly the final messages God intended to deliver to mankind. The resulting books represented closure of the Canon of Scripture (revelations of spiritual truth given to mankind by God). With completion of the Bible, the Lord inspired His writers to make it clear: no further books or revelations would be added to the Canon of Scripture. For example, the Apostle Paul warned the Christians in Galatia,

> But even if we, or an angel from heaven, preach any other gospel
> to you than what we have preached to you, let him be accursed.
> As we have said before, so now I say again, if anyone preaches
> any other gospel to you than what you have received, let him be
> accursed. (Galatians 1:8, 9)

In this passage, God has warned mankind to avoid any messages that differ from the plain gospel of Jesus Christ. Gospel is simply a word meaning "good news." God and Paul state that even a message supposedly delivered by "an angel from Heaven" should be rejected if it differs from the good news about Jesus Christ and His cross work. This passage of Scripture is significant because the rise of Islam began with "an other gospel" delivered by an angel. God has warned us to reject such teaching. We are even told to consider teachers of this message to be "accursed." The Greek word used here (ἀνάθεμα, *anathema*) is described in dictionaries as,[2] "devoted to God without hope of being redeemed." This is a dire prediction for Muslims and their teachers, because it points to a Judgment Day resulting only in doom and destruction.

A key statement in the above passage refers to the gospel Paul preached and the Galatians received. What was the good news? This gospel massage can be found throughout the pages of the New Testament. For example, Paul wrote:

> "...Christ died for our sins...He was buried, and that He rose again
> the third day..." (1 Corinthinas 15:3,4)

"Believe on the Lord Jesus Christ, and you will be saved, you and your household." (Acts 16:31)

Jesus Christ died for our sins and this is the gospel in Paul's revelations. These are certainly not the messages taught in the Islamic schools and mosques around the world. Islamic religious doctrines deny Jesus Christ died for our sins, deny that He was buried, and deny that He rose from the dead. Thus, the teaching of Islam does not fit with the previous revelations given by God through 1,500 years of writing by the prophets. This also means that Islam cannot be the final message of God's revelations, as it does not agree with the gospel or good news of Jesus Christ!

When the Apostle John wrote the book of Revelation (late first century), the prophet makes another a plain statement indicating that God had completed the Canon Scripture. In writing through this Apostle, God declares (Revelation 22:18b,19),

> ...If anyone adds to these things, God will add to him the plagues that are written in this book; and if anyone takes away from the words of the book of this prophecy, God shall take away his part from the Book of Life, from the holy city, and from the things which are written in this book.

Again, this is a Bible verse that Muslim scholars conveniently ignore. In the book of Revelation (the last book of the Bible), there are descriptions of future events involving Heaven, Earth, the nations, and judgments. At its closure in Revelation chapter 22, we see that God promises to judge and punish anyone who "adds to" or "takes away" from these prophecies. Islamic teachers do both.

Muslim scholars teach that Jesus will return to Earth, He will do away with the *jizyah* tax (imposed on non-Muslims), and He will demand that everyone converts to Islam.[3] This is certainly not taught in the Biblical book of Revelation and it obviously represents something that has been "added to" the statements from God. Moreover, Islamic traditions further state that Jesus will die a human death upon His return in the last days.[3] This clearly "takes away" the plain statement in Revelation (proclaimed by Jesus Christ Himself), "I am He who lives, and was dead, and behold, I am alive forevermore." When Jesus said "I am alive forevermore," He stated that He will never die. Muslim scholars and teachers boldly throw away this part of the prophecy in the book of Revelation. But they do so at their own peril, as God declared His judgment against those who do such things.

Again, the passage in Revelation 22 is a clear point of closure for God's revelation. His message to humanity was completed. It is important to notice that the Old Testament did not have a similar point of closure. When the prophets of Israel finished recording their revelations in about 500 B.C., they purposely left the Scriptures open ended, because God was not finished with His plan and His message for mankind. However, we do see a closure with the production of the New Testament. Both Paul and John described the closure of God's revelation in the above two Bible passages. After the completion of the Bible in 90 A.D., there could be no more added messages or prophetic books. This means that Islam could not have been the final message from God, as the Jewish and Christian prophets completed this revelation in the pages of the Bible.

A Consistent Message

Although Muslim apologists could points to a few minor items in the Quran that seem to be in accord with the 1,500 years of Biblical revelation, the most important spiritual topics form a sudden and terrible break. This means that Islamic teachings cannot be a continuation of God's message given by Moses, David, Isaiah, and all the Jewish prophets. Neither does the Islamic religion continue the message given by Jesus Christ and His Apostles. To demonstrate this truth, three important Bible doctrines will be examined and compared with the corresponding Islamic doctrines. This section will examine the attributes and character of God, the nature of sin, and the concept of reconciliation (being made "just" or "right") before God. One final note, it is understood that there are many variations in the beliefs/teachings between different Islamic schools and imams. No claim is being made here to speak for every teacher of Islamic theology.

The God of the Bible and the God Islam

Entire volumes have been written on the attributes, character, and names given to the God of the Bible and the God of the Quran.[4,5] Islam and Christianity are often lumped together in the same group, as monotheistic religions – or literally religious faiths that worship a single God. However, even a casual study can reveal that the two religions worship vastly different Gods. Suffice to say, a comprehensive treatment of this topic cannot be done in this book. The goal of this section is not to enumerate every difference between the God of the Bible and the God of the Quran. Rather, the purpose of this section is to show that the Quran cannot be adding to the messages given by God through the prophets of the Old and New Testaments of the Bible. This can be amply demonstrated by considering some of the descriptions of God in the Bible versus the God of the Quran.

186

Those who leave Islam for Christianity often describe a critical difference between the two faiths: the love from God. As noted by these men and women, Allah is generally not characterized as having love towards men and women. While there are two passages in the Quran that refer to Allah as the "loving" God (*Surah* 11.90 and 85.14), one finds Allah more often being described as "the merciful" God. Muslims are taught "99 beautiful names for Allah," however only one of these names makes reference to love. Indeed, one prominent Islamic scholar commented, "He (Allah) remains above the feeling of love" (Al-Maqsad Al-Asna, p. 91).[6]

This is contrasted with the descriptions of God in the Bible. The Bible repeatedly describes God as having a great love for mankind. Indeed, the Bible even states (1 John 4:8), "...God is love." Throughout the New Testament, God's love is declared and it is generally connected to the death of Jesus on the cross. We are able to see God's tremendous love for us in that He sent His Son to die on our behalf. For example, the Bible describes God's love in these terms:

> For God loved the world so much that He gave His only Son...John 3:16

> In this the love of God was manifested toward us, that God has sent His only begotten Son into the world, that we might live through Him. In this is love, not that we loved God, but that He loved us and sent His Son *to be* the payment for our sins.
> 1 John 4:9,10

In the passage from 1 John, the phrase "He loved us" is particularly striking. This and other Bible verses indicate that the God of the Bible loves you and I *personally*. He knows you and He loves you. This is clearly different than the God of Islam, whom according to one authority, "remains above the feeling of love."

Another important difference is revealed in 1 John 4:9,10 – that God's love for us is unconditional. It states that God loved us first, rather than His love coming as a result of our love for Him. Another often cited Bible verse echoes this idea:

> But God demonstrates His own love toward us, in that while we were still sinners, Christ died for us. Much more then, having now been justified by His blood, we shall be saved from wrath through Him. Romans 5:8, 9

Even more remarkable, the God of the Bible loves us despite the fact that we are sinners! God's love for us arises from His nature as a benevolent, loving God. This love is clearly not a reward for our own good behavior or righteous acts.

This is contrasted with the God of Islam, where Allah is said to love you - only when you love Allah, follow Muhammad, and do works of righteousness. This can be seen from the Quran:[7,8]

> Say: "If you love Allah, follow me: Allah will love you and forgive you of your sins." *Surah* 3:31

> On those who believe and do works of Righteousness, (Allah), the Most Gracious (Ar-Rahman) will bless (His) love upon them. *Surah* 19:96

Both of the passages declare that Allah's love for an individual depends on their conduct. There are no statements in the Quran describing God's love for sinners. This represents a huge change from the God described in the Bible, where we see God loves us even though we are all sinners!

Besides this attribute of God (His great love), the Quran makes another significant break from the Bible. Throughout the pages of the Bible, one finds descriptions of God's triune nature - sometimes called the Trinity. The Bible declares that God is Father, Son, and Holy Spirit. However, the Quran specifically denies this truth in several places. Before examining the messages from Old and New Testament prophets, we will first consider the teaching from the Quran. In the first part of *Surah* 5.73, we read:[9] "They surely lie who say, 'Allah is one of three in a Trinity.' There is no god except One Allah." This passage from the Quran clearly denies that God exists as the Father, Son, and Holy Spirit. It also claims that the doctrine of the "Trinity" is a "lie." With statements such as those in *Surah* 5.73, there can be no question or doubt, the Quran is not part of the same Divine revelation given by the Old and New Testament prophets. The message in *Surah* 5.73 contradicts plain statements made by Moses, Isaiah, David, Paul, and even Jesus Christ, where the Godhead is described as triune in nature or quality.

Foremost in this discussion, it must first be shown that Christians do not believe in three "gods." Both Old and New Testament prophets declare that there is only one God (Table 1). For example, both Moses and Isaiah affirmed this truth during Old Testament times. Their passages of Scriptures clearly deny the pantheism (worshipping many gods) that was common in ancient times, but it also refutes the idea that our universe is ruled by a triumvirate (a group of three gods). Likewise, the first century prophets James and Paul declare that there is only one

Table 1. A sample of Bible verses that declare monotheism – one God.

Author	Date of Writing	Reference	Bible Passage
Moses	1,400 B.C.	Deut. 4:35	…the LORD Himself is God; there is none other besides Him
Isaiah	800 B.C	Isaiah 45:5	I am the LORD, and there is no other; there is no God besides Me…
James	45 A.D.	James 2:19	You believe that there is one God. You do well. Even the demons believe—and tremble!
Paul	60 A.D.	Eph. 4:6	…one God and Father of all, who *is* above all, and through all, and in you all.

God. He is eternal, almighty, holy, and sovereign. The God of the Bible is indeed the center of a monotheistic faith. None of the Old or New Testament prophets ever taught the notion of "three gods."

Although the Bible teaches that there is only one God, it also teaches that He has the character of three personalities – described as the Father, the Son, and the Holy Spirit. This can be seen even from the very first revelations given to the prophet Moses, as he was inspired to name God using the plural form of Hebrew words. For example in Genesis 1:1 Moses wrote, "In the beginning, God created the Heavens and the Earth." The Hebrew word used for God is, *Elohim* - a word that is in the plural tense. Likewise, the prophet Isaiah describes the worship of God in Heaven by His mighty angels and they proclaim, "Holy, holy, holy is the Lord…" (Isaiah 6:3). A similar passage is found in the New Testament (Revelation 4:8), written about 900 years later by the New Testament prophet John. These worshipping angels declare God's holiness three times - not simply for the sake of emphasis - but they do so in reference to the Father, Son, and Holy Spirit in the person of God.

This doctrine is revealed consistently throughout the course of 1,500 years of Divine revelation. God's prophets spoke of the Father, Son, and Holy Spirit in both Old and New Testament revelations. For example, all three members of the Godhead are mentioned in the Old Testament:

God the Father
You, O LORD, are our Father; our Redeemer from Everlasting is Your name.
Isaiah 63:16b

Son of God

For unto us a Child is born, unto us a Son given...and His name will be called Wonderful, Counselor, Mighty God, Everlasting Father, Prince of Peace.
Isaiah 9:6

Holy Spirit

Create in me a clean heart, O God, and renew a steadfast spirit within me. Do not cast me from Your presence, and do not take your Holy Spirit from me.
Psalm 51:10,11

Remarkably, all three members are mentioned in a single Old Testament passage (Isaiah 48:16b), "...and now the Lord God and His Spirit have sent Me." From our perspective, we can see these are references to the Father, Holy Spirit, and Son of God. However, it is unlikely that the any ancient Jews would have understood this truth.

Likewise in the New Testament, multiple passages refer to the Father, Son, and Holy Spirit as God. More than 200 times God is called Father, including many times by Jesus Himself. For example, the Apostle John described an exchange between Jesus Christ and the Jewish leaders, where Jesus answered, "If I honor Myself, My honor is nothing. It is My Father who honors Me, of whom you say that He is your God. (John 8:54)." In this passage, Jesus refers to God as His "Father." Two members of the trinity are apparent here: the Father and the Son (Jesus Christ). A thorough treatment of the deity of Jesus Christ is presented in Chapter 12, and consequently it is not discussed at this point.

There are also many passages of Scripture that describe the Holy Spirit as God. He is said to have inspired the Old and New Testament prophets. For example, the New Testament prophet Peter described this process, "prophecy never came by the will of man, but holy men of God spoke as they were moved by the Holy Spirit." Likewise, Jesus describes (Mark 12:36) David's Old Testament Psalms as written "by the Holy Spirit." These same Scriptures are also called the "word of God" because God the Holy Spirit has inspired them. It is also important to note that the Bible describes God the Holy Spirit in terms of personality. He can be resisted and grieved by the sinful actions of men and women (Ephesians 4:30 and Acts 7:51). Moreover, He works to convince, guide, and make intercessions for men and women (1 Corinthians 2:10; Romans 8:16, 26; John 16:8; Galatians 5:18). These characteristics indicate that He is a personality, similar to the Father and Son.

Several New Testament passages include all three members of the Trinity. For example, Matthew described an event in which Jesus sent out His Apostles saying (Matthew 28:19), "All authority has been given to Me (Jesus) in heaven and on earth. Go therefore and make disciples of all the nations, baptizing them in the name of the Father and of the Son and of the Holy Spirit." Many other passages have two of the members of Trinity described together. The Apostle Paul often begins his letters with the greeting from the Father and Son, "Grace to you and peace from God our Father and the Lord Jesus Christ (Ephesians 1:2)." Likewise the Father and the Son are mentioned together by John, "and we have seen and testify that the Father has sent the Son as Savior of the world (1 John 4:14)." Taken together, this is compelling testimony. The Bible teaches the triune character of God or the Trinity.

Based on the Bible passages above, it is more than obvious that the message of Islam cannot be another step in God's progressive revelation. Islamic doctrines contradict the messages laid out so carefully in 1,500 years of Biblical revelations – that God has abundant love for us and He has eternally existed as Father, Son, and Holy Spirit. If the follower of Islam wishes to believe the Quran and its descriptions of God or Allah, then he or she must do so knowing that it contradicts those things taught by Moses, David, Isaiah, and all of the Jewish prophets. It also contradicts plain statements made by Jesus Christ Himself. The Muslim apologist might argue: these descriptions of a loving God with the character of a Trinity are actually the result of the corruption of the Scriptures. This is not the case. It was shown in previous chapters that both the Old and New Testaments of the Bible have been preserved through the centuries. Likewise, the Biblical revelations describing God must have also been preserved.

The nature of sin

Another example of a consistent teaching found in the Bible involves the concept of sin or transgression against the God of Heaven. With the fall of Adam described in Genesis chapter 3, sin entered into the human race and as the Lord states, "they now know good and evil." Throughout the Bible, we find several basic teachings regarding sin. These doctrines do not change and they are consistently developed throughout 1,500 years of revelation (Table 2).

During fifteen centuries of inspired writing, there were about 700 passages of Scripture written that mention sin or transgressions against the Law of Moses. Most of these Biblical teachings involve several human authors (often three or more) and these writers are sometimes recording their Divine revelations many centuries apart. For example, the Prophet Isaiah and the Apostle Paul both conveyed an important message from God, that our good deeds and righteous acts are considered filthy and worthless in front the infinitely Holy God. In particular with Paul's Scriptures, he tells us how we cannot approach God in our own "righteousness." Rather, we can

Table 2. Complimentary revelations or writings dealing with aspects of sin.

Biblical Concept of Sin	Scripture Reference(s)	Date(s) of Revelation(s)	Authors
Sin is a transgression against God.	Gen. 39:9; 1 Sam. 12:23; Ps. 51:3-4; Jer. 16:10; 1 Cor. 8:12	1,430 B.C., 1,000 B.C., 700 B.C., 56 A.D.	Moses, Samuel, David, Jeremiah, Paul
Sin(s) results in spiritual death..	Genesis 2:17; Ezekiel 18; Romans 6:23	1,430 B.C., 600 B.C., and 57 A.D.	Moses, Ezekiel, Paul
All men and women sin.	Eccl. 7:20; Isaiah 64:6; Rom. 3:23; Gal. 3:22; James 3:2; 1 John 1:8	1,000 B.C., 800 B.C., 45 A.D., 50 A.D., 57 A.D., 90 A.D.	Solomon, Isaiah, Paul, James, John
We became sinners with Adam's sin.	Gen. 5:3; Rom. 5:12	1,430 B.C, 57 A.D.	Moses and Paul
Even our good deeds are filthy and contaminated by sin.	Isaiah 64:6; Job 14:4, chap 15; Rom. 7:18	800 B.C., 57 A.D., and other date.	Isaiah, Paul, and other author.
Sin will be judged and punished by God.	Ps. 1:5; Eccl. 3:17, 12:14; Isaiah 1:28; Mal. 3:5; Rom. 4:15; 2 Cor. 5:10; Heb. 2:2-3	1,000 B.C.; 800 B.C, 450 B.C; 57 A.D.; 68 A.D.	David, Solomon, Malachi, Paul
Sin only forgiven or covered on the basis of a blood sacrifice.	Ex. 30:10; Lev. 17:11; 2 Chron. 29:23-4; Heb. 9:22	1,430 B.C.; 500 B.C.; 68 B.C.	Moses, Paul, and other author.
Sins of an individual placed on the innocent sacrifice, beginning with animals and then with Jesus Christ.	Lev. 8 and 18:21; Num. 8:12; 2 Chron. 29:23; Ez. 45:21-25; Isaiah 53:12; John 1:29; 2 Cor. 5:21; Heb. 13:11; 1 Peter 2:24	1,430 B.C., 800 B.C., 600 B.C., 500 B.C., 57 A.D., 68 A.D., 85 A.D.	Moses, Isaiah, Ezekiel, John, Paul, Peter, and other author.
All of our sins were punished at the cross.	Rom. 3:25; 1 Cor. 15:3; 2 Cor. 5:21; Gal. 1:4; Eph. 1:7; Col. 1:14; Heb. 9:28 and 10:12; 1 Peter 2:24; 1 John 2:2;	50 A.D., 56 A.D., 57 A.D., 60 A.D., 65 A.D., 68 A.D., 90 A.D., 95 A.D.	Paul, Peter, John
God cannot sin, and so Jesus Christ did not sin.	Psalm 11:7; Psalm 97; Isaiah 5:16; 2 Corinthians 5:21; 1 Peter 2:22; John 8:46; Hebrews 1:8,9;	1000 B.C., 800 B.C., 57 A.D., 65 A.D., 85 A.D., 68 A.D.	David, Isaiah, Paul, Peter, and John
Sinful men and women cannot stand before an infinitely Holy God.	Exodus 33:20; Isaiah 6:1-7; 2 Thessalonians 1:8,9; 2 Peter 2:1-10; Jude 1:14-15; Rev 1:17	1,430 B.C., 800 B.C., 51 A.D., 66 A.D., 68 A.D., 95 A.D.	Moses, Isaiah, Paul, Peter, Jude, and John
Sins forgiven if we trust in the work of Christ on the cross.	Luke 22:20; John 15:13; Rom. 3:21-26, 5:6-8; 1 Cor. 15:1,2; Eph. 2:8,9; Col. 2:5-14; 1 Peter 3:18	60 A.D., 56 A.D., 57 A.D., 60 A.D., 65 A.D., 85 A.D.	Luke, John, Paul, and Peter

only stand before God in the "gift righteousness" which He gives freely to Christians (those who have been saved from their sin). Remarkably, Paul and Isaiah wrote almost 1,000 years apart and their messages are in perfect agreement. This was not a coincidence. It is an example of progressive revelation and strong evidence for the Divine authorship of the Bible. The multiple-authored Bible doctrines are a miracle of ancient literature. Other aspects of the Biblical teachings on sin are outlined in the Table. It is important to notice that each of these doctrines is revealed by several writers of Scripture and the books are often separated many centuries.

Do the Islamic doctrines of sin agree with the Bible doctrines? Yes and no. While there are some minor areas of agreement, there are also very significant disagreements. These differences are so large that no one could possibly claim the Islamic doctrines continue earlier revelations from the Jewish and Christian prophets. For example, the Bible teaches that sin is the result of our own rebellion against the revealed will of God. It arises from a deeply imbedded sinful nature that we inherited from our distant ancestor Adam (Romans 5:12, ..."through one man sin entered the world, and death through sin"). Moreover, we are individually responsible for our own sins. According to some Islamic teachers, mankind sins because Allah willed it for us. This comes from several Quranic passages,[10] for example *Surah* 57.22:

> No misfortune can happen on earth or in your souls except that which is recorded in a command written before which we bring into existence: that is truly easy for Allah

This idea completely contradicts the message taught by Jewish and Christian prophets and even by Jesus Christ Himself. Nowhere does the Bible suggest that it is God's desire or will that men or women sin. Indeed, the Jewish prophet Ezekiel recorded (Ezekiel 33:11) this statement from the Lord GOD, "I have no pleasure in the death of the wicked, but that the wicked turn from his way and live." The God of the Bible does not travel the earth to inflict, cause, or tempt men and women with sinful deeds. As God declared in James 1:13, "...He Himself does not tempt anyone." Instead, His great desire is to give them forgiveness and eternal life. This is seen in the New Testament passage, Romans 6:23:

> For the wages (payment or result) of sin *is* death, but the gift of God *is* eternal life in Christ Jesus our Lord.

While the Islamic faith does teach that all men must hope for Allah's mercy regarding sin and punishment, the Islamic teachings are not at all consistent with the doctrines presented by Jewish and Christian prophets. For example, *Surah* 4.31 reads:[11]

> If you only avoid the most excessively evil of things that you are
> forbidden to do, We shall expel out of you all the evil in you and
> admit you to a Gate of Great Honor (the Paradise).

This passage is usually interpreted to mean that a man's sin can be forgiven, but only if he avoids the "excessively evil" sins. The Bible teaches that all sin is deserving of punishment. God even states:

> For whoever shall keep the whole law, and yet stumble in one
> point, he is guilty of all. (James 2:10)

> The good deeds of the righteous man shall not deliver him in the
> day of his sin (Ezekiel 33:12a)

The same God who revealed James 2:10 and Ezekiel 33:12 cannot be the same one who revealed *Surah* 4:31 to Muhammad, because the Quran and Biblical messages contradict. The Biblical revelation teaches that all sin is worthy of eternal punishment – small and large sins. Nowhere in the Bible do we find the message of Islam. Minor sins cannot be ignored or dismissed by the righteous judgment, perfect justice, and holiness of the Almighty God.

Clearly, Islam makes a sharp break from many of the long-standing Biblical revelations regarding sin. This includes the doctrines of the internal sin nature of mankind, the spiritual death inherited from Adam, the need for a new spiritual birth, and so on. The Bible has had a consistent message concerning sin. Moreover, God revealed this message through 1,500 years of progressive revelation. With its contradictory ideas about sin, we must conclude that the Islamic teachings cannot be part of God's previous revelations.

Reconciled: obtaining a right relationship with God

The Bible also has a very clear progressive revelation relating to the all-important issue of restoring our relationship with God Almighty (called reconciliation). However, we again find that Islamic doctrines make a sharp break from the 1,500 years of revelation given by Old and New Testament prophets. We have already seen how all sin is a grave offense to God. Yet, God gave mankind the sacrificial system to begin the reconciliation to Him. As discussed previously, an individual's sins were symbolically placed on an innocent animal and the creature was slain to cover or "pay for" the sins. As God stated through Moses (Leviticus 17:11), "it *is* the blood *that* makes atonement for the soul."

Atonement literally means covering or hiding of the sins. It is also worth noting, that in some Bible passages, atonement and reconciliation are used interchangeably. That is to say, they are two closely related principles. Covering of mankind's sins provided some measure of peace with God.

As described in Chapter 9, the sacrificial system (with innocent animals) was meant to be a foreshadow of the sacrifice made by the Savior Jesus Christ. Mankind's sins found complete atonement at the cross of Jesus Christ, as the blood of Christ did more than simply cover sins – it actually paid the penalty for our sins. God's righteousness, holiness, and justice could now be satisfied. The great sin debt had been paid. Our sins could be forgiven completely and our relationship with God could be fully restored. As the Apostle Paul states in Romans 5:10, "…we were reconciled to God through the death of His Son."

The Greek word used above for reconciled is καταλλάσσω, or *katallaso*. According to Vine's Dictionary of New Testament Words, this word carries the meaning "to change from enmity to friendship." As sinners, we have all been in a state of enmity - or war - with God. But an individual has *peace with God* when they become a Christian and receive reconciliation. God promises this reconciliation and He states it plainly in Romans 5:1, "…we have peace with God through our Lord Jesus Christ." Moreover, this reconciliation is freely given at the point of salvation. It is a present possession for those who complete the journey from Mecca to Calvary. Along with the forgiveness of sins, reconciliation, and the promise of eternal life in Heaven, the Christian has the promise of owning these blessings forever. Indeed, the great Apostle John wrote (1 John 5:13),

> These things I have written to you who believe in the name of the
> Son of God, that you may know that you have eternal life, and
> that you may *continue to* believe in the name of the Son of God.

Does Islam continue this doctrine of reconciliation? Does Islam point to the death of Jesus Christ as the basis for our *peace with God*? Does a Muslim ever know that he or she has eternal life? The answer to all of these questions is the same. No.

According to Islamic sources, sinful men and women receive forgiveness and mercy from God through the intercession of Muhammad. In fact, individuals are even said to appeal to Jesus for a rescue from Hell-fire - but according to the hadith

(Sahih Al-Bukhari 9.601) - Jesus must defer this act to Muhammad! The prophet of Islam then appeals to Allah for mercy towards the people. The individuals in Hell may then be removed from the torment as a result of Muhammad's intercession. The Bible states plainly that (1 Timothy 2:5) "there is one God and one Mediator between God and men, *the* Man Christ Jesus." Moreover, the hadith contains the blasphemous statement that Jesus Christ is not worthy to approach God on behalf of mankind.[12] It supposedly quotes Jesus saying, "I am not fit for that, but you'd better go to Muhammad."

This Islamic doctrine is in direct contradiction to messages from Christian prophets in the Bible. The Apostle John was inspired by God to write the book of Revelation. In the opening chapters of the book, John describes a future time in Heaven where a scroll must be opened – one that is associated with the judgments of God. He observed the scene in Heaven where (Revelation 5:4), "...no one was found worthy to open and read the scroll, or to look at it." But then it is Jesus – not Muhammad – who is able to take the scroll from God Almighty (Revelation 5:5). The creatures and elders who worship God are then described as singing a song (Revelation 5:9),

> You are worthy to take the scroll,
> And to open its seals;
> For You were slain,
> And have redeemed us to God by Your blood
> Out of every tribe and tongue and people and nation,

Only Jesus Christ is worthy to take the scroll because He is the unique Savior of mankind. The worshippers note the death of Jesus Christ redeeming and reconciling them to God. In the song above, the word "redeemed" is similar to "purchase" and His "purchase" relieves people of the great sin debt to God. This restores the peace between mankind and God. Yet, Islamic doctrines proclaim that Muhammad is worthy – and Jesus Christ is not worthy - to participate in these types of events in Heaven. Because of these great differences, we must conclude that the Quran and hadith cannot be part of the same progressive revelation that we find in the Bible!

It is also seen that Islamic doctrines of reconciliation are never associated with the death of Jesus Christ. In one hadith (*Sahih Al-Bukhari* 1.101), Muhammad is advising women on spiritual matters and he is quoted as saying, "A woman whose three children die will be shielded by them from the Hell fire." In this teaching from the hadith, we are told that God's judgment and wrath may be "shielded" if a woman loses three children (presumably by sickness or accident). This notion or idea cannot be part of the progressive revelation found in the Bible. The Bible's message is clear: a man or woman can only be justified and made righteous by the work of Jesus Christ on the cross. God declared this to be the only acceptable means of approach, so how can Islam then claim a life filled with hardship (such as losing children) can make someone more acceptable before the Almighty God?

Likewise, the Islamic doctrine of martyrdom contradicts 1,500 years of revelation from Christian and Jewish prophets - including the message of Jesus. Based on the teachings of the Quran and hadith, a Muslim martyr receives forgiveness and mercy as a result of his or her personal sacrifice.[13] Those who march to their deaths are given the confidence that a place in paradise is reserved for them. As an example, *Surah* 3:157 describes this method of reconciliation to God,[14] "And if ye are slain, or die, in the way of God, forgiveness and mercy from God are far better than all they could amass."

Yet, Jesus never tells His followers to take up arms, fight, and die in battle for God. He never states that martyrdom is a means of reconciliation with God. Indeed, this is one of the great differences between Islam and Christianity. Islam says that a man can find peace with God and eternal reward if he gives up his life for God. Christianity says that a man finds peace with God and eternal reward because the Son of God gave up His life for us!

Consider also the statements made by Jesus Himself. He never told His followers, "if you fight and die, Allah will reward you and you will have reconciliation" or some statement like this. Instead, Jesus tells His followers (Matt. 5:44), "but I say to you, love your enemies, bless those who curse you, do good to those who hate you, and pray for those who spitefully use you and persecute you." Nor do we find commands from Jesus where He tells His followers to "cut off the hands and feet from opposite sides" of enemies - as found in the Quran (*Surah* 5:33).[15] Instead, we see Jesus praying for the men who have crucified Him - as He prays from the cross (Luke 23:34), "Father, forgive them, for they do not know what they do." Even enemies and sinners find love, reconciliation, and salvation from the God of the Bible!

These contrasting ideas demonstrate the sharp break in the Islamic and Christian ideas of reconciliation to God. The Bible consistently teaches that we obtain peace with God through the cross work of Jesus Christ. His death clears our sin debt before God. Instead of "seeing" a sinful man or woman, the God of Heaven "sees" the perfect righteousness of Jesus Christ. Our reconciliation is never connected to the difficulty of our lives, our own martyr's death, and of course, not through the intercession of Muhammad. This again means that the Quran and hadith cannot be part of the revelation that began with the Jewish and Christian prophets.

Conclusions

The Quran does quote Jesus and Jewish prophets making statements in support of Islam. However, these quotes and statements are totally absent from the Biblical Scriptures. Since these statements do not appear in the Bible, the Muslim must decide which is the more reliable source of spiritual truth? We have seen that the Bible contains 1,500 years of divine revelation delivered to us by more than 40 prophets. And we have seen that the Quran contains an entirely different message presented by one man - Muhammad. With the break from Biblical theology, Muhammad stands alone with his revelations.

What does all this mean? As an illustration, imagine being lost in an unfamiliar city and you need to find your way to the airport. You ask 40 people for directions to the airport and they all tell you exactly the same directions. These people might include a policeman, doctor, fireman, bus driver, the city mayor, and others. However, one individual tells you a completely different course to the airport and the route would send you in the opposite direction. Whom would you believe...the lone person or the group of individuals with the consistent message? In a similar respect, multiple authors in the Bible have taught a consistent message,[16] that "...we were reconciled to God through the death of His Son." According to the teachings of Islam, however, one must discard these directions from the Bible and follow the new set of directions from the individual prophet named Muhammad.

References

(1)   Based on a published testimony, see:
        http://www.answering-islam.org/Testimonies/nadereh.html
        Downloaded February 26, 2011.

(2)   W. E. Vines, *Expository Dictionary of New Testament Words*, Thomas Nelson Publishers, Nashville, TN, 1985; pp. 141-142.

(3)   Zeki Saritoprak, *Islam's Jesus*, University Press of Florida, Gainsville, FL, 2014.

(4)   Ravi Zacharias, *Jesus Among Other Gods*, Thomas Nelson Publishers, Nashville, TN, 2002. Charles F. Baker, *A Dispensational Theology*, Grace Publications, Grand Rapid, MI, 1999. Thomas G. Brunswick, *Allah of the Qur'an and the God of the Bible: Are They the Same?*, Outskirts Press, Parker, CO, 2013.

(5)   Shems Friedlander and Al-HajjShaikh Muzaffereddin, *Ninety-Nine Names of Allah*, HarperOne, New York, NY, 1993

(6) See also, *Al-Ghazali on the Ninety-Nine Beautiful Names of God: Al-Maqsad Al-Asna Fi Sharh Asma' Allah Al-Husna*, D. B. Burrell and Nazih Daher (translators), Islamic Texts Society, Cambridge, UK, 1992.

(7) *Surah* 3.31

(8) *Surah* 19.96

(9) *Surah* 5.73

(10) *Surah* 57.22

(11) *Surah* 4.31

(12) Sahih Al-Bukhari 9.601

(13) Sahih Al-Bukhari 4.52-54, 4.72, 5.318

(14) *Surah* 3:157

(15) *Surah* 5:33

(16) Romans 5:10

Chapter 11

The message from God: more compelling evidence

The humble shall see this and be glad,
and you who seek God,
your hearts shall live. Psalm 69:32

In about 1932, Garba Adamu was born in Nigeria.[1] He was enrolled in Muslim schools as a young boy. Through his education, he learned to read and write his native language of Hausa in both the Roman and Arabic text. Along with his linguistic studies, he learned Islamic doctrines and he had read through the Quran many times. He was a devout follower of Islam and he even became secretary of a local Muslim mission. Soon he was promoted to the state executive committee of the Muslim mission.

With his expertise in the language of Hausa, some Europeans sought his help with the language and script. The Europeans were from a Christian missionary group. Garba made it clear that he would not read the Bible or study with the group. He felt so strongly about this that he decided to wash his hands with soap and water if he ever touched a Bible. Nevertheless, the work was only for six weeks, so he agreed to help the Christian missionaries.

Garba began his work teaching the Hausa language to the Europeans. There was an administrative assistant who worked with the Christian missionaries, a woman named Ms. Oliver. She helped Garba travel to and from the local mosque and she never criticized the Islamic faith. Garba was very impressed by Ms. Oliver, a woman known for her kindness and upstanding character. During the course of his work, Garba was given the task of checking the Hausa Roman and Arabic language of newly written Christian literature. Ms. Oliver first gave him a small Arabic-Hausa booklet describing the person and works of Jesus Christ. While checking the quality of the writing, Garba was astonished by the message. He read the booklet over and over. Something in the message touched his heart and he now wanted to read the Bible.

Garba started attending the Bible studies and prayers with the Christian missionaries. His knowledge of the Christian message became greater. Soon Ms. Oliver approached him with a newly written book to review. He checked the Hausa language. The book had a chapter on the Trinity, the Biblical description of God. The doctrine of the Trinity is often very difficult for Muslims to understand, nevertheless, it brought Garba to the point of prayer. He prayed to God,[1] "...remove the darkness from my understanding and show me His truth."

200

After some time, Garba believed the message of the Bible. He told Ms. Oliver,[1] "I repented of my sins and trusted in Jesus Christ," and immediately, he experienced a great joy and happiness. With his conversion to Christianity, Garba stopped participating in Muslim work, activities, and religious services. Following his journey from Mecca to Calvary, he continued to work for many years with Christian churches in Nigeria.

During Garba's journey from Mecca to Calvary, he read the Bible and saw descriptions of the miraculous events involving the Jewish and Christian prophets. He also read the gospel accounts of Jesus Christ and the descriptions of many, many miracles conducted by His hand. As described in this chapter, these miraculous events were done to verify God's messages in Jesus Christ and His prophets. But God provided even more compelling evidence to demonstrate the truth of the Bible. This chapter describes how God used Jewish and Christian prophets to endorse or confirm each other's messages. Jesus confirmed Moses' and David's books to be God's message, Peter confirmed Paul's books to be God's message, and John the Baptist testified that Jesus' ministry was from God. During the progressive revelation of the Bible, God included statements where the prophets confirm one another's ministries. This aspect of the Biblical message – along with the miraculous events – allows us to have confidence in the words of the Bible. We can be assured that it is the truth.

Confirmation of Jesus Christ's Ministry

As the unique Savior of mankind, Jesus Christ had the most important commission and ministry from God. A striking endorsement of Jesus Christ's teaching came directly from Heaven. God the Father declared that Jesus Christ was approved by Him and that we are required to listen to Christ's messages. The words and teachings of Jesus Christ were "certified" as authentic Divine revelation by several powerful lines of evidence. This includes the ministry of John the Baptist, the "mount of transfiguration," the lifetime of miracles and good works of Jesus Christ, and His resurrection from the dead. There are other important evidences to support Christ's message as the Word of God (such as fulfilled prophecies), but these were discussed in previous chapters. As a Muslim, one should consider whether Muhammad is able to offer similar credentials and evidences for his role as the pre-eminent of all prophets.

The witness of John the Baptist

Most Christian theologians believe that Jesus Christ began His public ministry at about 30 years of age. Just before the start of Christ's ministry in the nation of

Israel, a man called "John the Baptist" began preaching a message to the Jews. The ministry of John the Baptist was predicted in the Jewish Scriptures by the prophet Isaiah (Isaiah 40:3), more than 800 years earlier. Not to be confused with the Apostle John (author of the Gospel of John and the books of 1st John, 2nd John, and 3rd John), John the Baptist wrote no books of Scripture. His single purpose was to announce the arrival of Israel's Messiah, Jesus Christ. All four Gospel accounts describe the ministry of John the Baptist and there is perfect agreement between all four writers. He began his ministry by preaching and baptizing Jewish followers in the Jordan River.

Jewish religious leaders inquired of John the Baptist and asked him, who are you and why are you baptizing people? John states that he was sent to prepare a way or path for the Lord (John 1:23) and that God instructed him to watch for a particular sign as he baptized people. The God of Heaven told John: Israel's Messiah would be the one "upon whom you see the Spirit descending, and remaining on Him." John testified to the Jewish people that the Holy Spirit (in the form of a dove) came to rest upon Jesus Christ (John 1:32,33).

Importantly, John the Baptist did not know the identity of Israel's Messiah before beginning his ministry (John 1:31). His sole purpose was to identify Him "to Israel." By not knowing the identity of the Messiah, this rules out the possibility that John's witness was based on fraud or conspiracy. He did not have some prior agreement with Jesus (i.e., to promote Jesus as Messiah). John's witness and testimony was based entirely on the sign from Heaven. From John the Baptist's observations, he concluded (John 1:34,36) that Jesus Christ was the "Son of God" and the "Lamb of God." The first title connects Jesus Christ to His role as Israel's Messiah and it also speaks to the Divine nature of Christ. The second title addresses the work of Jesus Christ as redeemer and His future work on the cross.

John the Baptist eventually was arrested and put to death (beheaded). According to the Biblical accounts, King Herod of Israel had taken a relative's wife as his own. John the Baptist had proclaimed that this was against the Law of Moses, and therefore, it was a sin. Herod had John arrested and he was killed a short time later. It is important to note the reason for John's arrest. He was not arrested for misleading the Jews regarding the arrival of the Savior, nor was he jailed for some other unrighteous act. He was jailed for his comment regarding the immoral behavior of the king.

The God of Heaven provided us with many pieces of evidence to show us that Jesus Christ is the Son of God and that His message comes directly from Heaven. Among these pieces of evidence, there is John the Baptist. God sent this man to be a witness and to provide testimony regarding the arrival of Jesus Christ. This testimony also confirms the truth of the Bible and the messages about Jesus Christ.

The glory of Jesus Christ witnessed

Another spectacular event demonstrated that Jesus Christ came from God, and moreover, showed that we should believe His message. The event is generally called the "transfiguration" and it occurred on the "mount of transfiguration." The transfiguration occurred prior to His death on the cross and His resurrection. Importantly, it was an event that was witnessed by the Apostles Peter, James, and John.

Following their ascension to the top of a hill, Jesus was transformed to reveal the stunning glory of Christ's Deity, described as shining forth with a brilliant light. Two ancient Jewish prophets - Moses and Elijah - also appeared on the mount of transfiguration and they spoke with the glorified Jesus Christ. As described in Luke 9:35, a cloud then descended from Heaven and "a voice came out of the cloud, saying, "This is My beloved Son. Hear Him!" Similar written accounts are given by both Matthew and Mark. In all three descriptions of this event, the God of Heaven commands the Apostles to hear Him, or listen to the message delivered by Jesus Christ. Would the God of Heaven command the Apostles to listen to Christ's message, if it were not absolute truth? As such, we are also being commanded by the God of Heaven to "hear Him" and listen to the messages given by Jesus Christ. God confirmed the authority of Jesus Christ.

The resurrection of Jesus Christ

There is another event that provides even greater confirmation of the truth in the Christian message: the resurrection of Jesus Christ from the dead. As described in Chapter 4, the resurrection of Jesus Christ demonstrated that God the Father was satisfied with the life of Jesus Christ and His work on the cross.

Just prior to the death of Jesus on the cross, He uttered a word that is translated, "It is finished (John 19:30)." This particular Greek word, τελεω or *teleo*, was used commonly in the ancient marketplace. Merchants said it at the end of a purchase to indicate, "paid in full." With the death of Jesus Christ, our sin debt was in fact "paid in full." The word *teleo* is also a declaration of God's work being completed. Jesus Christ took all of our sin upon Himself and He was judged and punished by God the Father on the cross. He was buried shortly after His death on the cross. According to four independent accounts found in the Bible (Matthew, Mark, Luke, and John), Jesus Christ was raised from the dead by the work of His Father in Heaven. The resurrection of Jesus Christ is also discussed by other New Testament writers, including Paul and Peter. In the book of Romans, the Apostle Paul writes,

...declared to be the Son of God with power according to the Spirit of holiness, by the resurrection from the dead." Romans 1:4

From this passage of Scripture, God and Paul are telling us that the resurrection of Jesus Christ declares that He is the Son of God – a truth that Jesus Christ Himself claimed during His three years of ministry. The resurrection of Jesus Christ is evidence that verifies His claim to be God's Son.

The holy, righteous character of Jesus Christ is also declared by His resurrection. Hundreds of years prior to the arrival of Christ, King David wrote Psalm 16, in which he predicted, "...Nor will You allow Your Holy One to see corruption." It was in the eternal plan of God to send His only Son to die for our sins, and then raise Him from the tomb - alive and without any decay of His physical body. This was witnessed by the Apostles, as Peter testifies (Acts 5:30-32):

> The God of our fathers raised up <u>Jesus</u> whom you murdered by hanging on a tree. Him <u>God has exalted to His right hand to be Prince and Savior,</u> to give repentance to Israel and forgiveness of sins. And we are His witnesses to these things, and so also is the Holy Spirit whom God has given to those who obey Him.

Again, we find that God has "exalted" or glorified Jesus Christ following His resurrection. In other passages of Scripture, it is said that Jesus Christ has been raised and is now seated at God's "right hand." This term describes the position of honor and authority in Heaven. Peter also notes that the Apostles were "witnesses to these things."

The Apostle Paul summarizes the death of Christ and His resurrection in the book of Romans, where we read:

> ...but also for us, to whom God will credit righteousness-for us who believe in him who raised Jesus our Lord from the dead. He was delivered over to death for our sins and was raised to life for our justification. Romans 4:24,25

Jesus Christ died on the cross to pay for our sins and all of our sins were punished in Him. In the last part of the passage, God and Paul tell us that Christ's resurrection is "for our justification." Thus, God has accepted Christ's sacrifice on the cross and we are justified by His cross work. The physical resurrection of Christ can be considered evidence that we are justified (i.e. made just or right in God's judgment) as Christians. The God of Heaven has used the resurrection to demonstrate truth in the Biblical message of Christ.

The miracles by Jesus Christ

In reading the four Gospel accounts, one is immediately struck by the miraculous works done by Jesus Christ and His disciples. It is recognized that the miraculous works or signs were evidence or testimony that God Almighty was working in and through Jesus Christ. The signs confirmed that Jesus Christ was the Son of God and Messiah of Israel. John concludes his eyewitness account by stating (John 20:30-31):

> And truly Jesus did many other signs in the presence of His disciples, which are not written in this book; but these are written that you may believe that Jesus is the Christ, the Son of God, and that believing you may have life in His name.

Later in the New Testament, the Apostle John comments "that which we have seen and heard we declare to you (1 John 1:3)." The writers of the New Testament Scriptures have provided written testimony regarding the events related to Jesus Christ's life, death, and resurrection. This is an important point, because we have multiple eyewitnesses that describe the miracles of Jesus Christ. As mentioned previously, the evidence becomes overwhelming. With multiple eyewitnesses in agreement, we can be confident that the historical accounts are truthful and accurate. All of the writers of the gospel books (Matthew, Mark, Luke, and John) give similar descriptions regarding the miracles of Jesus Christ. These miracles confirmed that Jesus Christ came from God and spoke for God. As He declared to the religious leaders of Israel, "...the works which the Father has given Me to finish--the very works that I do--bear witness of Me, that the Father has sent Me. (John 5:36)."

Jesus Christ Himself conducted many different miracles or signs. His miracles confirmed that His message was from Heaven. Several types of miracles also attest to His position and authority as the Almighty God Himself. For example, three of the historical gospel accounts (Matthew, Mark, and Luke) describe how Jesus Christ calmed a storm on the Sea of Galilee. Jesus and His disciples were in a boat on the sea and a strong storm over took the boat. As the boat was beginning to sink, Jesus yelled out to the storm, "Be still," and the storm was immediately calm. The disciples understood the dangers of being caught in a storm on the open waters of the Sea of Galilee. When Christ calmed the storm with simply His word, they were astonished and afraid, as Mark records (Mark 4:41):

And they feared exceedingly, and said to one another, "Who can this be, that even the wind and the sea obey Him!"

Not only did the forces of nature obey His commands, it was also recorded that Jesus Christ raised several people from the dead. One individual named Lazarus had been dead for several days and he was already buried. When Jesus went to his tomb, there were many people mourning for Lazarus and his family. This group of people witnessed one of Christ's most amazing miracles. Christ commanded that the stone be moved away from the tomb and He yelled out, "Lazarus come forth!" Lazarus walked from the tomb, still bound in burial clothes. When word of this miracle reached the religious leaders in Jerusalem, one commented, "What are we accomplishing?" they asked. "Here is this man performing many signs. If we let him go on like this, everyone will believe in him…(John 11:47,48)." From that point onward, the religious leaders sought to kill both Jesus and Lazarus. Jesus Christ Himself stated the purpose of this extraordinary miracle. Prior to raising Lazarus, Jesus prays God the Father and He concludes by saying, "…that they may believe that You have sent Me." Thus, the miracle was meant to confirm that Christ came from Heaven and His message was directly from God.

The gospel accounts also describe countless events in which Jesus Christ healed people of all varieties of sickness, injuries, and disabilities. Among the recorded healings, He gave sight to the blind, healed withered hands and legs, cured leprosy, stopped chronic bleeding, stopped convulsions or epilepsy, cured deadly fevers, and made the deaf to hear. The writers of the gospel books describe these events as "great multitudes" being healed and it is noted by Luke that he healed "them all." In other words, everyone who came to Christ was healed, regardless of the severity of the illnesses. As described previously (Chapter 8), the Old Testament writers predicted - hundreds of years in advance – that the Messiah would heal people in this manner.

One of the most interesting healings occurred with a man born blind. Jesus and His disciples approached the blind man, Jesus mixed some dirt with spit, and He applied the mud to the man's dysfunctional eyes. After washing his eyes with water, the man was able to see with his own eyes. Christian theologians have noted the similarities between this method of healing and the original creation story in the book of Genesis. In the creation, God is said to have made man out of dirt or the "dust of the ground." In this healing, Christ uses mud to repair a man's body. Although Jesus could have chosen any method to heal the man, the mud was used to point to the Deity of Jesus Christ and His title as Creator. When the healed man was brought to the religious leaders in Jerusalem, he made an interesting statement regarding Jesus Christ. He said to the Jewish leaders,

> "Since the world began it was not heard that any man opened the eyes of one that was born blind. If this man were not of God, he could do nothing." John 9:32,33

This healed man understood the miracle from Jesus Christ. Later in the account, he professes his faith to Jesus and worships Him. Jesus Christ conducted these miracles to show the ancient Jews that He was indeed their long-awaited Savior and King. These great works also serve as evidence for us: Jesus Christ came from Heaven and His message is to be regarded as absolute truth.

This idea is further emphasized in Luke's book of Acts, where the Apostle Peter stands before a large group of Jews on the day of Pentecost (a Jewish feast day). Peter proclaims to them all (Acts 2:22-24),

> "Men of Israel, hear these words: <u>Jesus of Nazareth, a Man approved by God to you by miracles, wonders, and signs which God did through Him in your midst, as you yourselves also know</u> - Him, being delivered by the determined purpose and foreknowledge of God, you have taken by lawless hands, have crucified, and put to death; whom God raised up, having loosed the pains of death, because it was not possible that He should be held by it."

The key word in this passage is "approved," which is the Greek word αποδεικνυμι, or *apodeiknumi*. According to *Vine's Expository Dictionary of New Testament Words*, this word carries with it the idea of "proving by demonstration." Thus, the miracles done by Jesus Christ are to be considered proof that He was Israel's Messiah and He spoke for the God of Heaven. It is also important to notice that none of the Jews argued that, "Christ did no miracles!" or that "The miracles were all fake!" As Peter notes, Christ did the miracles in their midst and the Jews all appeared to have acknowledged this fact. Indeed, Jewish writers and rabbis completed a non-Biblical series of books called the Talmud (part one finished by 200 A.D. and part two finished by 500 A.D.). The Talmud described Jesus Christ as a "false messiah who practiced magic." While the unbelieving Jews clearly reject Jesus Christ as the Messiah of Israel, they do seem to acknowledge His working of miracles.

The Jewish Prophets and Old Testament Scriptures

The writer of the New Testament book of Hebrews makes a clear statement about the source of Old Testament writings (Hebrews 1:1), "God, who at various times and in various ways <u>spoke in time past to the fathers by the prophets</u>." Many of these messages from God were simply proclaimed to the Jews by the prophets. In some cases, God inspired the Jewish prophets to record their messages in written form and these documents became part of Scripture or the Bible. In the book of Romans (chapter 3, verse 2), the Apostle Paul notes that the Jewish nation of Israel was blessed "because to them were committed the oracles of God." Here the word "oracles" is the Greek word *logion*, a word that describes speaking, utterance, or communicating. Thus, the great Christian Apostle is noting in this passage that the old Jewish Scriptures were the result of God communicating through the prophets. Old Testament Biblical Scriptures are God's message to us. It is also important to notice the exclusivity of these revelations – that is to say God was only speaking through the Jewish prophets. Certainly, the pagan religions of the world had their prophets, priests, and holy men, but none of these individuals gave a truthful spiritual message. None of them were speaking or writing on behalf of the true God from Heaven.

Jesus Christ and the Prophets confirm the Old Testament

What evidence is there for the absolute spiritual truth being recorded in the Old Testament Scripture? As described previously, we have seen the miraculous prophecies contained in the Old Testament Scriptures. These foretold of the life and ministry of Jesus Christ centuries before His arrival. They described the history of the Israel and the Gentile nations thousands of years in advance. These prophecies could only have come from the eternal God in Heaven. Likewise, the Old Testament Scriptures were produced by 30 different writers - over a period of about ten centuries. With the agreement of their messages and writing, we have strong evidence that these Scriptures were produced through the oversight and control of God.

In the Bible, there is further confirmation of its spiritual truth: the different prophets endorse each others writings as inspired by God - or Holy Scripture. For example, Moses wrote the first five books of the Old Testament around 1,400 B.C. Several different writers (prophets) make reference to the writings of Moses as a product of God's inspiration or communication to Him (Table 1).

More significantly, Jesus Christ Himself makes many references to the writings of Moses and He quotes them as texts having the authority of God's message to mankind. For example in a discussion with Jewish leaders (Mark 12), Jesus refers to the books of Moses as Scripture. Why is this important? With Jesus

Table 1. Jewish prophets describing the books of Moses as God's revelation.

Descriptions of Moses' Revelation	Reference	Date of writing
Yes, all Israel has transgressed <u>Your law</u>, and has departed so as not to obey Your voice; therefore the curse and the oath <u>written in the Law of Moses</u> the servant of God have been poured out on us.	Daniel 9:11	600 B.C.
God speaking through Malachi: "Remember the <u>Law of Moses</u>, My servant, which <u>I commanded him</u> in Horeb for all Israel, with the statutes and judgments."	Malachi 4:4	450 B.C.
…this Ezra came up from Babylon; and he was a skilled scribe in <u>the Law of Moses, which the LORD God of Israel had given.</u>	Ezra 7:6	500 B.C.
…the book of the <u>Law of Moses which the LORD had given to Israel.</u>	Nehemiah 8:1	500 B.C.
Speaking of the God of Heaven: "<u>He made known His ways to Moses</u>, His acts to the children of Israel."	Psalm 103:7	1000 B.C.
But take careful heed to do the commandment and the law which Moses the servant of the LORD commanded you, to love the LORD your God, to walk in all His ways, to keep <u>His commandments</u>, to hold fast to Him, and to serve Him with all your heart and with all your soul.	Joshua 22:5	1,400 B.C.

acknowledging the books of Moses, we can be assured that these books of the Old Testament were messages from God. Additionally, the books of Moses are one of the oldest parts of the Bible but Jesus said nothing about them being corrupted or altered by Jewish scribes over the centuries.

Like the writings of Moses, other Old Testament Scriptures were endorsed by Jesus Christ and the Christian prophets. <u>Jesus Christ Himself made reference to - or quoted from - 24 of the 39 Old Testament books. He never questioned their integrity, preservation, or accuracy.</u> For example, Jesus commented on Psalm 110:1, "for David himself said by the Holy Spirit…(Mark 12:36)." Jesus Christ acknowledged that King David – and other Old Testaments writers – were delivering messages from God. On several occasions, Jesus made statements referring to the Law, the Prophets, and the Psalms or writings. While speaking with His Apostles, Jesus said (Luke 24:44),

> "...all things must be fulfilled which were written in the Law of Moses and the Prophets and the Psalms concerning Me."

The Law, Prophets, and Psalms were the three basic groups of Scripture in the Jewish Bible (i.e., the Old Testament). When Jesus makes reference to these three groups of Scripture, He is verifying the entire Old Testament!

The writers of the New Testament quoted from 34 of the 39 books of the Old Testament. Thus, the Christian prophets - such as John, Peter, Paul, and Luke - all endorsed the authority and accuracy of the Old Testament writings from the Jewish prophets. In particular, the Apostle Paul was one of the most well educated men in first-century Israel, and as such, he had perhaps the best knowledge of the Old Testament Scriptures in all of history. Paul never once questioned the integrity or accuracy of the messages from the Jewish prophets. Rather he verified that they are the source of Divine spiritual truth. As Paul wrote in the New Testament,

> "...the Holy Scriptures, which are able to make you wise for salvation through faith which is in Christ Jesus. All Scripture is given by inspiration of God, and is profitable for doctrine, for reproof, for correction, for instruction in righteousness, that the man of God may be complete, thoroughly equipped for every good work." 2 Timothy 3:15-17

In this passage of Scripture, the key word is "inspiration" and the original Greek word is rendered, τηεοπνευστοσ or *theopneustos*. This word literally means: "God breathed." This indicates that the Bible came about by God "breathing" in and through the writers of Scripture. The Greek word *theopneustos* carries with it a meaning similar to the Hebrew word found in the creation account described by Moses. Just as God breathed life into the man's body in the creation, so also God breathed life into the production of the Bible. As we find described in several places, only the Bible has a message that is capable of giving spiritual life to men and women.

The miracles of the Jewish prophets

In the Old Testament book of Exodus, Moses describes how the Jewish people were brought out of Egyptian slavery and eventually into the land of Canaan. God first appeared to Moses and told him to go into Egypt to free "His people" - the Jews. But Moses said to God (Exodus 4:1), "suppose they will not believe me or listen to my voice; suppose they say, 'The LORD has not appeared to you.'" With this concern, God promised to empower Moses to carry out signs or miracles before the Egyptian Pharaoh and the Jewish people. These were meant to be evidence for the divine mission of Moses. He was carrying a shepherd's staff and God said to Moses (Exodus 4:17), "And you shall take the rod in your hand, with which you shall do the signs."

These signs included turning the Nile River into blood and sending swarms of locusts/flies/frogs across Egypt. The signs also involved God sending illnesses upon the livestock and people of Egypt – all done in judgment of that nation. Since Pharaoh still refused to let the Jews have their freedom, God instructed Moses to raise his shepherd's staff and this caused a tremendous hailstorm. Egyptian people and livestock perished from the hail. Finally, the Lord God sent the Passover judgment – a final plague in which many Egyptians died. With this last devastating judgment and sign, the Pharaoh and his nation allowed the Jews to leave. They believed the message of Moses on the basis of the sings, miracles, and plagues that Moses accomplished by the power of God. In a similar respect, we can look to these miracles as evidence for the truth of Moses' books and messages.

Other Jewish prophets had similar confirmation of their messages. For example, the prophet Daniel authored the Old Testament book that bears his name. We have already seen that his messages contained stunning prophecies about the futures of Gentile nations. This alone should be confirmation that Daniel's writings were inspired by God. But Daniel was also involved in miraculous events to further support his divine mission, including having knowledge of King Nebuchadnezzar's dreams and surviving a night in a den filled with lions (Daniel 2 and 6). Likewise, the Jewish leader and prophet Joshua had a ministry and message confirmed by miracles of the Lord. God empowered him with a miraculous stopping of the Jordan River (Joshua 3:16), the outward collapse of the defensive walls around Jericho (Joshua 6:20), and the sun not move in the sky for a day (i.e., the Earth stopped its axial rotation; Joshua 10:13). As stated clearly in the book of Joshua (Joshua 6:27), these miraculous events demonstrated "the Lord was with Joshua."

The Christian Prophets and New Testament Scriptures
The death, burial, and resurrection of Jesus Christ had been planned by God in eternity past. It was the only means by which mankind could be saved from sin, judgment, and condemnation. It was predicted throughout the Old Testament Scriptures. Moreover, Jesus even told His first century followers that He would be

crucified and raised from the dead. Following these events, the Christian prophets wrote the books of the New Testament. These Christian prophets – eight different men - wrote the historical records in the four gospel books and they described the spiritual results that came from the crucifixion of Jesus Christ. The New Testament revealed the gospel: Jesus Christ died for our sins and God offers salvation to all mankind based on this sacrifice of the Savior. Like the Old Testament messages, the New Testament Scriptures are shown to be reliable spiritual truth based on the testimony of Jesus Christ and the testimonies of the Christian prophets/Apostles/disciples. The truth of their message also finds evidence in the miracles accomplished by the Christian prophets.

Jesus Christ and the Prophets confirm the New Testament

Shortly before giving His life on the cross, Jesus Christ prayed for His Apostles (John 17:20), "My prayer is not for them alone (the Apostles). I pray also for those who will believe in Me through their message." In this prayer, Jesus Christ was looking centuries ahead to the days when men and women would believe "their message" - that is the messages of the Christian prophets in the New Testament of the Bible. Through this prayer, Jesus Christ was endorsing the (still future) writings of the New Testament Scriptures.

Jesus further points to the truth of the gospel during one of His teaching sessions. Jesus told His followers (John 8:31-32), "If you abide in My word, you are My disciples indeed. And you shall know the truth, and the truth shall make you free." The "words" of Jesus are recorded in the New Testament of the Bible. By abiding in (or believing) the messages of Jesus, we are made free of the enslavement and penalties of sin. It should be emphasized that Jesus Christ knew His messages would be recorded and preserved in written form. In this He declared (Matthew 24:35), "Heaven and earth will pass away, but My words will by no means pass away." These statements reveal His confidence in the New Testament Scriptures - their preservation and quality as absolute truth.

Based on the quotes from Jesus Christ, He clearly endorsed the New Testament Scriptures in the Bible - even though the books had yet to be written. Christian prophets also verified that the New Testament books were accurate messages from God. For example, the Apostle Paul was given the task of revealing spiritual truths related to salvation in Jesus Christ. He wrote thirteen books of the New Testament. The Apostle Peter endorsed Paul's books and he encouraged his Jewish students to learn from Paul's letters (see, 2 Peter 3:15,16). Most importantly, Peter refers to Paul's letters as Holy Scripture (i.e., God's revealed message). In a similar respect, the Apostle Paul quotes a passage from the book of

Luke (Luke 10:7). Paul refers to this text as "Scripture" (see, 1 Tim 5:18). Thus, Paul is endorsing Luke's writings as the Scripture (i.e., God's revealed message).

As noted previously, Paul and Peter were inspired to communicate their messages from God at about the same time. Both men were martyred for their faith in Christ. A critic might argue that the two men were conspiring together - with Peter secretly agreeing to endorse Paul's letter for some dishonest intent. This argument was anticipated by God when He inspired Peter to write his letters in the Bible. Peter was moved by God to explain exactly how Biblical revelation occurred:

> "For we did not follow cunningly devised fables when we made known to you the power and coming of our Lord Jesus Christ, but were eyewitnesses of His majesty." 2 Peter 1:16

> "...knowing this first, that no prophecy of Scripture is of any private interpretation, for prophecy never came by the will of man, but holy men of God spoke as they were moved by the Holy Spirit." 2 Peter 1:20,21

Two important points are made by the Apostle in these passages. First, he addresses the critic's charge that they were "making this up" or that the Bible was the result of some grand conspiracy among the early Christians and the writers of the Bible. It seems particularly unlikely that these men would fabricate or "make up" the doctrines and stories in the New Testament. Most of the Apostles suffered violent deaths because of their testimonies for Jesus Christ. While men may give their lives for something they believe to be truthful, they will not give their lives for something they know to be false![2] Secondly, Peter describes exactly how the messages arrived on the pages of the Bible. He notes that the writers of Scripture were moved by God, or more precisely inspired by God the Holy Spirit. Thus, we can have utmost confidence in the New Testament Scriptures. They have been confirmed by the testimonies of Jesus Christ Himself and His prophets whom He inspired.

The miracles of the Christian prophets
Like the Old Testament prophets, writers of the New Testament also had their ministries confirmed by miraculous events. For example, the historical record of the Acts of the Apostles (written by Luke) describes how the Apostle Peter healed a man who had been paralyzed for 40 years. The healing occurred while Peter and

John approached the ancient Jewish temple. As recorded in the third chapter of the book of Acts, it reads:

> One day Peter and John were going up to the temple at the time of prayer—at three in the afternoon. Now a man who was lame from birth was being carried to the temple gate called Beautiful, where he was put every day to beg from those going into the temple courts.

> When he saw Peter and John about to enter, he asked them for money. Peter looked straight at him, as did John. Then Peter said, "Look at us!"

> So the man gave them his attention, expecting to get something from them. Then Peter said, "Silver or gold I do not have, but what I do have I give you. In the name of Jesus Christ of Nazareth, walk."

> Taking him by the right hand, he helped him up, and instantly the man's feet and ankles became strong. He jumped to his feet and began to walk. Then he went with them into the temple courts, walking and jumping, and praising God.

> When all the people saw him walking and praising God, they recognized him as the same man who used to sit begging at the temple gate called Beautiful, and they were filled with wonder and amazement at what had happened to him. While the man held on to Peter and John, all the people were astonished and came running to them in the place called Solomon's Colonnade.

> When Peter saw this, he said to them: "Fellow Israelites, why does this surprise you? Why do you stare at us as if by our own power or godliness we had made this man walk? The God of Abraham, Isaac and Jacob, the God of our fathers, has glorified his servant Jesus...you handed him over to be killed...but God raised him from the dead. We are witnesses of this. By faith in the name of Jesus, this man whom you see and know was made strong. It is Jesus' name and the faith that comes through Him that has completely healed him, as you can all see." Acts 3:1-16

It is important to note several aspects in this event of healing. Firstly, God carried out this healing to further verify that Jesus Christ is the long-awaited Messiah of Israel. The two Apostles also do not claim to have done the work of healing based on their own power. Secondly, there were apparently a large number of people around the Temple who witnessed the healing or saw the healed man. Thirdly, the miracle is presented as evidence from God Almighty that Peter and John were "witnesses" to all the events related to Jesus Christ. The miracle may be considered evidence for the authority of the messages of the Apostles and their books of Scripture. Notably, this account was not written by either Peter or John, but by a third person – the historian Luke.

As a consequence of Peter's preaching and the healing, many people believed that Jesus was the Savior. This prompted the religious leaders of Israel to arrest Peter and John and they were brought before a group of "rulers, elders, and scribes" of the nation of Israel. As we read further in this account,

> And when they had set them in the midst, they asked, "By what power or by what name have you done this?"

> Then Peter, filled with the Holy Spirit, said to them, "Rulers of the people and elders of Israel: If we this day are judged for a good deed done to a helpless man, by what means he has been made well, let it be known to you all, and to all the people of Israel, that by the name of Jesus Christ of Nazareth, whom you crucified, whom God raised from the dead, by Him this man stands here before you whole...Nor is there salvation in any other, for there is no other name under heaven given among men by which we must be saved."

> Now when they saw the boldness of Peter and John, and perceived that they were uneducated and untrained men, they marveled. And they realized that they had been with Jesus. And seeing the man who had been healed standing with them, they could say nothing against it. Acts 4:7-14

The Apostle Peter was an uneducated man (a fisherman by trade), so the Jewish leaders were amazed by his forceful speech. They were also directly confronted by clear evidence of a real miracle, as the healed man stood next the two Apostles. According to the text, Peter was "filled with the Holy Spirit" which indicates that his very words were being directed by God Almighty. He testified before the Jewish leaders that the healing of the "helpless man" occurred through the power of Jesus Christ. The miracle was meant to be sign to the Jews, that Jesus was the Messiah. Consequently, it was to support the message given by His Apostles, including the death, burial, and resurrection of Jesus Christ. This includes the gospel message of salvation in Jesus Christ.

The Apostles later prayed (Acts 4:29-30), "...grant to Your servants (the Apostles) that with all boldness they may speak Your word, by stretching out Your hand to heal, and that signs and wonders may be done through the name of Your holy Servant Jesus." These Apostles taught the message of Jesus Christ, to them were brought "multitudes" of sick people, and moreover "they were all healed. (Acts 5:16)." Again, the signs of healing were to demonstrate to the first century Jews that Jesus Christ was their Messiah and the Apostles were conveying spiritual truth.

Likewise, the Apostle Paul had his ministry confirmed by several miracles. As described in briefly in Chapter 2, Paul was known as Saul of Tarsus prior to his conversion to Christianity. He was greatly feared by the early Christian churches, as he led the persecution of Christians in his day. By his own account, he arrested these men and women and then voted for their deaths (Acts 26:10). Not only was Saul a leader in the persecution of the early Christian church, but according to Biblical accounts, he was also a prominent, well-respected, and highly educated Jew. He was a member of the Pharisees, perhaps the most fervent religious group in ancient Judaism. How did Saul go from being a prominent member of the Jewish elite to become the Apostle Paul, leader of the Christian church and author of a large part of the New Testament? His miraculous conversion is described in several places in the Bible. The most detailed account appears in the book of Acts, a book of the Bible written not by Paul, but instead by the historian Luke.

Following the stoning death of the Stephen (an early Christian), Saul obtained papers giving him authority to arrest Christians in nearby Damascus, bind them, and bring these people back to Jerusalem for punishment. However, his journey was interrupted by a visit from the risen Jesus Christ (Acts 9:1-31). A brilliant light "shined around him from Heaven" and Saul fell to the ground. A voice from Heaven said to him, "Saul, Saul, why are you persecuting Me?" When Saul asked, "Who are You, Lord?" The voice from Heaven responded, "I am Jesus, whom you are persecuting." After this encounter with the risen Christ, Saul lost his eyesight and consequently, he had to be led by the hand into Damascus.

How can we know that Saul really heard a message from the risen Jesus Christ? Skeptics have suggested that Saul probably just had some kind of heat stroke, so how do we know that this was a legitimate supernatural event? Unlike most people who have claimed to "hear voices," Saul's experience involved other people, it involved an event of physical healing, and it involved a dramatic change in this man's spiritual life.

As we read further into Luke's account of the events, a man named Ananias is given a dream or a vision from Jesus Christ. He is told by Christ to visit a particular house in Damascus and that he should heal Saul of Tarsus of his blindness. The Lord tells Ananias to find Saul (Acts 9:14):

> But the Lord said to him (Ananias), "Go, for he (Saul) is a chosen vessel of Mine to bear My name before Gentiles, kings, and the children of Israel.

Ananias locates Saul, and by Ananias "laying his hands on him," Saul was healed and received his eyesight. Most notably, Jesus Christ spoke to Ananias and endorsed the future ministry of Saul (later known as Paul the Apostle to the Gentiles). Paul's message and ministry is then further confirmed by his healing at the hands of Ananias.

The involvement of Ananias is important as evidence for the supernatural, miraculous conversion of Saul. Anyone can claim to "hear voices" or "speak with angels," but in Paul's case it also involved a simultaneous vision by a second person. Moreover, Ananias was skeptical and cautious, as Saul was leading the persecution of first century Christians. This makes it unlikely that Ananias was conspiring with Saul. Paul's encounter with the risen Lord Jesus Christ is further supported by the testimony of another early Christian, a man named Barnabas. When Paul tried to join the group of Christians remaining in Jerusalem, they would not accept him. However Barnabas said to the fearful and skeptical group of Christians in Jerusalem that Paul "had seen the Lord on the road, and that He had spoken to him, and how he had preached boldly at Damascus in the name of Jesus (Acts 9:27)."

In the following years, Saul of Tarsus would become the Apostle Paul. It was by this man that God revealed the greatest measure of Christian theology. Through the inspiration of the Holy Spirit, Paul eventually wrote 13 books of the Bible, more than any other ancient prophet. Paul is also thought to be the anonymous writer of the New Testament book of Hebrews. It is from Paul's revelations that we learn about the grace of God, a term describing how God loves us unconditionally.

God and Paul tell us how the love of God was expressed at the cross. God loved you and I so much, that He sent His only Son to the cross to die for us. Our sins were nailed to the cross with Christ and they were punished accordingly in His death. Paul's books go further to describe how a person can be saved from their sins. "Believe on the Lord Jesus Christ" and you will be saved, as Paul told his jailer in Phillipi (Acts 16:31). It was through this man that God would reveal and describe the full implications of Christ's death on the cross. Paul delivered these vital messages to us and they are described in more detail in Chapter 13.

In the end, the Apostle Paul was martyred for his faith and ministry to the early Christians. His lifetime of ministry can be followed through several of his books and the book of Acts. According to the description in 2 Corinthians 11:22-27, Paul was frequently in prison for his testimony about Christ, he was given 39 lashes with a whip on five occasions (men often died from a single whipping), he was beaten with rods three times, he was attacked with stones and left for dead once, and he suffered from lack food, shelter, and clothing. Despite these vicious attacks by Satan and his workers, Paul preached the good news of Christ throughout much of the civilized world. He established many local churches or assemblies of Christian believers, and of course, God also used this man to produce much of the New Testament Scriptures.

Like Moses and Christ before him, Paul's ministry was confirmed by a number of notable miracles. The miraculous healings at the hands of Paul are considered verification that God was working through this man. For example, we read about Paul and Barnabas traveling through Iconium (modern day Turkey) and teaching about Jesus Christ. Evidently, there were many miracles done during their ministry (Acts 14:3):

> Therefore they stayed there a long time, speaking boldly in the Lord, <u>who was bearing witness to the word of His grace</u>, granting signs and wonders to be done by their hands.

The key passage in this verse is, "who was bearing witness to the word of His grace," which indicates the purpose of these miracles (signs and wonders). The Lord Jesus Christ was granting that these signs be done to certify that Paul was speaking the truth of God. Paul and Barnabas were forced to flee Iconium and then traveled to Lystra (also in modern day Turkey). We find a more detailed description of the types of "signs and wonders" which were administered by God through these men (Acts 14:8-10):

> … a certain man without strength in his feet was sitting, a cripple from his mother's womb, who had never walked. This man heard Paul speaking. Paul, observing him intently and seeing that he had faith to be healed, said with a loud voice, "Stand up straight on your feet!" And he leaped and walked.

Later in Paul's ministry, he labored for about two years in the town called Ephesus preaching the good news of Jesus Christ. In Acts 19:10, we read of Paul's ministry, "...all who dwelt in Asia heard the word of the Lord Jesus, both Jews and Greeks." The author of Acts (Luke) continues to describe how "God worked unusual miracles by the hands of Paul, so that even handkerchiefs or aprons were brought from his body to the sick, and the diseases left them (Acts 19:11-12)." From these various accounts, two important points are made clear: Paul did miracles by the hand of God and the miracles or signs were meant to "bear witness" to the truth of Paul's message. This concept is further emphasized by the writer of Hebrews, where we read:

> ...how shall we escape if we ignore so great a salvation? This salvation, which was first announced by the Lord, was confirmed to us by those who heard him. God also testified to it by signs, wonders and various miracles, and by gifts of the Holy Spirit distributed according to his will. (Hebrews 2:3,4)

The offer of eternal life and salvation of our souls is made to everyone, and in this passage, God declares plainly that this message was proclaimed by Jesus Christ and by His Apostles. The message - Christian salvation - was confirmed by God with many miracles, signs, and wonders.

Other Apostles conducted miraculous healing in support of the gospel of Jesus Christ. Prior to the crucifixion, Jesus sent His twelve Apostles out to preach His message and empowered them to cast out demons and heal the sick. According to Mark's gospel (Mark 6:13), they healed many people of illnesses. This miraculous power continued after the death, burial, and resurrection of Jesus. For example, the Apostle Philip brought the good news of Jesus Christ to the land of Samaria (northern Israel) and Philip's message was confirmed by miraculous events. These were astonishing feats of healing - as noted by Luke (Acts 8:7), "...many who were paralyzed and lame were healed." This type of paralysis must have included spinal cord injuries, disfigured limbs, and other severe wounds. But through the power of God, these people were healed. These miraculous healings were meant to demonstrate that the Apostles of Jesus Christ were giving truthful spiritual messages. These messages were recorded by the Apostles in the books of the New Testament.

Islam and Its Sacred Writings

For the man or woman standing in Mecca, the testimonies and miracles described above pose a considerable problem. Firstly, there were no Islamic doctrines or theology in the original Jewish or Christian Scriptures. It has already been shown that the Old and New Testament books of the Bible have been very well-preserved through the ages. This is also evident from several Bible verses, for example, the Prophet Isaiah's Scripture (written in 800 B.C.) where he states, "...the word of our God stands forever (Isaiah 40:8)." Thus, the testimonies and miracles are demonstrating the truth of these Scriptures, even though there is a glaring absence of Islamic doctrines!

Upon inspection of the Quran and hadith, one finds many "Islamic" quotes by Jesus and the other prophets. These have never been present in the pages of Hebrew and Christian Scriptures. Rather, these statements and doctrines suddenly appeared with the rise of Islam in the period of 600-800 A.D. As described in previous chapters, these "quotes" from Jesus and the prophets - found in the Quran - often contradict the long-standing messages found in the Bible. So the man or woman standing in Mecca must again decide: which is the reliable message and what book has the credentials or character of divine revelation?

It must also be noted that none of the Jewish or Christian prophets or Apostles wrote passages of Scripture that verify or endorse the Quran as being part of God's revealed message, and no part of the ancient Scriptures predicted the arrival of an entirely new religious doctrine in the distant future. The all-knowing (omniscient) God of Heaven would have certainly been able to predict, and indeed know, if a new and different type of revelation would come six centuries after Jesus Christ out of the Arabian Peninsula. In such a case, God would have placed many prophecies in the Scripture regarding the arrival of the "greatest Prophet" and God would have endorsed Muhammad's teachings through other writers of Scripture (earlier Prophets). Moreover, if Muhammad is the pre-eminent of all prophets, then why did God send John the Baptist to announce the arrival of Jesus Christ? Why didn't God announce the arrival of Muhammad with a man preaching and "preparing the way" for Muhammad?

Finally, we have seen that Jesus Christ and His Apostles conducted spectacular miracles to prove their messages came from God, as did the ancient Jewish Prophets. Did Muhammad carry out similar miraculous feats? Did he raise anyone from the dead, cause storms to cease, heal blind or paralyzed men? No. If Muhammad is the greatest Prophet from God, then why didn't he perform at least as many miracles as Jesus Christ? If the God of Heaven showed His "approval" of Jesus Christ with "miracles, wonders, and signs," then why did not God also show approval of Muhammad with these demonstrations? These are indeed difficult questions. With careful consideration, they should lead one to turn from Mecca towards Calvary.

References

(1)   Based on the published testimony of Garba Adamu. Downloaded on April 7, 2011. See: http://www.answering-islam.org/Testimonies/garba.html

(2)   Lee Strobel, *The Case for Christ*, Zondervan, Grand Rapids, MI, 1998; p. 184.

Chapter 12

The Deity of Jesus Christ

I was watching in the night visions, and behold, One like the Son of Man, coming with the clouds of heaven! He came to the Ancient of Days, and they brought Him near before Him. Daniel 7:13

Sara was born in the capital city of Iran.[1] Her parents were Shiite Muslims and she was raised in this faith. Her father did work for the United States military, so he frequently travelled to the United States. She described her father as "a very devout Muslim who loved to please God."[1] He cared for his daughter Sara and he wanted her to have the best possible education, so he sent her to the United States.

As a teenager in the United States, Sara was far more conservative than her high school peers. Although she had casual friendships with guys in high school, she never dated. This was in contrast to the non-Muslim girls, who were often quite promiscuous and immoral. She attended a college in United States, as she hoped to be a medical doctor.

During her college years, she began dating a young man named Alex. He was not a Muslim, but he was a kind-hearted guy that reminded Sara of her father. After dating for about 4 months, they fell deeply in love with each other and they decided to get married. Sara made it very clear: although she was a nominal Muslim, she would always follow this faith. Alex had been raised a Catholic but he no longer practiced the faith, so he was perfectly fine with Sara's commitment to remain a Muslim. Sara's parents were initially upset that she married someone who was not a practicing Muslim. But after meeting her young husband, they were impressed by him and welcomed him into their family. Of course, Sara's father made it his goal to convert Alex to the Islamic faith!

Several years later, Sara's husband was transferred with his military unit. Since Sara was still in college, they were separated for this period of time. Sara was still in the United States while her husband lived far away in Asia. It was during this time that both Sara and Alex began developing friendships and working relationships with Christians.

Sara met a young woman named Mary in one of her college classes. They became close friends. Mary had recently learned about Jesus Christ and joined an evangelical church. Mary was very supportive of Sara during this time and she was a friend that truly cared for Sara. Sometimes Mary read interesting Bible passages to Sara, but there was never any "high-pressure sales pitch" to become a Christian.[1] About the same time, Alex had learned more about Christianity. He wrote a letter to Sara describing his own journey towards faith in Jesus Christ. He had undergone a "born again" experience and he was even baptized.

Sara's husband came home on a military leave to attend Sara's college graduation and spend time with her. She noticed that he was a different man. He was "very much at ease" and he seemed to have a great peace within him.[1] Alex was also caring and confident. In his love for Sara, he appealed to her to "know God through Jesus Christ."[1] She was a little annoyed by this request and Sara reminded him about her commitment to remain a Muslim, "...until I die," she said.[1] Alex prayed for his wife. But he also suggested that she should be more committed to Islam, if this was indeed her choice for life.

Soon Sara and her husband were able to settle down into a home. She prayed more frequently and studied her Quran. She began searching for the same spiritual peace that her husband knew. At the time she thought, since "we worshipped the same God, He must offer the same benefits in Islam as He has done in Christianity."[1]

Sara began her first job out of college and one of her new co-workers was another "born again" Christian. "How can I get away from these people?" she thought.[1] In God's sovereignty however, this was His way of reaching Sara with His truth. She immediately noticed the kindness of this fellow. He would offer his help in projects at work and always be ready with assistance if Sara needed it. Just like her husband Alex and her college friend Mary, Sara noticed a great peace in this man's spirit. She prayed, "Allah, show me how I can be like them in Islam."[1]

The struggle in her heart intensified. She read the entire Quran, but she could not find any similarities between the Christian and Islamic faiths. There was a stark contrast between the two faiths; the God was clearly different in each faith, and even the results of each faith seemed to differ. She started to see serious problems with Islam, including "hate, judgment, wrath, lies, (the) ungodly life of the prophet, etc."[1] But she also had problems with Christian doctrines. Sara did not feel as though she needed a Savior or that God's Savior was Jesus Christ. Most of all, she did not accept that Jesus Christ was God Himself! She concluded that this was blasphemy and it was so creepy that it literally "made the hair on her back stand straight."[1] She prayed every night that God would somehow reveal the truth to her.

Despite her problems with Christian doctrines, Sara and her husband attended Christian church together. They were friends with the pastor of the church and other married couples. On one occasion, Sara's husband was away on a trip. She went to church by herself on that day. Although she had been attending the church for months, she never participated in the worship and she was not open to the Christian messages. During the church service, Sara found herself singing the famous old hymn, *Amazing Grace.* She was shocked to hear the words coming from her mouth and she stopped singing in the middle of the hymn.

Then it happened. The hand of God reached into her spirit and she believed. She awoke the next morning and she knew the truth. She told her husband, "I believed Jesus to be God himself, and that I needed Him to forgive me for my sins, and become my Savior."[1] Her husband was in total shock. He began crying out for joy. Sara finished the journey from Mecca to Calvary on that day. With great happiness, she also became a born-again Christian.

Although her father had already died, Sara shared her new faith with her mother and brother. Even though her mother was a non-practicing Muslim, she took the news badly. The family "turned against" her and treated Sara as if she had died.[1] Nevertheless, Sara had a new family now. This family included the Father of Jesus Christ, and moreover, God had "surrounded my life with many sisters and brothers" in Christian fellowship.[1]

Like many former Muslims, Sara struggled with the doctrine known as the deity of Jesus Christ. This Bible message reveals that Jesus Christ is co-equal with God the Father and God the Holy Spirit. Sometimes referred to as the Trinity, this topic was thoroughly treated in Chapter 10. In this chapter, we will specifically examine the deity of Jesus Christ. It will be shown that Jesus Christ Himself made unmistakable claims to be the eternal God of Heaven. It will also be shown that Jesus Christ was given the same names of God from the Old Testament Scriptures and He had the same attributes as God. Moreover, it will be shown that Jesus Christ did things in accord with Him being the very Son of God – such as, accepting the worship of men and the forgiving of sins.

What did Jesus Christ claim about Himself?

According to Islamic apologists, Jesus Christ never claimed to be God.[2] While this may be true of the "Jesus" described in the Quran, it is not true of the individual described in the Bible. Upon inspection of the New Testament gospel books, one finds very clear statements by Jesus Christ where He claims to be the same as the God of the Old Testament Scriptures. For example, in an exchange with the Jewish religious leaders (John 10:30-33), Jesus said, "I and My Father are one." After making this statement, the Jews picked up stones to throw at Him and Jesus said, "Many good works I have shown you from My Father. For which of those works do you stone Me?" The Jews answered Him, saying, "For a good work we do not stone You, but for blasphemy, and because You, being a Man, make Yourself God." The Jewish leaders correctly understood Jesus Christ's statement – He claimed to be the same as God.

Important concepts in the Bible are often repeated. After the resurrection of Jesus Christ, one of His Apostles (Philip) asked Jesus (John 14:9), "show us the Father." To this request Jesus Christ answered, "Have I been with you so long, and yet you have not known Me, Philip? He who has seen Me has seen the Father; so how can you say, 'Show us the Father'?" In both of the above Bible passages, Jesus Christ explicitly claimed to be equal with God the Father.

Likewise, Jesus Christ takes the name that God gave Moses – the name "I AM." When God first spoke to Moses and sent him to rescue Israel from Egyptian slavery, Moses asked God for His name (Exodus 3:13). The God of Heaven said (Exodus 3:14), "I AM WHO I AM." And He said, "Thus you shall say to the children of Israel, 'I AM has sent me (Moses) to you.' " About 1,400 years later, Jesus Christ began His ministry in Israel. During one encounter with the Jewish leaders, Jesus told the Jews that Abraham "rejoiced" over Jesus Christ. Abraham lived about 2,000 year earlier, so the Jewish leaders asked Jesus (John 8:57), "You are not yet fifty years old, and have you seen Abraham?" To this question Jesus said to them (John 8:58), "Most assuredly, I say to you, before Abraham was, I AM." In this statement by Jesus Christ, He is taking the exact name of Him who spoke to Moses – that is the God of Abraham, Isaac, and Jacob. This claim prompted the Jewish authorities to pick up stones in order to put Jesus Christ to death. They sought to stone Jesus Christ to death because He was claiming to be the God of the Old Testament Scriptures!

Names of God in the Old Testament: seen in Jesus Christ

Speaking to the nation of Israel, Moses declared (Deuteronomy 6:4), "Hear, O Israel: The LORD our God, the LORD is one!" This passage of Scripture is one of the most well-known verses to ancient and modern Jewish people and it is completely consistent with deity of Jesus Christ. There are two words for deity used here: "LORD" comes from the Hebrew word rendered *Jehovah*, while "God" comes from the Hebrew word rendered *Elohiym*. The word *Elohiym* is a frequently used name for God in the ancient Jewish Scriptures, appearing over 2,200 times. Remarkably, this word is the plural form. The use of a plural name is no accident, but rather it points to the Trinity of the Godhead – Father, Son, and Holy Spirit. It should also be noted that other Old Testament passages (see Deuteronomy 4:35 and Psalm 100:3) indicate that *Jehovah* is identified as *Elohiym*.

Throughout the Old Testament Scriptures, the God of Heaven is also called by several compound names, composed of *Jehovah* and *Elohiym*, or *El*. For example, two compound names describe God's tremendous power, *Jehovah Saboath* (LORD of hosts or armies) and *El Shaddai* (Almighty God). There are many other names given to God in the Old Testament Scriptures. As a testimony to the deity of Christ, these same names are either given to Jesus Christ or they are apparent in His death, burial, and resurrection. In one such case, the Jewish prophet Jeremiah described the age in which Israel's Messiah would appear (Jeremiah 23:6), "In His days Judah will be saved, and Israel will dwell safely; now this is His name by which He will be called: THE LORD OUR RIGHTEOUSNESS." In this context, Jeremiah refers to the Messiah as *Jehovah-zidkenu*, which is translated "the LORD our righteousness."

How does God become "our righteousness?" Jesus Christ went to the cross to die for our sins, and the New Testament Scriptures declare that His righteous act (the cross-work) and His righteousness can be "applied" or credited to us. The Apostle Paul wrote of this in Romans 4:3, where it is declared, "...to the man who does not work but trusts God who justifies the wicked, his faith is credited as righteousness." The cross-work of Jesus Christ is the basis of our righteousness. Thus, Jesus Christ is our righteousness. This means that Jesus Christ is the same as the LORD in Jeremiah's passage of Scripture.

In a passage from another Old Testament book (Judges 6:23-24), the God of Heaven is given a title rendered from the Hebrew, *Jehovah-shalom* or the "LORD our peace." This name is a beautiful picture of the deity of Jesus Christ and His work on the cross. As described previously, every man and woman is under the condemnation of sin. We all face the judgment and wrath of God. Sin must be punished. Moreover, our sin is considered to be rebellion and warfare against God Himself. So how can God become "our peace," when we are at war with Him? God the Son became "our peace" when He went to the cross. The punishment for our sins was placed on Christ and God was fully satisfied with this sacrifice. As explained by the Apostle Paul (Romans 5:1), we have "been justified by faith, we have peace with God through our Lord Jesus Christ." Rather than God "seeing" you and I as filthy, unrighteous, rebellious sinners, God "sees" the perfect righteousness of our Savior Jesus Christ. In this regard, we have peace with God. Jesus Christ is our peace, and in this name, we again see His deity.

Attributes of God seen in Jesus Christ

God spoke through the prophet Isaiah, declaring (Isaiah 43:11), "I, even I, am the LORD, and there is no Savior besides Me." About 800 years later, Jesus Christ came and died on the cross to save us from our sins. He is our Savior. Indeed, the Christian Apostle Paul wrote (Titus 2:13,14),

> Looking for that blessed hope, and the glorious appearing of the great God and our Savior Jesus Christ; Who gave himself for us, that He might redeem us from all iniquity..."

226

If Jesus Christ is referred to as the God and Savior in the New Testament, and the LORD (*Jehovah*) is the only savior, then clearly Jesus Christ and *Jehovah* are the same individual. Interestingly, the Apostle Paul refers to Jesus Christ as the "great God and our Savior." Archaeological evidence - inscriptions dating to the time of Christ - have shown that this Greek phrase was used in its day as a declaration of deity.[3] Consequently, the deity of Christ is being proclaimed in this New Testament verse. Also notable from this verse, Paul reminds us that Christ "gave Himself for us" and in doing so, His work would "redeem us from all iniquity." This describes how Jesus Christ serves as the Savior.

The same Old Testament passage also describes God (Isaiah 43:14a), saying, "Thus says the LORD, your Redeemer, The Holy One of Israel..." What did Paul say about Jesus Christ? He said that Christ would "redeem" us from all iniquity. To an approximation, redeem is a word describing a purchase. Jesus Christ purchased you and I when He died on the cross. Payment was made with the precious "blood of the lamb." Thus, the attributes of God – the Savior and Redeemer - are clearly fulfilled in Jesus Christ.

What did the Prophets say?

Both Jewish and Christian prophets were inspired by God to convey the message – Jesus Christ is the Son of God. In the case of Old Testament Jewish prophets, these messages came in the form of predictions regarding future events. About 800 years before the birth of Jesus Christ, the prophet Isaiah made many predictions regarding the birth of Israel's Savior. The passage in Isaiah 9:6 reads:

> For unto us a Child is born, unto us a Son is given; and the government will be upon His shoulder. And His name will be called Wonderful, Counselor, Mighty God, Everlasting Father, Prince of Peace.

Most notably, it is clear from Isaiah's prophecies that the Messiah of Israel was to be more than just another man or prophet. Isaiah clearly states that their Messiah would be born as a Son in Israel and that He would also be the "Mighty God, The Everlasting Father." This prediction was only fulfilled by the person of Jesus Christ - who was born of humanity and also possessed full deity as God the Son. The passage speaks of the government being ruled by Israel's Messiah, however it is understood that this event is still in the future. As described previously, the Father, Son, and Holy Spirit are all co-equal and co-eternal and they are one God. It was God the Son that came here two thousand years ago to die on the cross for our sins. Jesus Christ is the Son, but He is also known as the "Mighty God" and "Everlasting Father." This is consistent with Jesus Christ's own statement where He said (John 10:30), "I and My Father are one."

Likewise, King David recorded a prophecy in Psalm 110:1 describing God, speaking to God and honoring God. The passage reads: The LORD said to my Lord, "Sit at My right hand, until I make Your enemies Your footstool." In this verse, King David describes how the LORD (*Jehovah*) tells David's Lord (*Adonai*) to "sit at My right hand" until the day when His enemies are subdued. The name *Adonai* is another common Hebrew name used for God the Bible. The phrase "sit at My right hand" is in reference to a place of honor and power. This was common in courts of ancient kings. So how is it that God speaks to God? When this Psalm is examined in the light of New Testament Scriptures, it becomes clear that this is a description of God the Father honoring and speaking to God the Son, Jesus Christ.

Prior to His crucifixion, Jesus Christ was put on trial in front of the leaders of Israel and Jewish authorities. At one point, the High Priest asked Him (Luke 22:67), "are you the Christ (i.e., the Messiah)?" As part of His answer, Jesus said (verse 69), "hereafter the Son of Man will sit on the right hand of the power of God." By assuming the title of "Son of Man," Jesus claimed to be the Messiah. As described previously, this was a title or name for the Messiah that was given by the ancient Jewish prophet Daniel (Daniel 7:13). Jesus also states that He would be sitting "on the right hand of the power of God." This part of His answer points directly to King David's prophecy (Psalm 110:1, see above). By sitting at God's "right hand," Jesus Christ claimed to be *Adonai* or the Lord from David's prophecy. This claim to deity lead the Jewish leadership to condemn Jesus Christ to death, where upon He was brought to the Roman leadership for crucifixion. Following His death, burial, and resurrection, Jesus Christ indeed was seated at God's "right hand." This was confirmed by the testimonies of the Christian prophets, Paul and Peter, who described Jesus Christ as being seated in glory at God's "right hand" (see, Ephesians 1:20, Colossians 3:1, Romans 8:34, Peter 3:22).

Further testimony can be found from the Christian prophets and New Testament authors, that Jesus Christ is God. For example, the disciple named Thomas met Jesus Christ shortly after His resurrection (John 20:28). As a result of seeing the resurrected Christ, Thomas declares, "My Lord and my God!" The Apostle Peter began his second book with the phrase (2 Peter 1:1), "...our God and Savior Jesus Christ." This phrase is a clear statement regarding the deity of Jesus Christ. The same phrase is used by the Apostle Paul and it likewise points to Jesus as the Son of God. More significantly, the Apostle Paul describes Jesus Christ in the unmistakable terms of the Creator of the world. In describing Jesus Christ, the Apostle Paul states (Colossians 1:16), "by Him were all things created" and "all things were created through Him and for Him." The Apostle John declared a similar testimony regarding Jesus Christ (John 1:3), "All things were made through Him, and without Him nothing was made that was made." These statements could only be describing the Almighty God and Creator. Yet, they are being made in reference to Jesus Christ.

Only God Could...

As further evidence for the deity of Jesus Christ, one finds that He assumes the responsibilities, duties, and roles that could only be done by God Himself. These include forgiving sins, accepting worship, and receiving prayer. Most significantly, Jesus Christ is found to be the Eternal and Almighty Judge at the great Judgment Day. These things clearly point to Jesus Christ as God.

Forgive Sins

During His ministry in first century Israel, Jesus Christ demonstrated the ability to forgive sins. This is a particularly important point, because it is understood that sins are foremost an offense to God. Therefore, only God Himself could actually forgive men of their sins. The priests of the ancient Jewish religion were never given the authority to forgive sin, but rather they were given sacrificial rituals by which sin could be covered or hidden (by the blood of innocent animals). The ancient Jewish temple provided a place for men and women to pray for forgiveness of sin, but forgiveness was always the result of God's mercy. Forgiveness of sin was always at God's pleasure.

In Mark's gospel account, a fascinating event is described in which Jesus Christ demonstrated His ability to forgive sin. Christ was teaching a group of people in a crowded house or lodging. Four men wished to bring in a paralyzed man for Jesus to heal, but they could not enter the crowded room. The account continues (Mark 2:2-12):

> And when they could not come near Him because of the crowd, they uncovered the roof where He was. So when they had broken through, they let down the bed on which the paralytic was lying. When Jesus saw their faith, He said to the paralytic, "Son, your sins are forgiven you."

> And some of the scribes were sitting there and reasoning in their hearts, "Why does this Man speak blasphemies like this? Who can forgive sins but God alone?"

But immediately, when Jesus perceived in His spirit that they reasoned thus within themselves, He said to them, "Why do you reason about these things in your hearts? Which is easier, to say to the paralytic, 'Your sins are forgiven you,' or to say, 'Arise, take up your bed and walk'? But that you may know that the Son of Man has power on earth to forgive sins," He said to the paralytic, "I say to you, arise, take up your bed, and go to your house."

Immediately he arose, took up the bed, and went out in the presence of them all, so that all were amazed and glorified God, saying, "We never saw anything like this!"

This same event is also recorded in the gospel book written by Luke. In this passage, Jesus calls Himself the "Son of Man" – an unmistakable title of Israel's Messiah (Daniel 7:13,14). Evidently, the crowd of people at this event included scribes, who were some of the most well-educated, religious elite. When Jesus told the man, "your sins are forgiven you," the scribes immediately recognized that Jesus Christ was assuming a role that only God Himself could take: the forgiveness of sin. However, Jesus Christ confirmed His ability to forgive sins by the healing miracle. In other words, the God of Heaven would not have allowed Jesus to heal the man, if Jesus did not have the ability to forgive sins.

Besides the ability to forgive sins, another important aspect of the Deity of Jesus Christ is revealed in this passage. Only God has the ability to see into a person's mind or heart and "read their thoughts" as Jesus Christ does so here. Theologians refer to this as God's omniscient abilities, or His ability to know everything. According to the account of both Mark and Luke, Jesus Christ knew the thoughts of the scribes and directly answered their concerns.

Accept Worship

In the gospel accounts, we find several examples where Jesus Christ accepted the worship from men and women (Matt 2:11; Matt 8:2; Matt 9:18; Matt. 14:33; Matt 15:25; Matt 28:9,17; Mark 5:6; Luke 24:52; John 9:38). If Jesus were simply a prophet from God, then He would not have accepted the worship of these men and women. Rather, He would have exhorted these people to follow the great commandment written by God and Moses (see Luke 4:8 and Matt 4:10), which stated "You shall worship the LORD your God, and Him only you shall serve."

A typical case of Jesus Christ being worshiped is found in Matthew's gospel book. According to Matthew's account, Jesus Christ had just finished delivering His famous "Sermon on the Mount" and He came down from the top of the hill:

When He had come down from the mountain, great multitudes followed Him. And behold, a leper came and worshiped Him, saying, "Lord, if You are willing, You can make me clean." Then Jesus put out His hand and touched him, saying, "I am willing; be cleansed." Immediately his leprosy was cleansed. And Jesus said to him, "See that you tell no one; but go your way, show yourself to the priest, and offer the gift that Moses commanded, as a testimony to them." Matt. 8:1-4

There are two aspects of this passage that are notable. First, the leper came and worshiped Jesus. He was not rebuked or corrected for worshipping Jesus. It appears to be perfectly appropriate for Jesus Christ to be worshiped. Secondly, the leper calls Jesus Christ by His title of "Lord." Again, the man was not corrected for using this term. This particular term is the Greek word κυριοσ, or *kurios*, which is translated 650 times in the New Testament as a title of deity. According to Scofield, it is the Greek equivalent to the Hebrew words *Adonai* and *Jehovah*.[4] Both of these words were used by the Hebrew prophets as terms to describe the God of Heaven in the Old Testament. As a result of this man's faith, he was immediately cleansed of this horrible disease. The miracle also shows that it is appropriate to worship Jesus Christ as Lord!

If Jesus Christ were not God, He would have rejected the worship of men and women. Indeed, both the Christian Apostles Peter and Paul were worshipped by men and they promptly stopped it. Likewise, the Apostle John was overwhelmed by the glory of an angel and he fell down to worship - only to be halted by the angel.

Peter rejects the worship of man, Acts 10:25,26:
As Peter was coming in, Cornelius met him and fell down at his feet and worshiped him. But Peter lifted him up, saying, "Stand up; I myself am also a man."

Paul and Barnabus reject being worshiped as gods, Acts 14:11, 14-15:
Now when the people saw what Paul had done, they raised their voices, saying in the Lycaonian language, "The gods have come down to us in the likeness of men!"

But when the Apostles Barnabas and Paul heard this, they tore their clothes and ran in among the multitude, crying out and saying, "Men, why are you doing these things? We also are men with the same nature as you, and preach to you that you should turn…to the living God, who made the heaven, the earth, the sea, and all things that are in them…"

<u>An angel from Heaven refuses worship from the Apostle John, Revelation 19:9-10a:</u>
(The angel speaking to the Apostle John)....Then he said to me, "Write: 'Blessed are those who are called to the marriage supper of the Lamb!' " And he said to me, "These are the true sayings of God." And I (John) fell at his feet to worship him. But he said to me, "See that you do not do that! I am your fellow servant, and of your brethren who have the testimony of Jesus. Worship God!"

However when men and women fell to the feet of Jesus Christ and worshiped Him, it was perfectly appropriate, because He is the great God of Heaven. He never corrected these individuals and Jesus never halted their worship.

Receive Prayer
Jesus Christ not only accepted worship and forgave sins, but Scripture tells us that holy men prayed to Him (and they still do so!). Unquestionably, this is a role that can only be assumed by the great God of Heaven. An example of Jesus Christ receiving prayer may be seen in the account of Stephen, an early Christian. Luke's book of Acts describes how Stephen was endowed by God with powerful speech and spiritual understanding. His ministry was also confirmed by "wonders and signs," according to Luke. These miracles were a visible demonstration to the nation of Israel that Stephen was speaking the truth.

Because of the impact of his ministry, the religious leaders of Israel had Stephen arrested and brought before the ruling council for a trial. After being questioned by the High Priest, Stephen speaks to the council and confronts the Jewish leaders with the fact that they "always resist" God the Holy Spirit, they persecuted and murdered the prophets in centuries past, and they betrayed and murder their own Savior Jesus Christ. This brought about an uncontrollable fury in the Jewish leaders. The trial then reached a climax (Acts 7:55-60),

> (Stephen), being full of the Holy Spirit, gazed into heaven and saw the glory of God, and Jesus standing at the right hand of God, and said, "Look! I see the heavens opened and the Son of Man standing at the right hand of God!"

> Then they cried out with a loud voice, stopped their ears, and ran at him with one accord; and they cast him out of the city...and they stoned Stephen as he was <u>calling on God</u> and saying, "<u>Lord Jesus, receive my spirit.</u>" Then he knelt down and cried out with a

loud voice, "Lord, do not charge them with this sin." And when he had said this, he died.

It says that Stephen called on God, but Whom is he addressing in his prayer? The Lord Jesus is being asked to receive his spirit and forgive the men of this sin. Stephen was praying to Jesus Christ, who is also identified as God. By the account in Acts, it is clear that Stephen was a remarkable man of God and his ministry was verified or confirmed by "wonders and signs" from God. Would this spiritually gifted man pray to Jesus Christ if Jesus were not God? Why would Stephen ask Jesus to forgive their sin, if Jesus was not able to forgive sin? These things again proclaim the deity of Jesus Christ.

Jesus Christ on Judgment Day

The vast majority of Muslims (as well as Christians and Jews) believe that the great God of Heaven will one day judge the souls of all men and women. Very few Muslims, however, realize that Jesus Himself taught that judgment was given to Him from God the Father. In other words, the Bible teaches that Jesus Christ will be seated on God's throne in Heaven to judge the condemned souls and the redeemed souls. As Jesus told the religious leaders of Israel,

> For the Father judges no one, but has committed all judgment to the Son, that all should honor the Son just as they honor the Father. He who does not honor the Son does not honor the Father who sent Him. Most assuredly, I say to you, he who hears My word and believes in Him who sent Me has everlasting life, and shall not come into judgment, but has passed from death into life (John 5:22-24).

The role of Jesus Christ as judge is a doctrine not only taught by Jesus Himself, but it was also taught by other writers of New Testament Scriptures. For example, Paul speaks of this when he warns us (Romans 14:10), "For we shall all stand before the judgment seat of Christ." This teaching is also seen in his second letter to Timothy, where he declared,

> I charge you therefore before God and the Lord Jesus Christ, who will judge the living and the dead at His appearing
> 2 Timothy 4:1

In the book of Revelation, the Apostle John also describes judgment and wrath brought by God upon the Earth in the last days. Often John refers to Jesus Christ in His glory as God Almighty. For example, John describes a terrible series of judgments on the Earth wherein the mightiest men on Earth flee in terror (Revelation 6:16). They pray to rocks and mountains, saying, "Fall on us and hide us from the face of Him who sits on the throne and from the wrath of the Lamb! For the great day of His wrath has come, and who is able to stand?" It is clear from the previous chapter in Revelation that Jesus Christ is He who "sits on the throne." Jesus Christ is the great God of Heaven - a doctrine that is consistently taught throughout the New Testament.

With respect to Judgment Day, the Bible states in several places that every knee shall bow to the Almighty God. Most Muslims will likely agree with this teaching. In the Old Testament, the Jewish prophet Isaiah described this event,

> Look to Me, and be saved, all you ends of the earth! For I am God, and there is no other. I have sworn by Myself; the word has gone out of My mouth in righteousness, and shall not return, that to Me every knee shall bow, every tongue shall take an oath. Isaiah 45:22,23

About 900 years later, the Apostle Paul revealed that every knee would bow to Jesus Christ!

> ...He humbled Himself and became obedient to the point of death, even the death of the cross. Therefore God also has highly exalted Him and given Him the name which is above every name, that at the name of Jesus every knee should bow, of those in Heaven, and of those on Earth, and of those under the Earth, and that every tongue should confess that Jesus Christ is Lord, to the glory of God the Father. Philippians 2:8-11

In this passage (and in a companion verse, Romans 14:11), the Apostle Paul describes the day in which "every knee" will bow to Jesus Christ. This event is evidently part of a day of judgment given to Jesus Christ. The verse also notes that "every tongue" will confess that Jesus Christ is Lord. The word rendered "Lord" is the Greek word *kyrios*. As described previously, this is one of the Greek words conveying the meaning, God or deity. Not only will every soul bow down before the Lord Jesus Christ, but everyone will declare that He is Lord and God. This includes everyone who was Muslim.

Conclusions

It has been noted by theologians and Bible scholars, that there are three possible ways a person could interpret the statements made by Jesus Christ and His actions. In the words of C. S. Lewis,[5]

> "Either this man was, and is, the Son of God, or else a madman or something worse. You can shut him up for a fool, you can spit at him and kill him as a demon or you can fall at his feet and call him Lord and God, but let us not come with any patronizing nonsense about his being a great human teacher. He has not left that open to us. He did not intend to."

This quote has been summarized to say that Jesus was one of these: a liar, a lunatic, or the Lord. With His claims to be God, Jesus Christ could have only been one of these three. Muslim clerics refer to Jesus Christ as one of God's major prophets, however this cannot be true. A true prophet would not claim to be God. Men who claim to be "God" are insane or delusional. Or they are lying with the hope of deceiving people. This leaves us with one other option – Jesus Christ is God Almighty.

Finally, it should be noted that the deity of Jesus Christ was known to be a fundamental doctrine at the very beginning of Christian church history. Among the writings of the church fathers, for example, Ignatius referred to Jesus Christ as God more than 15 times in his letters – written in about 110 A.D.[6] Similarly, a Roman ruler named Pliny the Younger wrote a letter to the Emperor Trajan in about 111 A.D.[7] and he describes Christians as worshipping Jesus Christ "as though he were a god." In accord with this doctrine being taught in the Old and New Testament Scriptures, the doctrine of the deity of Jesus Christ was basic truth from the very beginning.

Again, how do we know that Jesus Christ is the God of Heaven? He Himself claimed to be God. He supported His claim with miraculous acts, including rising from the dead. During His ministry on Earth, Jesus forgave sins and accepted worship. These are both actions only God could carry out. Moreover, Jewish and Christian prophets plainly endorsed His deity. The deity of Jesus Christ is among the most stunning messages of Bible, because we also know that Jesus Christ died on the cross for our sins. Thus, the Almighty God of Heaven came here as a man and He had one expressed purpose. He came to be nailed to a Roman cross and accept the punishment for your sins and mine. In doing so, He provided a way of salvation for every man, woman, and child. Jesus Christ demonstrated the endless love of God - a love that reaches out to every person standing in Mecca.

References

(1) Based on the published testimony. Downloaded from the Internet on February 26, 2011.

http://www.answering-islam.org/Testimonies/sara.html

(2) Ahmeed Deedat, *Christ in Islam*, Amazon Digital Services, Inc., p. 35. Ron Rhodes, *The 10 Things You Need to Know About Islam*, Harvest House Publishers, Grand Rapids, MI, 2007; pp. 111-124.

(3) A similar statement was also made by the Apostle Peter (2 Peter 1:1); a very thorough analysis of this Greek phrase is done in an article by Sam Shamoun. An excerpt reads "that Paul and Peter "employ a Greek grammatical construction known as Sharp's (first) rule to identify Jesus as both God (in fact, the great God!) and Savior. According to this rule, when singular nouns that are not proper names are connected together by the conjunction *kai* ("and"), with the definite article ("the") only appearing before the first noun, then both nouns refer to a single person." See the original article and references cited therein (downloaded June 24, 2014):

http://www.answering-islam.org/authors/shamoun/great_god_and_savior.html

(4) C. I. Scofield, *The Scofield Study Bible III*, Oxford University Press, Oxford, UK, 2002; p. 1313.

(5) C. S. Lewis, *Mere Christianity*, Collins, London, UK, 1952; pp. 54-56.

(6) James A. Kleist, *Ancient Christian Writers. The Epistles of St. Clement of Rome and St. Ignatius of Antioch.* Paulist Press, Mahwah, NJ, 1978.

(7) Ramsey MacMullen and Eugene N. Lane, Eds., *Paganism and Christianity 100-425 C.E. A Source Book.* Fortress Press, Minneapolis, MN, 1992.

Chapter 13

Getting Started as a New Christian

Therefore if the Son makes you free, you shall be free indeed. John 8:36

Anwar's story is described in Caner and Pruitt's book, *The Costly Call, Book 2.*[1] He grew up as a nominal Muslim in Jaipur, India. His family attended the local mosque, but with the demands of earning a living, he stopped attending during his teenage years. He was a cultural Muslim, but not much more. Anwar first learned about Jesus Christ when he was in his twenties. He heard the good news from an American tourist named Thomas.

Anwar made his living driving an auto rickshaw through the streets of Jaipur. Like other rickshaw drivers, he knew that tourists were good passengers. They paid well and often gave him generous tips. Anwar picked up Thomas outside one of the hotels in Jaipur. The American tourist asked Anwar to guide and drive him for the entire day - promising to pay one thousand rupees (about $25) for Anwar's services. This was far more than his income for a typical day, so Anwar happily accepted the offer. Little did Anwar know, he would be receiving something significantly more valuable than the thousand-rupee fare. Thomas would soon possess the priceless treasure of salvation in Jesus Christ and the eternal blessings found in Him!

Thomas brought Anwar to one of the finest restaurants in Jaipur and shared dinner with him. As a rickshaw driver from a low caste group, he had never eaten at such a restaurant. It was quite better food than the typical bowl of rice that he ate on a daily basis. Thomas questioned Anwar about his religious background and his beliefs. Since he had not been to the mosque regularly for many years, Anwar could only describe his Islamic faith in general and vague terms. Later in the evening, Thomas began to describe Christianity. He found a Bible and began reading the gospel accounts of Jesus Christ - Anwar was astonished by the ministry and life of Jesus Christ.

The next day, Thomas again paid Anwar to drive him through Jaipur. Since it was a Sunday morning, Thomas requested a drive to the local Christian church. He invited Anwar into the church to attend a morning worship service. Having never attended a Christian church service, Anwar was struck by two notable observations. Upon entering the church, a man from the highest caste in India greeted Anwar with a handshake and kind words. This man was from the Brahman caste and Anwar was not even supposed to touch him or look at him in the eyes. Yet, the social, cultural, and religious barriers were seemingly nonexistent in the Christian church!

As Anwar explained this encounter, "I later found out that he had become a follower of Jesus, and he believed that God created all people equal."[1]

Anwar was also surprised to see the worship service with singing and music. As he described it, the music was "upbeat and loud" with "even people playing guitars." Anwar's initial reaction was to think that the worship was irreverent, as he had never seen such activities at his mosque. However, Thomas explained to him that Christians are filled with joy. He added, "they are just so happy that their sins have been forgiven that they love to sing praises to Jesus."

The following day, Anwar brought Thomas to the airport for his departure from Jaipur. He gave Anwar a gift in a plastic bag – it contained a Bible written in the Hindi language. Thomas then departed for a flight to New Delhi. Later that evening, Anwar opened the Bible to find a letter written by Thomas. It was placed at the beginning of the gospel of John. Thomas wrote, "Anwar, my dear friend. Please take time to read this book, as it will change your life. This book, the Bible, contains the keys to peace, joy, and eternal life. May Jesus give you understanding as you read."[1] With the letter, Thomas also enclosed three thousand rupees. Anwar spent several hours reading the New Testament Scriptures. He became overwhelmed as he read about the beatings of Jesus Christ and His crucifixion. He began to cry and had to close the Bible.

The very next Sunday morning, Anwar parked his rickshaw outside the Christian church and he debated whether or not to attend the worship service. As he thought about it, one of the church members came up and said, "Anwar, are you going to join us today? Please come in and sit with me."[1] Anwar joined the group inside the church. Soon he found himself singing with the other people and then listening to a message (or teaching) from the pastor. The message was related to forgiveness. Prompted by feelings of peace and curiosity, Anwar spoke to the pastor after the service. They talked about the Bible and Jesus Christ for more than two hours. The pastor finally asked Anwar, "What will you do this day with the Son of God who died on the cross for you?"[1]

Anwar professed his new faith in Jesus Christ. He completed his journey from Mecca to Calvary on that day. During the next few weeks, Anwar worried about many things. He was concerned about his family's reaction when they learned of his conversion to Christianity. He worried about his Muslim friends abandoning him. These concerns and worries were suddenly forgotten one day, when he was told that his mother was diagnosed with cancer and she only had a short time to live.

Anwar was deeply concerned for mother and her eternal destiny. When he visited his parents' home, Anwar begged his mother to hear the good news about Jesus Christ. She agreed and listened for a while. Then Anwar's father arrived home and he was furious. He grabbed Anwar's Bible and threw it across the room.

Anwar's mother pleaded, "No wait! I want to hear more about this Jesus." But a few minutes later, Anwar's father returned with some policemen and he had Anwar arrested. He spent the next two days in jail and then the police dropped the charges.

Following the disclosure of his Christian faith, Anwar's life became more difficult. His daily income from driving the rickshaw had dropped from about five hundred rupees to one hundred rupees. Local Muslims refused to ride with this man who had left Islam for Christianity. Then one day, a flaming bottle of gasoline was thrown into his rickshaw by two Muslim thugs. The rickshaw burst into flames and Anwar barely escaped with his life, as the fuel had also splashed onto him. When the crime was reported to the local police, he was arrested and thrown in jail for two weeks!

The persecution followed Anwar. On the following Sunday, he attended the worship service at the Christian church. In the middle of the service, the local police raided the church and arrested the pastor. The police charged the pastor of the church with proselytizing (sharing the good news of Jesus Christ). The doors of the church were chained shut. When members of the church – including Anwar - visited their pastor in jail, they were all arrested and thrown in jail. Still more church members came to the jail to visit the pastor and their fellow Christians. With this large group of Christians at the local jail, the police decided to drop all of the charges and released the group. They promptly returned to their church, broke the lock and chain, and gratefully worshipped the Lord.

Anwar's faith had grown through the years. He was fortunate enough to again meet the American tourist, Thomas. Both men rejoiced in Anwar's faith and love for Christ. Nevertheless, Anwar is still "haunted" by the words of his sick mother - "No wait! I want to hear more about this Jesus."[1] His family refused to let Anwar attend his mother's funeral. Two of his relatives confronted Anwar at the funeral and he was then beaten with an iron rod. Anwar still hopes and prays for his family members. He hopes to also hear them say, "I want to hear more about this Jesus."

Anwar made the journey out of Islam and into Christianity. Likewise, some readers of this book may also have been guided from Mecca to Calvary. The truth of the Bible has led you to eternal life in Jesus Christ. Now what? For some individuals, they might be completely isolated from other Christians. Many Muslim countries have outlawed Christian churches, while in other nations, the Christian churches are being burned down almost on a daily basis. Some individuals may also be in a hostile environment, where an open proclamation of their new life in Christ would end with a violent death or perhaps years of torture at the hands of Muslim "security forces." These individuals will face great challenges in their new faith and growth will be a difficult task. There may not be a good church, Bible study, or Bible class accessible. They may not have access to good reference books or study guides to the Bible. In many situations, it may not even be possible to obtain a copy of the Bible for personal study. Other individuals may be in a situation where there are many Christian churches and Bible studies, but they are eager to learn more about their Savior and the Bible.

This chapter is intended to introduce new Christian believers to some basic doctrines and ideas presented in the Bible. Regardless of an individual's situation, this chapter will provide an overview of important teachings from the Scriptures. Some points need to be made at the start. Firstly, an entire lifetime of study cannot exhaust the supply of wisdom and truth in the Bible. In the Old Testament, the Holy Scriptures are referred to as a "great deep" and "mighty ocean." These descriptions were meant to describe the endless supply of truth and knowledge in the Bible. This is to be expected. The Bible describes the Almighty God – infinite and holy, righteous and wise, loving and just. As the glory of God has no end, the book that describes Him has a similar type of character – endless in its truth and wisdom. Thus, an introductory chapter can barely "scratch the surface" of such a profound and deep subject matter.

Secondly, the ultimate authority for spiritual truth is the Bible and the Holy Spirit of God. No man or group of men can replace the Word of God as our guide. From the very beginning, Christians have been encouraged to test every doctrine, teaching, and belief, against the plain statements in the Bible. Although this chapter presents some of the basic teachings of Biblical Christianity, the reader is called upon to verify all of the doctrines and messages. If a Bible is available to the reader, then he or she is invited to confirm the truth presented in this chapter.

Finally, the reader is encouraged to pray for wisdom and guidance. As a new Christian, the Lord will feed you and help you grow in your new faith. The Lord Jesus Christ told (John 4:10,14) the women at the well in Samaria,

> Jesus answered and said to her, "...who ever drinks of the water that I shall give him will never thirst. But the water that I shall give him will become in him a fountain of water springing up into everlasting life."

Just as the Lord promised to give the woman at the well "living water," so also, He will teach us from the Bible. Many spiritual truths are difficult to understand, especially for sinful men and women. It is only through God's help that we are able to grasp His wisdom and truth.

Knowledge and Assurance

The most exciting sections of the Bible describe our salvation in Jesus Christ. These Scriptures reveal the great blessings given to those who have travelled from Mecca to Calvary - or any other individual who has brought their sins to the cross. As the Apostle John stated (1 John 5:13),

> These things I have written to you who believe in the name of the
> Son of God, that you may know that you have eternal life, and that
> you may continue to believe in the name of the Son of God

The absolute assurance of our salvation is unique to Biblical Christianity. As John points out, Christians can "know" with certainty that Heaven is their eternal reward. Christians not only have the words of God to verify their salvation, but God Himself confirms this truth by His power in the Holy Spirit:

> ...our gospel did not come to you in word only, but also in power,
> and in the Holy Spirit and in much assurance...1 Thessalonians
> 1:5

Saved by Faith

The most important question for a man or woman: how is someone actually saved from their sins? As described previously, this very question was asked of the Apostle Paul by a jail guard. Paul replied, "Believe on the Lord Jesus Christ and you will be saved...(Acts 16:31)." A person receives salvation upon believing the good news – Jesus Christ died for our sins. Two equivalent words are used in Scripture for this process – faith and trust. Eternal life is meant to be a completely free gift to you and I, but it depends on our faith, trust, or belief. In Paul's book of Ephesians, God reveals exactly how a person is saved,

> For it is by grace you have been saved, through faith—and this is
> not from yourselves, it is the gift of God— not by works, so that
> no one can boast. For we are God's handiwork...(Eph. 2:8-10a)

In this passage, we see that salvation from sin occurs by grace through faith. The term "grace" refers to God's favor and kindness that He has shown to mankind. The original Greek word (χάρις, *charis*) also gives us our modern English word charity.[2] This idea reflects the exact nature of our salvation, that "it is a gift of God" or an act of charity towards us.

We are also reminded in this passage that our good works do not contribute to our salvation. No one in Heaven will be able to boast, "I gave a billion dollars to a good cause" or "I fought and died in a war," and "so for these noble acts, God rewarded me with eternal life." Instead, every person in Heaven will simply claim, "God saved my soul through the work of Jesus Christ on the cross." As God's Word declares (Titus 3:5),

> "not by works of righteousness which we have done, but according to His mercy He saved us, through the washing of regeneration and renewing of the Holy Spirit"

Here again we find that our good works do not contribute to our salvation. Although people generally like to believe that their own deeds have been noble and good, it was God's mercy and love saved our souls!

Eternal Security

The new Christian must also come to know that his or her salvation is eternally secure. Once a person has been saved from their sins, then they will always be considered set apart and destined for eternal life in Christ. Paul was able to proclaim (Romans 8:1a), "There is therefore now no condemnation to those who are in Christ Jesus." The Apostle John declared (1 John 1:9) similar good news, "If we confess our sins, He is faithful and just to forgive us our sins and to cleanse us from all unrighteousness." All of our sins were punished on the cross – past, present, and future - so they can never lead to condemnation for the true Christian.

"What if I commit a really terrible sin after becoming a Christian," some might ask "wouldn't God take away my salvation?" No. Our salvation is based entirely on the blood of Christ and the righteous work done by our Savior at the cross. Although sinful conduct is always discouraged in the strongest of terms in the Bible, acts of sin cannot nullify God's infinite grace and mercy. The sinful Christian is stupid and disobedient - but he or she is still preserved blameless in Christ. The Apostle Peter addresses this important truth:

> Praise be to the God and Father of our Lord Jesus Christ! In his great mercy he has given us new birth into a living hope through the resurrection of Jesus Christ from the dead, and into an inheritance that can never perish, spoil or fade--kept in heaven for you, who through faith are shielded by God's power until the coming of the salvation that is ready to be revealed in the last time
> 1 Peter 1:3-5

As a believer in Jesus Christ, you have "an inheritance that can never perish, spoil or fade." God's power preserves and keeps your salvation secure. If you were saved by trusting in the cross, then you can rest assured in your salvation. Your salvation will never be lost, as you are a treasured possession of the Savior Jesus Christ.

Peter's declaration also points to our "new birth" – a strong argument for the security and permanence of our salvation in Christ. When you completed the journey from Mecca to Calvary, you became a born-again Christian. This new spiritual birth was a work of God done for you. It was not something that you earned or accomplished through any effort of your own. Moreover, your new spiritual birth is permanent. No verses of the Bible describe us being "unborn." Eternal security for the saved individual was taught by Jesus Christ Himself, when He proclaimed (John 10:27-29):

> "My sheep hear My voice, and I know them, and they follow Me. And I give them eternal life, and they shall never perish; neither shall anyone snatch them out of My hand. My Father, who has given them to Me, is greater than all; and no one is able to snatch them out of My Father's hand."

The Bible gives us a confident knowledge of our salvation. Moreover, it reminds us that this great gift can never be taken away from us – even if we fail to serve our Lord with faithfulness and due diligence.

Counting Our Blessings

In the business world, it is often important to take an inventory. This may be done for planning, or tax purposes, or for other reasons. The business owner counts the items on the shelves or in the storage warehouse. Christians should also consider their "inventory" of blessings in Christ. Since they are permanent gifts from God, we are encouraged to consider them, to number them, and to be thankful for them. They are all evidence of God's tremendous love for us. It is vitally important for new Christians to be aware of these truths, because they are a source of unlimited joy and they will provide the foundation for spiritual growth. With knowledge of these blessings, one should have a growing love for the Savior Jesus Christ. Some of the more important blessings are described below.

Redemption

Redemption often carries the meaning of something being purchased or bought. The Old Testament Scriptures have many examples of redemption or someone being redeemed. For example, God made a provision for a slave to be purchased out of slavery by a family member (see, Leviticus 25). This was an example of redemption. Even when God led Israel out of Egyptian slavery, this was considered an act of redemption. This act of redemption involved God's own work or labors, as Moses himself recorded,

> God redeemed the Jews from Egyptian slavery. This was not done with money or through the blood of a sacrifice, but it was done through the mighty works and judgments of God...Exodus 6:6

Other Old Testament passages indicate the need for redemption in the spiritual realm. As we are all born sinners, our debt involves countless sins. We are literal slaves to sin (John 8:34). With each sin, we incur a debt – judgment and punishment from the almighty and infinite God of Heaven. It is only through power and mercy of God that this sin debt can be redeemed. King David wrote of this redemption in his Psalms:

> But God will redeem my soul from the power of the grave, for He shall receive me. Psalm 49:15

> The works of the LORD are great, studied by all who have pleasure in them...He has sent redemption to His people; He has commanded His covenant forever: Holy and awesome is His name. The fear of the LORD is the beginning of wisdom; a good understanding have all those who do His commandments. His praise endures forever. Psalm 111:2, 9-10.

The New Testament Scriptures explain how God is able to redeem sinful mankind. Using the language of the marketplace, it is said that we were purchased or redeemed by the blood of Christ. This truth is seen in the last words uttered by Jesus Christ upon the cross of Calvary (John 19:30), "It is finished." This particular Greek word, teléw, *teleo*, was used in the ancient marketplace when a purchase was paid in full.[2] Jesus Christ Himself proclaimed that our sin debt was paid in full when He gave His life upon the cross. This truth is further explained by Paul (Colossians 1:13,14):

(God) has delivered us from the power of darkness and conveyed us into the kingdom of the Son of His love, in whom we have redemption through His blood, the forgiveness of sins.

How were you redeemed? It was through the blood of Jesus Christ that you were redeemed and all of your sin was forgiven! Many other passages of Scripture describe God's redemption towards Christians, see for example Galatians 4:4-5, Romans 3:25-26, and Hebrews 9:12-14. Redemption involves payment or purchase. Like a slave bought from the slave market, God purchased you from slavery to sin and He set you free to serve Him as a new creation in Christ. The price of redemption was indeed great, as the death of His Son paid for your freedom.

Propitiation

After Israel was brought out of Egyptian slavery (or redeemed), God instituted the Divine ordinances of the Law and the Tabernacle. Moses was instructed to build Israel's first Tabernacle according to specific guidelines provided by the Lord. One day each year (Day of Atonement) the High Priest was to enter the most Holy place of the Tabernacle – the location where God's glory appeared above the Ark of the Covenant – and apply the blood of animal sacrifices to the Mercy Seat on the Ark of the Covenant. The blood was from two animal sacrifices, a bull and a goat. This was done as a covering for the sins of Israel and of the High Priest himself. This elaborate yearly ritual is an example of propitiation.

There are several elements of propitiation that are particularly important for us to see in the Day of Atonement. First, the word propitiation is used to describe the idea of an offended God and a sacrifice that covers or hides the offense. There is great significance in the High Priest placing the blood of the sacrifice of the Mercy Seat of the Ark. The Lord had instructed Moses to place the two stone tablets of the Law within the Ark. Thus, the sins of Israel are evident from the inscribed commandments on the stone tablets. These offenses represented a barrier between sinful man and the infinitely holy and righteous God. When the High Priest applied the blood of the sacrifices to the Mercy Seat, their sins were covered and mankind (the High Priest) could be in the presence of the Lord God. This was a powerful foreshadow - as the Day of Atonement pointed ahead to the day when the innocent blood of Jesus Christ paid for our sins (not merely covered them).

Secondly, propitiation represents an appointed place of meeting between God and man. Whereas the Tabernacle was the only such place in Old Testament times, the cross is the only place of propitiation in this day. Access to God is no longer limited to a High Priest, but all men and women are able to meet with the God of

Heaven at the cross.

Finally, propitiation is entirely an act of God done on man's behalf. The propitiation of sin in Old Testament times depended entirely on the mercy of our loving God. Since the blood of bulls and goats could not fully pay the penalty of sin, God's love and mercy for the sinner was the true basis for the covering of the sins. God was able to look ahead to the day when He would provide an acceptable sacrifice for sin – the Son of God, Jesus Christ. Salvation includes complete propitiation for our sins against God. Our sins have been covered by the blood of an innocent Sacrifice - our Savior Jesus Christ. With our filthy sins covered, we are now able to stand before the infinitely holy God of Heaven.

Reconciliation

As described in Chapter 10, our salvation includes reconciliation. This spiritual blessing relates to the "peace" made between mankind and God. As sinners, you and I were at war with God. The Bible even describes men and women as enemies of God! This includes people who do good works, pray, and actively follow their favorite religion.

One only needs to look at the cross to see how the human race is at war with their God and Creator. Jesus Christ ministered to the nation of Israel for about three years, blessing the nation with wholesome spiritual teaching and miraculous works. How did the law-abiding religious men respond? They had Jesus crucified! Mankind's violence towards God was on full display with the cruel beatings, mocking, and brutal murder of Jesus Christ upon the cross of Calvary.

While we were actively at war, nevertheless, God was responding with love and mercy. God Almighty saves hopelessly lost sinners at the cross and He reconciles – or makes peace - in the relationship between Him and us. This truth is made very clear in Paul's New Testament books (for example, Colossians 1:20-21):

>...having made peace through the blood of His cross. And you, who once were alienated and enemies in your mind by wicked works, yet now He has reconciled.

As a Christian, your relationship with the God of Heaven has been restored. God no longer considers you to be a rebel and enemy, but rather He is now able to look upon you as a beloved son or daughter in Christ. You have been "reconciled" to God.

Forgiveness of Sin

The Bible message is often called the "gospel" of Jesus Christ. The word "gospel" means "good news." We have many reasons to consider the news to be good, because among our blessings, Christians have the forgiveness of sins. All of your sins – past, present, future, big and small – were forgiven at the moment of your salvation. When you completed the journey from Mecca to Calvary, God credited you with complete forgiveness. Your sins will not keep you from Heaven and eternal life. The same cannot be said for those who reject Christ. These unfortunate souls will die with their sins and they will face a lost eternity.

It is important to realize that all of your sins were forgiven completely at the moment of salvation. Immature Christians sometimes feel that their salvation might be lost if they commit a terrible sin. However, consider the passage of Scripture written by Paul,

> And you, being dead in your trespasses...He has made alive together with Him, having forgiven you all trespasses
> Colossians 2:13

One should be careful to note how God describes our forgiveness - that He has "forgiven you all trespasses." The word "all" means that no sin remains unforgiven. Although we commit many sins each day, they are forgiven instantly on the basis of the cross work of Jesus Christ.

Critics of the Bible have been known to hurl insults and accusations related to this idea. Their criticisms often state, "If all of your sins are forgiven, then you are encouraged to keep sinning. You can live an unrighteous life style." Unfortunately, these critics do not themselves understand the gospel of Jesus Christ or the power of God's love. As Christians, we have received tremendous mercy and blessings from the God of Heaven. This is not a motivation to commit unrighteous acts, but rather it pushes us towards good works. This can be clearly seen in Paul's letter (Ephesians 4:31-32):

> Let all bitterness, wrath, anger, clamor, and evil speaking be put away from you, with all malice. And be kind to one another, tenderhearted, forgiving one another, even as God in Christ forgave you.

As Christians, we are to have good conduct and we are motivated by God's blessings given to us. Elsewhere in the New Testament, we are told that "the love of Christ compels us" (2 Corinthians 5:14). The word "compels" means to control or push us forward. So when God forgives all of your sins, it actually motivates you to live for Him in all righteousness.

Freedom from Condemnation

For Christians, God declares (Romans 8:1), "There is therefore now no condemnation to those who are in Christ Jesus." With the total forgiveness of sin, Christians are blessed with a freedom from condemnation. This means that your sins will not be punished by the fires of Hell, because God already judged and punished your sins (all of them) on the cross of Calvary. For those unfortunate souls who do not journey to Calvary, their sins will be judged by God and they will be found "guilty." The infinite righteousness and perfect justice of God will lead to eternal punishment for the guilty sinner. The Bible describes how these individuals will be cast into the "Lake of Fire" where they will experience extreme anguish and pain. Jesus Christ Himself described (Matt. 13:49-50) people in this place as "weeping" and "gnashing" their teeth.

In this we see the two categories of people in the world: the saved and lost. The saved people have been to Calvary's cross where the blood of Jesus Christ has paid for their sins. The lost people have rejected this great gift and they remain in a terrifying state of condemnation. God describes their situation (Hebrews 10:26b-7,31):

> ...no sacrifice for sins is left, but only a fearful expectation of judgment and of raging fire that will consume the enemies of God...It is a dreadful thing to fall into the hands of the living God.

This passage explains that no animal sacrifices – or even good works – can be a means to avoid condemnation for sins. None of these acts can replace the perfect sacrifice of God's own Son on the cross in payment for sin. This passage also describes the future for the lost human being – judgment, punishment, and great fear of the Almighty God.

Christians have been thankfully saved from this eternal condemnation. Rather than seeing God in "dreadful" fear, we will see Him and experience tremendous joy. Our joy will center on Jesus Christ the Son of God, because we will know that His sacrifice on the cross saves us from condemnation. Although non-Christians (including Muslims) cling to the hope that their good works and own religion will save them from condemnation and wrath, this is not so. The Apostle Peter presented this fact to the Jewish leaders of the first century when he declared (Acts 4:10,12) "Jesus Christ of Nazareth...salvation is found in no one else, for there is no other name under heaven given to men by which we must be saved."

248

Heaven Bound

Christians are told in the Bible that our eternity will be spent with the Lord in heaven. The Biblical view of heaven is vastly different than the Islamic view of heaven. Unlike the Quran (see 78:31; 54:51-55), the Bible does not describe heaven as a place where men will receive beautiful women to satisfy their sexual desires. Nor is heaven described in terms of a "gushing fountain" or "rivers" of wine (see Quran 37:40-48; 47:15). The Bible describes heaven as the dwelling place of the Almighty God. The book of Revelation describes it as a place where everyone continuously worships God, especially as He is manifest in the person of Jesus Christ. This is done with great joy, excitement, and satisfaction.

In the New Testament, God makes an exclusive promise to Christians - we will spend their eternity with the Lord in heaven. This is a promise only made to individuals who have been to Calvary – men and women who have been redeemed by the blood of Jesus Christ. Even now, the Bible refers to Christians as citizens of heaven, as seen in Philippians 3:20:

> For our citizenship is in Heaven, from which we also eagerly wait
> for the Savior, the Lord Jesus Christ.

As citizens of Heaven, we are simply travelling abroad at this time and we will be heading home upon our deaths. We should have complete confidence in our salvation and we can know as a matter of fact that God will keep us with Him for all eternity. God's promises are dependable and true, even the promise of spending eternity in Heaven. This truth is confirmed by other passages of the New Testament:

> ...knowing that you have a better and an enduring possession for
> yourselves in Heaven. Hebrews 10:34b

> We are confident, yes, well pleased rather to be absent from the
> body and to be present with the Lord. 2 Corinthians 5:8

> For the Lord Himself will descend from heaven with a shout, with
> the voice of an archangel, and with the trumpet of God. And the
> dead in Christ will rise first. Then we who are alive and remain
> shall be caught up together with them in the clouds to meet the
> Lord in the air. And thus we shall always be with the Lord.
> 1 Thessalonians 4:16,17

249

New Spirit and New Birth

What is death? Although we are all familiar with the painful event known as physical death, what is happening in the spiritual realm? When God spoke with Adam in the Garden of Eden, He warned Adam that "you shall surely die" if he ate the forbidden fruit (Genesis 2:17). The Hebrew implies two deaths and so it can be rendered "dying you shall die" if Adam were to become a sinner. Bible scholars often define death as a "separation." So our physical death involves separation of our soul and spirit from the body. The second death of Genesis 2 is considered the spiritual death, where Adam's spirit became separated from God and the life that He provides. As children of Adam, we were born physically alive but dead spiritually.

Nevertheless, God is able to make us alive spiritually. This is another blessing we have as Christians. New spiritual life is also essential. In a conversation with a Jewish leader, Jesus declared (John 3:3) its importance:

> Jesus answered and said to him, "Most assuredly, I say to you,
> unless one is born again, he cannot see the kingdom of God."

In this passage, Jesus is referring to a new spiritual birth. Although the Bible does not describe all the reasons why a new birth is necessary, there are some indications. For example, Jesus also said, "that which is born of the flesh is flesh, and that which is born of the Spirit is spirit (John 3:6)." Thus, spiritual life cannot be produced by things we do in our body (i.e, good works or religious activities). Spiritual life is a work of God done for mankind. The Lord produces this new life in Christians when they are saved. The Apostle Peter declares this truth:

> Since you have purified your souls in obeying the truth…having
> been born again, not of corruptible seed but incorruptible, through
> the word of God which lives and abides forever (1 Peter 1:22,23)

For those who have traveled from Mecca to Calvary, they are able rejoice in "having been born again" by an incorruptible seed. This new birth provides us with a new spirit – one that will be always please God (1 John 3:9).

Even though Christians have experienced the new birth (or regeneration as it is sometimes called), we must still deal with our old sinful nature as human beings. The Apostle Paul contrasts the old sinful nature (called the old man) with the new spirit (called the new man). The old sinful nature still resides in the Christian and it can lead to occasional sins. But we are encouraged to live through our new nature or man, as Paul wrote (Eph. 4:24), "…put on the new man which was created according to God, in true righteousness and holiness."

250

Eternal Life

"For the wages of sin is death, but the gift of God is eternal life in Christ Jesus our Lord (Romans 6:23)." This passage says it all. Mankind's sin results in death or separation from God. But God will provide eternal life to those who are Christians, or those "in Christ Jesus." This is a stark contrast. Sinful, unsaved mankind is destined for eternal separation from God, while Christians will receive eternal life through the love and kindness of God! This truth is echoed throughout the New Testament, as it was a message spoken by Jesus Himself. Some of these passages are shown below:

> "And these will go away into everlasting punishment, but the righteous into eternal life." Matt 25:46

> "And as Moses lifted up the serpent in the wilderness, even so must the Son of Man be lifted up, that whoever believes in Him should not perish but have eternal life. John 3:14,15

In these statements from Jesus, He contrasts those who will perish with "everlasting punishment," and those who have eternal life. This statement also describes clearly how we obtain eternal life: "whoever believes in Him."

For those who have truly been from Mecca to Calvary, their belief or faith results in eternal life. What about the Muslims who only "believe" in the Jesus described in Islamic Scriptures? The "Jesus" of Islamic Scriptures did not die for their sins, and of course, the "Islamic Jesus" is never described as the Son of God. These men and women may acknowledge Jesus as a prophet, but they reject His role as their Savior. Unfortunately, these men and women are rejecting the one message that saves us – that Jesus Christ died for our sins and He was risen on the third day. *For those Muslims who refuse to travel from Mecca to Calvary, they will not inherit eternal life.* This truth is stated in clear terms by the Apostle John, an eyewitness to the death, burial, and resurrection of Jesus (1 John 5:11-12),

> And this is the testimony: that God has given us eternal life, and this life is in His Son. He who has the Son has life; he who does not have the Son of God does not have life.

As the inspired Word of God, this passage represents a guarantee and assurance that Christians have eternal life. But it also represents a warning to those who reject the Savior Jesus Christ. Tragically, such individuals do "not have life."

Holy Spirit

As described previously, the Bible describes God as a Trinity. He is the one Almighty God, but He is described in terms of three co-eternal and co-existing personalities. Each member of the Trinity is described as having roles and functions. The Holy Spirit serves very important roles in the salvation of Christians and He continues to minister to us during our growth in this faith. A brief summary of His work is presented in Table 1. The New Testament describes at least ten blessings we have through the Holy Spirit's work. These are blessings freely given to Christians upon their salvation in Jesus Christ. When you were saved through Christ, God sent His Holy Spirit to indwell you. He also placed you into the "body of Christ." This is a collective group of all of the saved individuals from the present age. The Holy Spirit gives us life and helps us live a life that is pleasing to God.

The Holy Spirit also opens the lines of communication between us and God – helping us pray and helping us understand the truth of God's messages. This provides us with an access to God the Father - something that the unsaved world cannot enjoy. Most important, the Holy Spirit "seals" us for our eternal destiny. The writers of Scripture use language similar to a financial transaction, wherein the Holy Spirit represents a very significant "down payment" on a purchased item. Having indwelled you with the Holy Spirit Himself, you can be assured that God will complete His redemption or purchase.

The Christian also benefits in other ways from the ministry of the Holy Spirit. As an outgrowth of your faith in Christ, the Holy Spirit can produce tangible blessings in your life. These are called "fruit" in Scripture, as they are comparable to fruit growing from a healthy tree. When a Christians reads the Bible, believes its teachings, lives the Christian lifestyle, and continues in prayer, the Holy Spirit produces these qualities. The Apostle Paul describes this truth in the books of Romans (see Table 1) and the book of Galatians where we read (Galatians 5:22-23), "But the fruit of the Spirit is love, joy, peace, patience, kindness, goodness, faithfulness, gentleness, self-control."

Adoption into family of God

As described previously, our salvation leads to a new spiritual position. This spiritual position is also described in terms of adoption. In ancient times, a ruler or king would occasionally adopt a slave or servant to be their son or daughter. This was sometime done out of love for the slave. Needless to say, the adoption could elevate the slave from a very low position to a very high position. One could go from having no guaranteed rights as a slave to a position having rights, privilege, and wealth, as a son of the king! When you made the journey from Mecca to Calvary, you were adopted into the family of God. Like the adoption of a beloved

252

Table 1. The role of the Holy Spirit of God in a Christian's salvation and life.

Blessing	Scripture
Holy Spirit given to us; indwells us	•…the love of God has been poured out in our hearts by the Holy Spirit who was given to us. Romans 5:5 •Do you not know that you are the temple of God and that the Spirit of God dwells in you? 1 Corinthians 3:16 •By this we know that we abide in Him, and He is in us, because He has given us of His Spirit. 1 John 4:13
Holy Spirit sets us apart from lost mankind	•But we are bound to give thanks to God always for you, brethren beloved by the Lord, because God from the beginning chose you for salvation through sanctification by the Spirit and belief in the truth. (Paul's prayer for the Thessalonian Christians) 2 Thessalonians 2:13
Holy Spirit baptizes - or places us into - the body of Christ	For by one Spirit we were all baptized into one body--whether Jews or Greeks, whether slaves or free--and have all been made to drink into one Spirit. 1 Corinthians 12:13
Holy Spirit gives us life and enables us to serve God	•But if the Spirit of Him who raised Jesus from the dead dwells in you, He who raised Christ from the dead will also give life to your mortal bodies through His Spirit who dwells in you. Romans 8:11
Holy Spirit gives us spiritual power and strength	•For this reason I bow my knees to the Father of our Lord Jesus Christ, from whom the whole family in heaven and earth is named, that He would grant you, according to the riches of His glory, to be strengthened with might through His Spirit in the inner man. Ephesians 3:14-16 •For our gospel did not come to you in word only, but also in power, and in the Holy Spirit and in much assurance…1 Thessalonians 1:5
Holy Spirit gives us access to God the Father	•For through Him we both have access by one Spirit to the Father. Ephesians 2:18
Holy Spirit helps us pray	•Likewise the Spirit also helps in our weaknesses. For we do not know what we should pray for as we ought, but the Spirit Himself makes intercession for us with groanings which cannot be uttered. Romans 8:26
Holy Spirit reveals truth to us.	•But God has revealed them to us through His Spirit. For the Spirit searches all things, yes, the deep things of God. 1 Corinthians 2:10
Holy Spirit produces in blessings in us.	•for the kingdom of God is not eating and drinking, but righteousness and peace and joy in the Holy Spirit. Romans 14:17
Holy Spirit certifies or seals us - saved from sin and Heaven bound.	• Now it is God who makes both us and you stand firm in Christ. He anointed us, set his seal of ownership on us, and put his Spirit in our hearts as a deposit, guaranteeing what is to come. 2 Cor. 1:21-22 •In Him you also trusted, after you heard the word of truth, the gospel of your salvation; in whom also, having believed, you were sealed with the Holy Spirit of promise, who is the guarantee of our inheritance until the redemption of the purchased possession, to the praise of His glory. Ephesians 1:13-14 •And do not grieve the Holy Spirit of God, by whom you were sealed for the day of redemption. Ephesians 4:30

slave, God's adoption of you was prompted by His love for you. It has elevated you from a lowly position as a slave to sin and to the lofty position of being called a son or daughter of God. Our adoption is described in several place in the New Testament, for example in Ephesians 1:3-6:

> Blessed be the God and Father of our Lord Jesus Christ, who has blessed us with every spiritual blessing in the heavenly places in Christ, just as He chose us in Him before the foundation of the world, that we should be holy and without blame before Him in love, having predestined us to <u>adoption as sons</u> by Jesus Christ to Himself, according to the good pleasure of His will to the praise of the glory of His grace, by which He made us accepted in the Beloved.

Though the Scripture reads adoption as sons, the literal meaning includes men and women. Our adoption says much about our future, as the term "predestined" speaks to our future blessing. We will forever be the objects of God's love and we will be kept in a position close to Him.

Adoption also means that we are free to love God. With the great salvation and blessings from Him, it is natural for us to throw ourselves down at the Savior's feet and express our love for Him. Indeed, this aspect of adoption is revealed through Paul's letter to the Galatians, where he wrote (Galatians 4:6,7):

> And because you are sons, God has sent forth the Spirit of His Son into your hearts, crying out, "Abba, Father!" Therefore you are no longer a slave but a son, and if a son, then an heir of God through Christ.

This aspect of Biblical Christianity is an entirely new experience for ex-Muslims. The religion of Islam says little about Allah's love for mankind (see Chapter 10). The God of Islam is almighty, but he is also distant and impersonal. However, the God of the Bible knows you and loves you. He desires you to learn about Him and He wants you to enjoy His love. In return, He enjoys your praise, worship, and love.

Free from bondage to sin

When our adoption is considered, it is often contrasted with our former position. Our new position in Christ offers a dramatic contrast to the lost condition we had as sinners. The Bible describes several aspects of our state prior to being saved at the cross of Calvary. Not only do we have great blessings given to us as Christians, but we were also removed from a horrible situation as lost men and women. Prior to being saved by God through Christ, we were under "the power of darkness." As the Apostle Paul described (Colossians 1:12-14):

> ...giving thanks to the Father who has qualified us to be partakers of the inheritance of the saints in the light. He has delivered us from the power of darkness and conveyed us into the kingdom of the Son of His love, in whom we have redemption through His blood, the forgiveness of sins.

Note the contrast of your position as a Christian versus the non-Christian: inheritance as a saint, redeemed, forgiven, placed in the Son's kingdom, versus being under "the power of darkness." Other passages of Scripture indicate that "the power of darkness" refers to the spiritual blindness of non-Christians or unsaved individuals. Thus, Jesus Christ was able to tell the first century Jews (John 8:12), "I am the light of the world. He who follows Me shall not walk in darkness, but have the light of life."

Even more ominously, the un-saved person - who resides in "the power of darkness" – is also under the influence and power of Satan. This sad truth was revealed by Jesus Christ Himself when He gave the commission and Apostleship to Paul, saying (Acts 26:18), "I now send you, to open their eyes, in order to turn them from darkness to light, and from the power of Satan to God, that they may receive forgiveness of sins and an inheritance among those who are sanctified by faith in Me."

But we can be thankful for our deliverance! As Christians, we have turned from "darkness to light" and from the "power of Satan" to the blessings and power of God. Virtually every non-Christian would deny being under the "power of Satan," despite the plain statement from Jesus Christ Himself. Yet as sinners, human beings are in Satan's camp rebelling against their Creator and God. Moreover, the non-Christian religions seek to undermine God's truth revealed in His book, the Bible. They deny God's power and glory. And ultimately, they lead people away from the love and mercy of God. These acts are in accord with Satan's goals and desires. God declares that salvation is free to everyone who believes: Christ died for your sins. Satan will always try to hide this truth from mankind and he often does this using other religious systems.

Nevertheless, our salvation frees us from our slavery to sin. Jesus Christ Himself told us, "most assuredly, I say to you, whoever commits sin is a slave of sin (John 8:34)." Unsaved men and women are incapable of living free from sin. The term "slave" indicates that they do not have their own will or ability to avoid sins. What about all the good deeds mankind seems capable of doing? What about the good husband and father or good wife and mother? What about the person who feeds the poor and cares for the sick? Are these the acts of an a "slave to sin?" The Bible answers this question. It says, "but we are all like an unclean thing, and all our good deeds are like filthy rags (Isaiah 64:6)" and "there is none righteous, no, not one (Romans 3:10)." While our goods deeds may satisfy us and impress others, they are "filthy rags" when brought before the infinitely righteous God of Heaven. Moreover, we are warned that even one sin makes us unfit to stand before God. This concept was revealed through the Apostle James, who wrote (James 2:10), "For whoever shall keep the whole law, and yet stumble in one point, he is guilty of all."

As a Christian, you have been freed from the slavery of sin. You will occasionally sin, as long as you live in this body. However, God has made you capable of serving Him with a pure heart and pure motivations. You have also been made free of the penalty of sin because all of your sin was punished on the cross of Calvary. The Bible presents many spiritual truths in the form of "contrasts." Your freedom from sin is contrasted with your former the slavery to sin. God proclaims this truth in the book of Ephesians, where Paul wrote (Ephesians 2:1,4):

> And you were dead in your trespasses and sins...but because of
> His great love for us, God, who is rich in mercy, made us alive
> with Christ...

We see here that God has made you "alive" as a Christian, while unsaved individuals (non-Christians) are "dead in trespasses and sins." But the good news continues! Elsewhere in the New Testament, we find another great contrast. We are no longer "slaves" to sin, but we are now considered sons and daughters with a great inheritance from God through Christ. The Apostle Paul also wrote (Galatians 4:7), "you are no longer a slave but a son, and if a son, then an heir of God through Christ."

We can give thanks to God for His kindness and love for us. While we were once slaves to sin and dead in our trespasses, we are now made free from sin and alive in Christ. Our legal status has been forever changed – from slaves to sons and daughters of the Most High God.

Conclusions

In summary, you have been given many, many eternal blessings as a new Christian. No one can take them from you and they have immeasurable value! One only needs to consider the state of wealthy and powerful men who have died in their sins – without Christ. They will be banished from God's presence and punished for their sins. Upon death, these miserable souls will immediately learn about the great value of God's grace and love. Unfortunately, they will be tormented by the knowledge that they rejected the great gift from God - salvation in Jesus Christ. But this is not so with you! Your spiritual blessings have immeasurable value for you - with an eternal inheritance in Christ!

Finally, the Apostle Paul often prayed for his new converts to Christianity. He prayed that Christians of his day would have "wisdom and revelation in the knowledge" of Jesus Christ. Indeed, Paul's prayer for the Ephesians still resonates to this day. It is especially appropriate for those who have made the trip from Mecca to Calvary. This is also my prayer for you.

Paul's prayer (Ephesians 1:15-19):

Therefore I also, after I heard of your faith in the Lord Jesus and your love for all the saints, do not cease to give thanks for you, making mention of you in my prayers: that the God of our Lord Jesus Christ, the Father of glory, may give to you the spirit of wisdom and revelation in the knowledge of Him, the eyes of your understanding being enlightened; that you may know what is the hope of His calling, what are the riches of the glory of His inheritance in the saints, and what is the exceeding greatness of His power toward us who believe.

References

(1)   Caner and Pruitt, *The Costly Call, Book 2.* Kregel Publications, Grand Rapids, MI; pp. 43-50.

(2)   W. E. Vine, *An Expository Dictionary of New Testament Words*, Thomas Nelson Publishers, Nashville, TN, 1985; p. 239.

Index

Crucifixion, continued:

Nebuchadnezzar,
    conquering Jerusalem, 107-108
    destruction in Judah, 107-108
    dream related to future empires, 130-132
    fall of Israel, predicted in covenant, 107-108
New Testament,
    ancient copies available, 82
    church fathers confirm, 71-72
    conformation of its truth,
        by the miracles of the Christian prophets, 213-219
        by the testimony of Jesus Christ, 212
        by the testimony of Peter and Paul, 212-213
    corroborating accounts, 72-74
    dates of authorship, 14; 167
    preservation, 66-83
    written by eyewitnesses, 69-70; 80
Old Testament,
    archaeological evidence for
        age of a divided kingdom, 101-104
        age of Babylonian captivity, 104-107
        age of Moses, 94-96
        age of the monarchy, 100-101
        age of the patriarchs, 92-94
        conquest of Canaan, 97-98
        fall of Jericho, 99
        judges period, 99-100
        return from captivity,108-111
    comments of Jesus, 88-90; 111-112; 209-210
    confirmed as truth, 208-210
    dates of authorship, 14; 88; 166
    oracles of God, 90; 208
    preservation, 86-111
    verified by Dead Sea Scrolls, 90-92; 129
Passover, 148; 171
persecution of Christians by Muslims, 67-68; 155-157
Philip the tetrarch, 77
Philistines, 99-100
plagues on Egypt, 95-96
Pontius Pilate, 19; 30; 41; 71-73; 76-80
prophecy,
    as evidence for Divine inspiration, 13; 128-129
    Daniel's dream, 132-134
    in the Passover, 148-149
    Jesus Christ
        of His birth, 13; 139-143

Printed in Great Britain
by Amazon